Apprenticeship Companion

Level 3: Customer Service Specialist

Tim Webb
PGCE, FBII, FInstLM

THE CHOIR PRESS

Titles in the Apprenticeship Companion series

Level 3: Business Administrator

Level 3: Customer Service Specialist

Level 3: Team Leader/Supervisor

Level 5: Operations / Departmental Manager

Copyright © 2022 Tim Webb

All rights reserved. No part of this publication may be reproduced or transmitted in any form or by any means, electronic or mechanical including photocopying, recording or any information storage or retrieval system, without prior permission in writing from the publishers.

The right of Tim Webb to be identified as the author of this work has been asserted by him in accordance with the Copyright, Designs and Patents Act 1988

First published in the United Kingdom in 2022 by
The Choir Press

ISBN 978-1-78963-286-6

Foreword

Foreword

Having already written a couple of books you might think the endless hours of writing, researching and proof reading would deter any attempt to repeat the process. Given that this is now the third book in the series, that clearly hasn't happened! This time the challenge has been a little easier. The benefit of 20:20 hindsight and a great deal of the research done previously, whilst it has been no walk in the park, it has certainly been very rewarding.

The time, effort and endeavour will all be worth it though, if just one of today's Business Administrators finds it a beneficial and effective support resource as they work towards the End Point Assessment of their Apprenticeship.

I have taken the materials and resources I have used and developed over the years I have taught management studies and recompiled it into a format which, I hope, will be of benefit to all who have the stamina to wade through the detail it contains. I have tried to steer clear of the traditional, drab, textbook style and have striven to lighten what can be a rather mundane subject being so entrenched in theory.

It is no coincidence the book follows the Standard for the Level 3 Customer Service Specialist Apprenticeship and has been designed to provide the reader with support through each module of the programme.

I hope that everyone who delves into this documents finds something of interest and reward and for those who use it to support their efforts to develop themselves and their career, I wish you every success.

Remember – you only get out, what you put in!

Contents

Contents
Chapter 1: Personal Development 7
   Personal and Professional Development 8
      Professional Development 8
   Personal Development 10
   Personal and Professional Development Activities 12
      Difference between Personal and Professional Development 12
      Key Stages in Development Planning 13
   Identifying Personal and Professional Development Requirements 14
   Self-Reflection 17
      Identifying Personal Development Needs 18
      Preparing a Skills Audit 19
      SWOT Analysis 22
      SMART Objectives 23
   Learning Styles 27
   Learning and Development Activities 28
   Personal Development Plan (PDP) 29
   Continuing Professional Development Log (CPD) 32
      For Individuals 32
      For Organisations 32
      How CPD is Recorded 33
Chapter 2: Business Knowledge and Understanding 35
   The Customer 36
      Types of Customer 37
      External Customers 37
      Internal Customers 37
      Other Customer Classifications 38
   Needs and Expectations 39
      Customer Needs 39
      Customer Expectations 40
      Customer Satisfaction 42
      Customer Experience 43
      Service Delivery 43
      Expectations of Internal Customers 45
      Failure to Meet Expectations 45
   Delivering Customer Service 45
   The Importance of Customer Service 47
   Providing Exceptional Service 57
   The Importance of Consistency in Customer Service 58
      Creating Consistency in Customer Service 59
      Focus on Continuous Improvement 60
      Continuous Improvement 60
      The Concept of Continuous Improvement 62
      Improving Quality 63
      Customer Focus is Key 64
   The Continuous Improvement Model 65
   Types of Process Improvement 66
      Getting Started with Continuous Improvement 66

Contents

Implementing Continuous Improvement 68
Benefits of Continuous Improvement 68
Models of Continuous Improvement 70
Total Quality Management Model (TQM) 73
Six Sigma 76
The Six Sigma Methodology 78
Crosby's 14 Steps 80
Crosby's Four Absolutes 83
Lean Production 84
Kaizen 85
Organisational Mission, Vision and Value Statements 88
The Vision Statement 88
The Mission Statement 89
The Values Statement 90
Customer Service Statement 91
Organisational Strategy 93
Strategic Plans 94
SWOT Analysis 94
PESTLE Analysis 95
A Customer-Focused Business Strategy 96
Feedback 98
Feedback Channels 103

Chapter 3: The Customer Journey 109

Customers 111
Customer Profiles 112
Multiple Customer Profiles 117
Brands and Branding 118
Brands are an Asset 120
The Five Stages of a Customer's Journey 122
Customer Journey Map 127
Producing a Customer Journey Map 129
Generate a customer profile 129
Identity the Touchpoints 130
Presenting the results 131
Customer Emotions 136
Why Emotions Matter 137
Map the Emotional Journey 138
Types of Customer Journey 140
Customer Service Issues 140
Customer Questions 141
Frequently Asked Questions 143
Dealing with routine customer service problems 143
Stimulus and response 144
The Emotional versus the Rational Response 144
Fight or Flight Response 145
The Escalation to Violence 146
Communication Skills 148
Blocks to Communication 150
Dealing with angry customers 153

Contents

- Complaints.. 154
- Working Within the Limits of Authority 155
- Service Breakdowns 158
  - *Refunds* *159*
- Managing Customer Related Problems 161
  - *Escalation* *161*
  - *Service Level Agreements* *162*
- Legal Implications When Delivering Customer Service 163

Chapter 4: Teamwork and Leadership 167
- Teams 168
- Teamwork 172
  - *Performance Monitoring* *173*
  - *Teamwork in Customer Service* *174*
  - *Customer Service in the Wider Organisation* *178*
- External Customers 178
- Internal Customers 179
- Developing a Team 180
  - *Team Development Stages:* *180*
- Leadership 182
- Leadership in Teamwork 185
- Leadership Styles 186
  - *Lewin's Leadership Styles* *187*
  - *Other Leadership Styles and Models* *195*
  - *Strategic Leadership Style* *195*
- Identifying a Leadership Style 209
  - *Benefits of Effective Teamwork in Customer Service* *210*

Chapter 5: Governance and Compliance 213
- Compliance 216
  - *Health and Safety – Employer Duty* *218*
- Equality and Diversity 221
  - *Equality* *221*
  - *Diversity* *221*
  - *Inclusion* *221*
  - *Equality & Diversity at Work* *221*
  - *Employee Rights* *223*
- Equality, Diversity and Employment Laws 228
- Employment Legislation 230
- Operational Legislation 233
  - *Other Legislation and Regulations* *238*
- Consumer-Related Legislation in Customer Service Delivery 239
- The Consumer Rights Act 239
- Governance 241
  - *Implications of Unresolved Governance and Compliance Issues* *248*

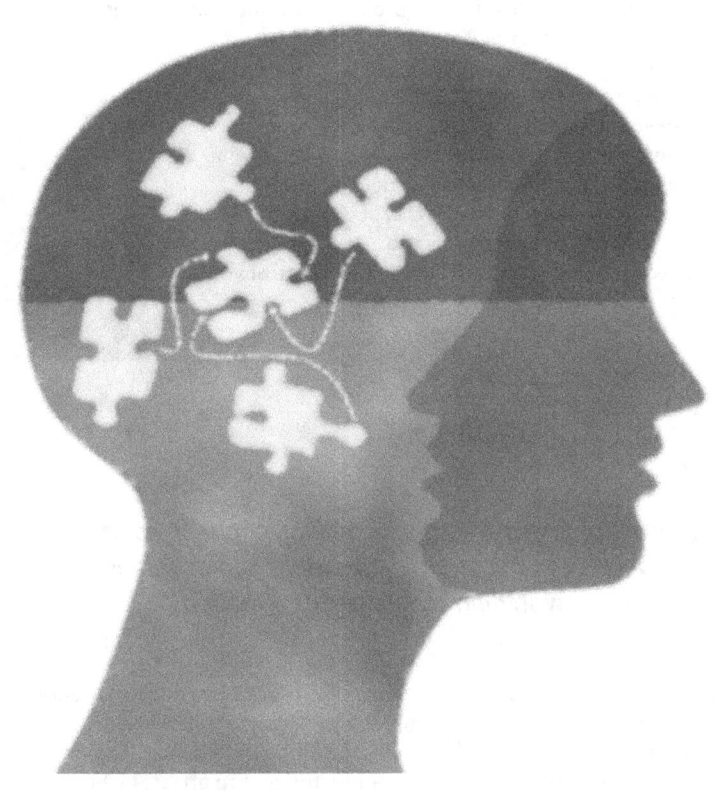

Chapter 1: Personal Development

Personal and Professional Development

Personal and Professional Development

There was a time when personal and professional development was provided and managed by the employer. You went on a few courses chosen by your employer, said yes when you were offered the chance to take on a new project and waited until the time was right to move up, or move on. But it is not like that anymore.

These days, **you** are responsible for your personal and professional development and **you** need to look for your own opportunities. In order to achieve this, you need to know what needs to be changed and what needs to be developed. The only way to do this is to take a deep and thorough look at yourself, not just at work, but personally too. How can you manage and direct others if you do not have knowledge of your own weaknesses and inadequacies?

Professional Development

Can be defined as:

> *"the process of improving and increasing capabilities of employees through access to education and training opportunities or through watching others perform the job."*

Professional Development is focused on gaining new capabilities and experience and improving the knowledge and skills that improve potential in the work environment. These skills make staff more efficient and effective at their job. It is also suggested that it helps build and maintain the morale of employees and is thought to attract higher quality staff to an organisation.

> *"professional development is either related to a current role or a role you want to do in the future".*

With changes to our working lives happening every day, it is important to develop your skillset to remain effective in your career.

Effective professional development involves ensuring your knowledge and understanding of your area of expertise is always at the highest possible level. It is the acquisition of skills and knowledge for career advancement, but inevitably, it also includes an element of personal development.

Personal and Professional Development

Broadly speaking, it may include formal types of vocational education or training that leads to a career related qualification. It can also include informal training and development programmes, which may be delivered on the job in order to develop and enhance skills.

Some examples of professional development are:

- IT training
- Health and Safety Risk Assessment
- Accountancy or budgeting
- Legal knowledge or expertise

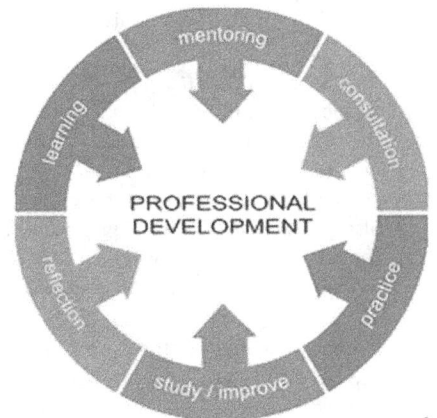

Benefits of Professional Development

Investing in workers is beneficial to the whole organisation and can boost the bottom line. Listed below are some of the organisational benefits which can be expected because of effective professional development training initiatives:

1. **Increase the collective knowledge of the team.**
   Encouraging staff to train in relevant subjects and applications — an advanced course in a software package they use daily, can have an immediate effect on productivity. Professional development can also help raise overall staff expertise when employees with vastly different backgrounds and levels of experience are required to work together such as on projects.

2. **Boost employees' job satisfaction**
   When staff members can do their jobs more effectively, they become more confident. This leads to greater job satisfaction and improved employee retention. There are a range of low-cost professional development training options to choose from, including mentorships, job shadowing and cross training.

3. **Makes a company more appealing.**
   When providing training and development opportunities, it builds a positive reputation as an employer that cares about its workforce and wants to employ only the best. Customers and clients will benefit too, from the high level of efficient service they receive. Employees are brand ambassadors. When they attend conferences and seminars, they represent and reflect all that is good about the organisation.

Personal and Professional Development

4. *Attract the right kind of in-demand candidates.*
   Organisations want to attract the most highly driven and career-focused candidates when they advertise a job. By offering them an enticing picture of how they can grow professionally or expand the career avenues available to them if they join the organisation is an attractive add on to an attractive salary.

5. *Aids a retention strategy.*
   Employees want to feel like they are appreciated and making a difference. But they also want to feel like they are developing expertise and becoming more well-rounded. If team members do not feel challenged, or they sense stagnation in their careers, they will look for advancement opportunities elsewhere. Lifelong learning exposes employees to new experiences and keeps them engaged in their work. Professional development helps build and maintain enthusiasm, but it also inspires loyalty.

6. *Make succession planning easier.*
   Professional development programs are tools for developing future leaders for the organisation. The ability to promote existing staff to managerial positions in the future using targeted training now, can help ensure the best and brightest are readied to move up.

Personal Development

"the process of improving oneself through activities such as enhancing employment skills, increasing consciousness and building wealth."

Personal development is about improving talents and potential, both in and out of the workplace.

Personal development sits alongside professional growth —to progress in a career, personal; development will be needed first.

It helps with handle fears, take on more responsibility, and succeed with greater challenges.

Personal Development requires broadening of knowledge, improvement and development of skills and develop and refinement of behaviours to ensure performance with the utmost professionalism.

You may have experienced something like this:

> There are two people in your team, both of whom are great at managing budgets. They are both accurate, detail-oriented and deliver the results needed. However, one of them is a real people person. Their interpersonal and communication skills are fantastic, and, because of this, they have no problem getting the information

Personal and Professional Development

they require quickly from colleagues at any level. The other person does not have this skill and often encounters conflict from colleagues, for many possible reasons.

Which of these people do you think needs personal development?

Both can do their jobs. Both have the skills required on a professional level to deliver results, however, with the benefit of excellent relationship building skills one of them will always be one step ahead.

Some examples of personal development are:

- *Leadership training*
- *Management training*
- *Time management*
- *Handling difficult situations and conflict management*
- *Communication skills*

Personal development relates to life skills. These are what is needed to achieve life goals. It focuses on helping to improve talents, whether they are related to work or not.
Benefits of Personal Development

Personal development offers many different benefits.

- *Boosting self-awareness*
- *Increasing self-knowledge*
- *Developing your existing skills or learning new ones*
- *Renewing or building your self-esteem or identity*
- *Developing pre-existing talents or strengths*
- *Enhancing your employability*
- *Improve the quality of your life.*
- *Positively affecting your social status and wealth*

All these activities can help make a major difference in life. When feeling helpless, these are skill sets which can help turn the odds in your favour. By focusing on personal development, it ensures the right skill sets are available.

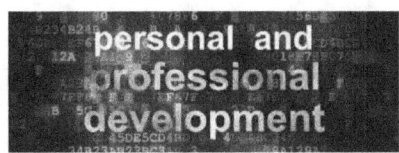

Personal and Professional Development

Personal and Professional Development Activities

Personal Development	Professional Development
Emotional Wellbeing	Management Training
Health and fitness	Skill-based training
Communication	Internal Assessment
Motivation	Conflict Resolution
Spirituality	Online Education
Self-belief	Networking
Journaling	Research

Difference between Personal and Professional Development

It is clear from the definition that professional development relates to enhancing the workforce and/or an individual within that workforce. The objectives will usually be specific to the organisation and its goals at a specific time and the skills that would be required to deliver the products/services.

The definition of personal development suggests it is used when individuals, seek to update their own knowledge and learn skills that they would like to have. This means the activities are more unique to the individual and their personal objectives.

When contrasting personal development against professional development, it is easier to see that there is a connection rather than trying to identify differences.

Both professional and personal development are similar in that they both represent a drive towards improvement, greater understanding and increased effectivity (either an individual or a group).

Both require effort, time and resources (often money) to get involved in and both regularly reoccur for all individuals and not just professionals.

Whilst personal development might seem to be separate from the professional life, it could be a great way to achieve career objectives. It is not just what is learnt that could help at work; making a commitment to personal development clear to an employer, will demonstrate dedication and the ability to learn and grow.

Personal development makes a difference in life on a daily basis. At almost every stage of life, something new will be learnt which will help development as a person.

Personal and Professional Development

The key to managing personal development is knowing one's strengths and areas for improvement. Knowing these can help you to develop your weaknesses and turn them into strengths.

Finally, neither Personal nor Professional development can be completed satisfactorily without a depth of self-awareness which is far greater than we currently have. By having a thorough understanding of what you need to achieve and how to achieve it, you can develop the necessary skills by way of a solution.

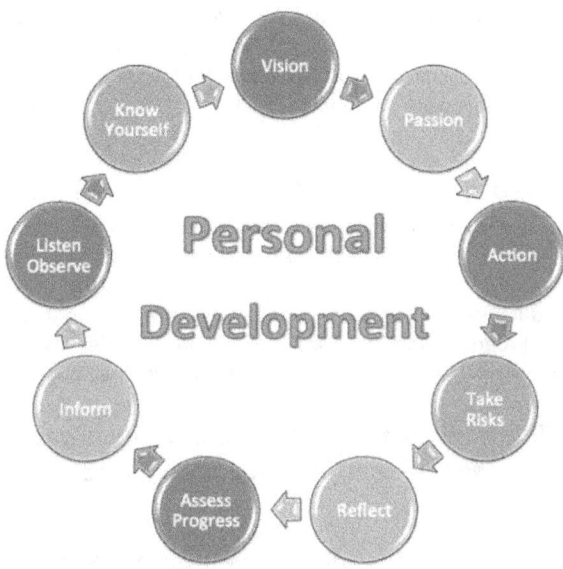

Key Stages in Development Planning

There are several stages to go through to plan personal and professional development. These can be defined as:

- *analyse current skills, knowledge and experience* – to identify skills gaps and where we are now.
- *identify development needs and set objectives* – to focus on where we need to be.
- *identify learning styles.*
- *arrange resources and support mechanisms to meet the objectives* – the basis of how we are going to achieve our goals.
- *monitor and review progress and overcome barriers to learning* – to make sure we are still going the right way.

Personal and Professional Development

At the heart of the process, there are three questions:

1. *Where am I now?*
   To answer this question, we need to have a look at our current, personal, situation – e.g., our skills, knowledge and experience; qualifications; job description and tasks; salary package; grade or position at work.

2. *Where do I want or need to be?*
   Where we would like to be in the future. This can be six months ahead, a year, five years or a period that fits into our future plans. We need to consider our goals, the things we want or need to achieve – e.g., a higher salary; promotion; increased knowledge and skills in specific areas at work; greater job satisfaction; improved job security; improve employability prospects.

3. *How will I get there?*
   The route achieving this is what will be recorded in our Personal Development plan. We need to identify the steps we need to take to begin to work towards our goals.

   This may include qualifications, a career review, do voluntary work to gain specific experience, ask to broaden experience within current work role, shadow colleagues to learn from them, consider the best learning options for you personally.

Remember! This is about focussing on your personal goals and set targets that are specific to you and your needs.

Identifying Personal and Professional Development Requirements

The Concept of Self-Awareness

Self-awareness is your ability to recognise your own emotions and their effects on you and others. Without being aware of, and understanding your own emotions, it will be difficult for you to deal with the other emotional competencies like self-management, social awareness, or team leadership.

Self-awareness is:

the conscious knowledge of ourselves – our character, desires, beliefs, qualities, motives and feelings

When you look in a mirror – what do you see?

- *Do you see the person you are?*
- *The person you want to be?*
- *The person you think other people see?*

Personal and Professional Development

The first step on the road to self-development is to recognise that the image we see is simply a reflection of the packaging we come in! That packaging is about as relevant as the cardboard box your breakfast cereals are delivered in!! – You don't eat the box – it is what is inside the box that matters!!

We seldom look inside the packaging because we are afraid of what we might find. Without absolute honesty, you will never recognise what is really inside.

We are not inclined to spend much time on self-reflection. Even when personal feedback is presented to us, we are not always open to it, because honest feedback is not always flattering. Consequently, many of us have a pretty low level of self-awareness.

Self-awareness is being aware of oneself including one's traits, feelings and behaviours.

It is quite difficult today to find time to think about who we are, what our strengths and weaknesses are, personality type, habits and values. We are just not inclined to spend much time on self-reflection.
Consequently, many of us have low level of self-awareness. An increased level of self-awareness is the essential first step toward maximising management skills. It can improve judgment and help identify opportunities for professional development and personal growth.

This first step on the road to personal development, therefore, is to take a long hard look at ourselves and be brutally honest about our true targets and expectations in life.

If you cannot be totally honest with yourself – you will never be honest with anyone.

Self-awareness is also associated with soft skills – There are thought to be five elements to this – Personality, Values, Habits, Needs and Emotions.

These are considered below:

> ***Personality:*** – Personalities cannot be changed, but values and needs are based on what we learn about ourselves. Understanding our own personality can help us find in what environment we can be successful. Awareness of our personality helps us analyse such a decision.
>
> ***Values:*** – It is important that we know and focus on our personal values. When we focus on our values, we are more likely to accomplish what we consider most important.

Personal and Professional Development

Habits: – Our habits are the behaviours that we repeat on a daily basis and often, automatically. Although we would like to possess the habits that help us interact effectively with and manage others, we can all identify at least one of our habits that decrease our effectiveness.

Needs: – Maslow and other scholars have identified a variety of psychological needs that drive our behaviours such as needs for esteem, affection, belonging, achievement, self-actualisation, power and control.

Emotions: – Understanding your own feelings, what causes them, and how they impact our thoughts and actions is emotional self-awareness. Persons with high emotional self-awareness understand the internal process associated with emotional experiences and, therefore, has greater control over them.

Having a good sense of these aspects of ourselves can help us in the workplace, and in our private lives.

We can assess personal growth and understanding through self-awareness by, for example:

- *being aware of how people and other things influence us.*
- *learning how to influence and interact with others.*

Developing self-awareness, and understanding our own psychology, is a skill that is part of our personal and professional development.

Self-awareness can be applied in our working lives to help us to, for example:

- *understand emotions more clearly* – ours and other people's
- *improve our communication skills* – and interact with others in the workplace and resolve conflict more effectively
- *improve leadership skills* – and our general operational performance
- *improve job satisfaction* – by focusing on job roles and tasks that truly motivate us
- *maximise career development opportunities*

Techniques that can help us learn about how to reveal, recognise, evaluate and understand the different attributes and qualities that make us unique include, for example:

- *psychometric tests*
- *management tools*
- *coaching tools*
- *self-reflection tools*

Personal and Professional Development

Self-Reflection

Self-reflection helps to develop skills and review their effectiveness, rather than just carry-on doing things as you have always done them. It is about questioning, in a positive way, what you do and why you do it and then deciding whether there is a better, or more efficient, way of doing it in the future.

In any role, whether at home or at work, reflection is an important part of learning. You would not use a recipe a second time around if the dish did not work the first time! You would either adjust the recipe or find a new one.

When we do our job, we can become stuck in a routine that may not be working effectively. Thinking about your own skills can help you identify changes you might need to make.

Reflective questions to ask yourself:

> **Strengths** – *What are my strengths? Am I well organised? Do I remember things?*
> **Weaknesses** – *What are my weaknesses? Am I easily distracted? Do I need more practise with a particular skill?*
> **Skills** – *What skills do I have? What am I good at?*
> **Problems** – *What problems are there at work/home that may affect me? For example, responsibilities or distractions that may impact on study or work.*
> **Achievements** – *What have I achieved?*
> **Happiness** – *Are there things that I am unhappy with or disappointed about? What makes me happy?*
> **Solutions** – *What could I do to improve in these areas?*

Although self-reflection can seem difficult at first, or even selfish or embarrassing, as it does not come naturally, you will find it becomes easier with practise and the end result could be a happier and more efficient you.

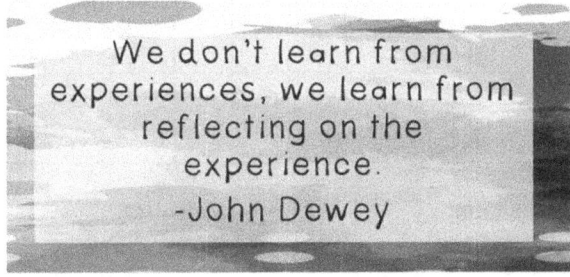

We don't learn from experiences, we learn from reflecting on the experience.
-John Dewey

Personal and Professional Development

Identifying Personal Development Needs

Skills audits can be used to list the skills that are relevant to a role, then assess one's ability using a scoring system. The skills tested can be for a current role, to see where improvement is needed, or on a role we want to aim for in the future.

In this example, an experienced departmental manager in a supermarket wants to apply for promotion to deputy store manager. The following skills audit is based on the skills and attributes shown in the organisation's job description for the deputy manager position. This helps them to identify skills gaps that will need to be addressed if their application for promotion is to be successful. They show their current skills in these areas, with 1 = poor and 5 = excellent

Skills and attributes	*Current ability rating*					*Action to be taken*
	1	2	3	4	5	
Experience of all departments within the store			✓			Need to work in other store areas – see line manager
Evaluating competitors' stores and managing advantage			✓			OK for fresh produce, useful to try other areas competitive
Leadership skills				✓		OK
General staff management skills				✓		OK
Communication skills			✓			Usually very good, but need more at senior management level – ask line manager
Training and coaching skills					✓	One of my strengths
Purchasing and negotiating delivery and discounts	✓					Do not have to do this in current role – ask! procurement team if I can shadow them for a day/week?
Ability to promote and generate sales – demonstrations, displays				✓		One of my strengths
Customer service skills				✓		One of my strengths
Budgeting/finance skills			✓			Only have to do a bit – need to shadow someone
Working to the organisation's and industry's standards				✓		OK

Personal and Professional Development

Skills and attributes	Current ability rating					Action to be taken
Maintaining health and safety in the store -e.g., fire evacuation, first-aid cover, risk awareness, minimising hazards, dealing with dangerous chemicals correctly			✓			OK in my area, do not really need to worry about chemicals here – find out a bit more for rest of store
Quality management – e.g., store cleanliness, customer satisfaction, quality of produce					✓	OK

The audit now reveals the areas that this manager needs to address before or when preparing to apply for promotion.

Analyse your current skills, knowledge and experience.

The normal process for analysing current skills, knowledge and experience is to use a skills audit. This is a simple process which identifies what you are good at what you are not so good at as well as things you may not have done before.

An audit is:

a simple process to identify your strengths and weaknesses.

The skills audit will help to analyse your current position – where I am I now? – and reveal areas that are strong and those that need attention. These can be entered onto a Personal Development Plan, so that we can see our strengths and skills gaps, then start to decide what we need or want to consolidate or improve.

Preparing a Skills Audit
A definitive and comprehensive list is made of the skills that are relevant to the role covering all the relevant criteria. When deciding what skills are necessary to audit, the details can be taken from a variety of sources – the job description and person specification should go some way to providing most of the criteria for this, but can be supplemented by criteria from the organisation's own policies, procedures and standards; national occupational standards; essential standards; professional bodies' standards, etc. The final list should be checked by all parties concerned or involved.

Personal and Professional Development

The existing skill set is then compared to the list and a simple rating system applied which shows the level of skill for each criterion. The rating can be from self-evaluation or be done with someone else, such as the line manager.

Below are two examples of skills audits:

	Personal Audit	1	2	3	4	5
1	Lack confidence in expressing my needs		✓			
2	Manage time effectively			✓		
3	I am competent to lead		✓			
4	I cope with stress well				✓	
5	I do not have the confidence to give presentations			✓		
6	I am patient when teaching and coaching others		✓			
7	I can handle a number of tasks		✓			
8	I do not have the confidence to influence others			✓		
9	I can motivate others			✓		
10	I do not make people do tasks			✓		

Personal and Professional Development

Professional Skills Audit		
Skills required	Rating (1–5)	Action to be taken
Computing skills	4	Undertake short courses (if possible) to enhance computing skills
Leadership skills	4	Get more involved in communities/societies
Numeracy skills	4	Discuss with lecturers and fellow students on ways to improve
Revision and exam techniques	3	Learn from lecturers and fellow students on techniques to revise and answer exam questions.
Time-management and organisation skills	2	Jot down all activities that need to be done accordingly in a diary
Oral presentation skills	4	Learn to fully utilise and use other presentation aids that are available besides PowerPoint
Critical analysis and logical argument skills	3	Get more involved in group discussions
Selecting and prioritising information when reading	3	Listen to lectures and identify which are the important points
Referencing skills	3	Write more essays and get used to the Harvard referencing style
Summarising skills	4	Need to fully understand the topic
Developing appropriate writing style	3	Read more articles and journals to get used to the writing style so that it can be implemented
Search skills (library and e-resources)	3	Fully utilise the library's 'resources and support' section
Utilising and comprehension	5	Listen more to the way people converse with each other and try and pick up whatever necessary
Proofreading and editing	3	Take another look at the work

Personal and Professional Development

SWOT Analysis

As well as doing a skills audit and reflecting on your choices, you can also do a SWOT analysis to focus your attention on your strengths and weaknesses. These are the things which you are good at and things you are not so good at or need additional support or training to achieve a higher level of competence.

SWOT stands for Strengths, Weaknesses, Opportunities, and Threats.

The strengths and weaknesses are factors which affect you personally. Strengths are things you are good at, things you can do without support or help. This could include literacy or numeracy. It could include being well organised, etc.

Weaknesses are things you need help or support to achieve. It may be that you can happily read a newspaper, but a textbook may be more challenging. You can maybe deal with personal finance including paying bills and managing credit cards, but departmental budgets and cost management you find difficult and need help with. It may also be that you are simply disorganised! These are your strengths and weaknesses!

Opportunities and threats are not about you personally, but about society in general. Opportunities are the things that help you to achieve your targets such as free training courses, help with childcare whilst studying, work shadowing opportunities, etc. Threats are the things which may prevent you from achieving your targets such as the economic climate, lack of opportunities, etc. Both opportunities and threats are matters outside of your control, but you should be aware of these issues.

- S   *Strengths*
- W *Weaknesses*
- O   *Opportunities for improvement*
- T   *Threats to such progress – things that may stop progress.*

The next stage is to prepare a SWOT analysis to identify development needs in more detail. This shows what is needed to be able to develop skills, experience and knowledge to be in a good position to apply for promotion or a new role.

Personal and Professional Development

SWOT

	Strengths	*Weaknesses*
	Personal finance Paying bills Managing credit cards	Departmental budgets Cost management Disorganised
	Free training courses Help with childcare. Work shadowing opportunities	Economic climate Lack of opportunities
	Opportunities	*Threats*

Setting Objectives.

Having analysed where you are now, you can then work out where you want to be and set personal objectives to plan how to improve your performance at work.

When setting personal and work objectives, it is important to have a realistic number of goals. If overloaded, people feel overwhelmed and are more likely to fail, give up and lose confidence. Honesty about achievements and expectations is important.

It can be useful to support this process with personal reflection and discussions with senior colleagues, maybe during the appraisal process. Once you have established your needs, you can set objectives that support your strengths, address your weaknesses and help you to improve your performance.

SMART Objectives

Once areas for personal development have been identified, it is important to set targets.

By having our goals and objectives clearly in mind, there is a much greater chance of success. One good way to set goals is to use SMART objectives:

SMART is an acronym that you can use to guide your goal setting.

Personal and Professional Development

To make sure your goals are clear and reachable, each one should be:

*S*pecific (simple, sensible, significant).
*M*easurable (meaningful, motivating).
*A*chievable (agreed, attainable).
*R*elevant (reasonable, realistic and resourced, results-based).
*T*ime bound (time-based, time limited, time/cost limited, timely, time-sensitive).

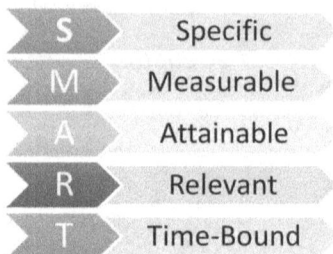

Some authors have expanded it to include extra focus areas.

SMARTER, for example, includes Evaluated and Reviewed.

Set SMART objectives

1. **Specific**
   Your goal should be clear and specific, otherwise you will not be able to focus your efforts or feel truly motivated to achieve it. When writing your goal, try to answer the five "W" questions:

   - *What do I want to accomplish?*
   - *Why is this goal important?*
   - *Who is involved?*
   - *Where is it located?*
   - *Which resources or limits are involved?*

   Example:
   Imagine that you are currently a marketing executive, and you would like to become head of marketing. A specific goal could be, "I want to gain the skills and experience necessary to become head of marketing within my organisation, so that I can build my career and lead a successful team."

2. **Measurable**
   It is important to have measurable goals, so that you can track your progress and stay motivated. Assessing progress helps you to stay focused, meet your deadlines, and feel the excitement of getting closer to achieving your goal. A measurable goal should address questions such as:

   - *How much?*
   - *How many?*
   - *How will I know when it is accomplished?*

Personal and Professional Development

Example
You might measure your goal of acquiring the skills to become head of marketing by determining that you will have completed the necessary training courses and gained the relevant experience within five years' time.

3. **Achievable**
   Your goal also needs to be realistic and attainable to be successful. In other words, it should stretch your abilities but still remain possible. When you set an achievable goal, you may be able to identify previously overlooked opportunities or resources that can bring you closer to it. An achievable goal will usually answer questions such as:

   - *How can I accomplish this goal?*
   - *How realistic is the goal, based on other constraints, such as financial factors?*

   Example
   You might need to ask yourself whether developing the skills required to become head of marketing is realistic, based on your existing experience and qualifications. For example, do you have the time to complete the required training effectively? Are the necessary resources available to you? Can you afford to do it?

4. **Relevant**
   This step is about ensuring that your goal matters to you, and that it also aligns with other relevant goals. Everyone needs support and assistance in achieving our goals, but it is important to retain control over them. So, make sure that your plans drive everyone forward, but that you are still responsible for achieving your own goal. A relevant goal can answer "yes" to these questions:

   - *Does this seem worthwhile?*
   - *Is this the right time?*
   - *Does this match our other efforts/needs?*
   - *Am I the right person to reach this goal?*
   - *Is it applicable in the current socio-economic environment?*

   Example
   You might want to gain the skills to become head of marketing within your organisation, but is it the right time to undertake the required training, or work toward additional qualifications? Are you sure that you are the right person for the head of marketing role? Have you considered your spouse's goals? For example, if you want to start a family, would completing training in your free time make this more difficult?

Personal and Professional Development

5. **Time-bound**
   Every goal needs a target date, so that you have a deadline to focus on and something to work toward. This part of the SMART goal criteria helps to prevent everyday tasks from taking priority over your longer-term goals. A time-bound goal will usually answer these questions:

   - *When?*
   - *What can I do six months from now?*
   - *What can I do six weeks from now?*
   - *What can I do today?*

   Example
   Gaining the skills to become head of marketing may require additional training or experience. How long will it take you to acquire these skills? Do you need further training, so that you are eligible for certain exams or qualifications? It is important to give yourself a realistic time frame for accomplishing the smaller goals necessary to achieve your final objective.

SMART is an effective tool that provides the clarity, focus and motivation you need to achieve your goals. It can also improve your ability to reach them by encouraging you to define your objectives and set a completion date. SMART goals are also easy to use by anyone, anywhere, without the need for specialist tools or training.

When you use SMART, you can create clear, attainable and meaningful goals, and develop the motivation, action plan, and support needed to achieve them.

Questions to ask when setting SMART objectives

S	Specific	What are the details of the learning activity, task or training course that I want to do? What qualifications do I need for that promotion? Which job am I aiming for?
M	Measurable	Is there a certificate or report that can show my progress? Can I count the number of units I am covering so that I can see my progress?
A	Achievable	Can I do it? What support do I need to find to make sure that I can achieve these goals?
R	Realistic	Is it realistic to do the training or tasks in the time that is allowed? Is it realistic to work full time and do all of this study quickly, or do I need to study over a longer period of time?
T	Time-bound	What are the deadlines? Do I need to have completed this task before my tutor comes next time, or in time for my annual review?

Personal and Professional Development

Learning Styles

Once objectives have been set and agreed, it helps to be aware of different learning styles so that we can focus on the most suitable learning activities.

Everyone has a preferred learning style that they use to develop their skills, experience and knowledge. Some like to learn by reading about things, others need to see a demonstration to understand something, and others need to try the activity themselves before they remember everything.

People have favourite ways of learning and training needs to be adapted to accommodate these preferences where possible.

A common model used to assess peoples preferred learning styles is the VARK model. This asserts that learning can be broken down into four preferred styles

These four styles are:

- **Visual** – *seeing and watching* – e.g., seeing pictures of how to make the product, or watching instruction videos.
- **Auditory** – *listening and speaking* – e.g., being told how to make the product.
- **Reading** – *Reading and Writing e.g. listening to a lecture and writing notes*
- **Kinaesthetic** – *touching and doing* – e.g., touching the components and actually making the product under supervision.

According to this model, people have a dominant or preferred learning style.

When training team members, the trainer must be prepared to use a combination of all four skills so that everyone's learning style needs can be met.

A visual learner will learn about a subject by looking at graphs, pictures and diagrams, or watching videos or demonstrations. Just being told about what to do will not register. Touching and doing the new activity will help to reinforce the learning at a basic level, but they will need to observe and read up on the details.

An auditory learner will absorb the information by listening to their tutor or colleague, asking questions, then listening carefully to the answers.

A reading/writing learner will learn best from reading instructions, research and information about the subject, and writing notes to help them remember important details.
A kinaesthetic learner needs to touch and do the activity. They may absorb a reasonable amount of information from listening to the tutor or watching a demonstration, but they will not truly understand the subject or activity until they do it for themselves.

Personal and Professional Development

Learning and Development Activities

We can use a variety of learning and development activities, based inside or outside the workplace. It is better to choose a learning activity which is more closely associated with your preferred learning style. A combination of activities can be put together to suit the individual's needs, goals and areas of weakness. Activities may include, for example:

- **delegation** – e.g., offering tasks to challenge the individual and give them the opportunity to develop their skills and experience.
- **demonstrations** – e.g., watching demonstrations about how a new piece of equipment is used, then trying it out
- **role-play** – e.g., to practise how to deal with angry customers' complaints.
- **job rotation** – e.g., training people in a wide variety of tasks to aid flexibility and motivation.
- **shadowing** – e.g., arranging for a trainee to follow an experienced member of staff for a week.
- **coaching and mentoring** – e.g., giving intensive one-to-one support and guidance; having a senior member of staff as a role model
- **project work** – e.g., expanding knowledge and experience by following through all aspects of a project, and not just isolated tasks.
- **classroom-based training courses** – e.g., a first-aid course at the local college
- **computer-based training** – e.g., induction courses to give an overview of the organisation and its policies and procedures.
- **Internet-based e-training** – e.g., food safety knowledge, followed by an exam at an assessment centre to gain the full certificate.
- **blended learning** – a mixture of different methods – e.g., a computer-based course in Spanish as well as conversation lessons at the local college
- **distance learning** – e.g., a course done at work or at home, with the assistance of an assessor or a tutor who may be based miles away.
- **workplace training** – e.g., internal training sessions on equality and diversity given by colleagues or external trainers.

You should identify the activities which suit your learning style and then identify the development opportunities available including the cost, duration, level, availability, etc.

Personal and Professional Development

Personal Development Plan (PDP)

A PDP is a document that is based on awareness, values, reflection, goal setting and planning for personal development. This can be at work, in education or in the context of self-improvement.

Employees who are taking part in personal, professional, development are typically asked to record their development by completing a PDP.

A Personal Development Plan is a written account of self-reflection and improvement, which doubles up as a detailed action plan used to identify ways to achieve academic, personal, or career-based goals.

It is usually created within the workplace or when studying (with guidance from your manager or tutor), and works by allowing you to establish your aims, recognise your strengths and weaknesses, and identify the need for improvement.

Objectives are put in place, based on the areas you would like to improve, and the plan consists of your own personalised actions that will help you to achieve them.

When creating a Personal Development Plan, it is essential to make sure it accurately outlines your personal goals, why they are important to you, and how you plan to achieve them.

Although all PDPs are specific to each individual, the plan will generally detail your ideal future based on your short and/or long-term ambitions. Areas of development will be specific to you, and could be centred on work, education, or self-improvement.

It should also always recognise the potential obstacles you might face, and how you propose to overcome them – and if the roadblocks cannot be tackled, include a contingency plan to help your career keep moving forward.

The PDP can also contain SWOT analyses, SMART objectives and other action plans about how to develop skills, knowledge, understanding and experience in the future.

When preparing a PDP, you will need to have identified:

- **clear SMART objectives** – *Specific, Measurable, Achievable, Realistic and Time-bound*
- **resource requirements** – *e.g., learning activities, training materials or courses.*
- **timescales and finances** – *e.g., work and study deadlines or course fees*
- **support mechanisms** – *e.g., line manager, course tutor, workplace mentor or coach*

Here is an example of a PDP for Alex Smith, a customer services senior supervisor:

Personal and Professional Development

Personal Development Plan	
Name: *Alex Smith*	**Job title:** *Customer Service Senior Supervisor*
Relevant professional and vocational qualifications: - A level business studies, GCSE economics. - Qualified first aider - PTTLS (training qualification), qualified H&S induction trainer - Level 2 team leading - Level 2 customer service - Level 3 diploma in management (part of the way through)	

Date: *1 April 2021*

Part 1 – Personal analysis

Strengths	Weaknesses
- Good listener, good communicator with team and customers - Organised and able to meet deadlines. - Planning and allocation of tasks - Training – new and established team members - Coordinating and planning resources needed by team. - Confident following recruitment process - Dealing with customer complaints (when team members need to escalate)	- Can get distracted by interruptions – e.g., colleagues wanting something. - Do not enjoy repetitive routine. - Get frustrated when people waste my time. - Feel that team members take advantage of me sometimes. - Spending too much of my free time doing work jobs to catch up – e.g., emails and reports for 1-2 hours each evening at home
Opportunities	Threats
- This is a good role to show my ability to work under pressure, solve problems and make decisions. - Can demonstrate a good range of management and leadership skills. - Team has 30 members now (24 last year), further 10-15 to be recruited and trained at end of 2017 – good opportunity to develop my M&L skills further, especially strategy and planning. - Can consolidate current role and skills and start to think about going for promotion next year. - I can ask for coaching and mentoring from line manager. - My annual appraisal will give focus and be a source of guaranteed feedback	- Time-management skills - Work-life balance

Personal and Professional Development

Part 2 – Setting objectives

Objective	Action	Resources and support mechanisms	How to measure success	Timescale and review dates
Finish L3 apprenticeship in Customer Service	5 more elements to go – complete 1 per week	Approx. 70 hours of study needed to finish – plus review time. Computer and Internet access Ask course tutor for extra feedback and support if necessary	Finish each assessment. Tutor feedback – work on weak areas & resubmit if necessary. L3 awarded	10 study hours per week if possible – so end of May, mid-June at the latest. Course tutor review booked next week
Improve my time management	Arrange coaching and self-study	Next unit on L3 course covers this. Ask line manager for coaching afterwards if needed	Less chaotic diary Reduction in stress Less work at home in the evenings	Next L3 unit will be done by mid-April. Review & ask for coaching if needed end June
Develop planning and strategy skills	Review records and data to track team changes. Develop plan for next stage of change	Recruitment, training and performance records for last 12 months Recruitment & training plans for next 12 months Customer and team feedback reports Line manager for support and feedback	Smooth transition to next stage with new staff Team members' performance records – to check quality, output and skills gaps	Review past records – by mid-June. Develop plan – by end June. Review team's progress & performance – ongoing

Part 3 – Personal objectives

Short-term goals (next 3 months)
Finish L3 Customer Service Start to prepare for having larger team. Improve time management and stop working at home so much

Medium-term goals (next 12 months)
Consolidate current role this year and develop management skills with the larger team. Start to discuss and plan promotion opportunities for next year

Long-term goals (beyond 12 months)
Promotion to Customer Services Manager Do a level 5 course – check funding nearer the time

Personal and Professional Development

Continuing Professional Development Log (CPD)

CPD stands for Continuing Professional Development (CPD) and is the term used to describe the learning activities professionals engage in to develop and enhance their abilities. It enables learning to become conscious and proactive, rather than passive and reactive. It may include life-long learning, maintaining the currency of skills and knowledge, developing occupational effectiveness, impact and achievement.

> *CPD is the holistic commitment of professionals towards the enhancement of personal skills and proficiency throughout their careers.*

A CPD log combines and records the different methodologies undertaken for learning, such as training workshops, conferences and events, e-learning programs, best practice techniques and ideas sharing, completed by an individual over a period of time.

Development recorded in the PDP is transferred to the CPD Log when it has been satisfactorily completed.

Engaging in Continuing Professional Development ensures that both academic and practical qualifications do not become out-dated or obsolete, allowing individuals to continually 'up skill' or 're-skill' themselves, regardless of occupation, age or educational level.

Benefits of CPD

For Individuals
Continuing Professional Development helps individuals to regularly focus on how they can become a more competent and effective professional. Training and learning increase confidence and overall capability, and compliments career aspirations.

CPD enables individuals to adapt positively to changes in work/industry requirements. Recording CPD properly provides evidence of professional development (this can be useful for supervision and appraisals).

CPD log shows the individuals commitment to self-development and professionalism.

For Organisations
Providing learning benefits the organisation by promoting a healthy learning culture leading to a more fulfilled workforce and retaining valuable staff.

Staff may have CPD obligations as members of professional bodies.

Personal and Professional Development

Allocating Time for CPD

Most institutes provide their members with Continuing Professional Development requirements generally as a minimum annual number of hours. These targets are defined by the accrual of CPD hours through training, seminars & workshops, events & conferences as well as other structured forms of CPD learning. These CPD hours are sometimes converted to points, units or credits. Most institutions allow members to choose subjects of relevance to them as individuals, a minority also require their members to seek CPD on a range of core subjects.

How CPD is Recorded
An individual must keep a track of their annual Continuing Professional Development activities on a CPD log and must ensure it is correct, up to date and meets the requirements of their professional body or association.

The CPD activity is recorded in terms of learning outcomes and practical application of the knowledge obtained.

The Cost of Personal and Professional Development

Anything which is beneficial in our lives almost always comes at a cost and that is also true of Development. There can be a personal cost as well as a cost for the organisation. It is, however, true to say that the cost of development is often far outweighed by the benefits it brings.

The costs of development can include any or all of the following:

- *Financial cost of the training*
- *Time spent on training.*
- *Expenses involved in attending the training.*
- *The cost of providing mentors and coaches.*
- *Loss of production whilst training.*
- *Cost of replacement staff.*

There may also be additional cost regarding resources. It maybe that new software or machinery needs to be purchased to facilitate the development. It may be that structural alterations may be needed to facilitate this or additional resources such as PPE may need to be purchased. It may require that other staff need to be trained first to bring them to a standard whereby they can perform the task being left vacant by another staff member taking up their development.

Chapter 2: Business Knowledge and Understanding

Business Knowledge and Understanding

The Customer

Before any study of customer service can be undertaken, it is important to identify exactly who the customer is.

- *The customer is the most important person whether they visit the organisation in person, write or telephone.*
- *The customer is not dependent on us; the organisation is dependent on them, for its income.*
- *The customer is not an interruption to work; they are the purpose of it. They are doing us a favour by giving us the opportunity to serve them.*
- *The customer is not someone with whom to argue or match our wits. No one has ever won an argument with a customer.*
- *The customer is someone who uses an organisation because they need certain products or services. It is the role of the organisation to provide them in a mutually profitable way.*
- *The customer is not a cold statistic; they are flesh and blood human beings with emotions and prejudices.*
- *The customer is the most important person in the business, for without them there would be no business.*

All customers are different, they come from different age groups, cultural and social backgrounds and may have health, language or learning issues. Customers may also have different attitudes e.g., assertive, angry, or confused. Customers will have different timescales, some will want to grab and go, others will want to take their time to ensure they buy the right item or service. We must also remember that what is good customer service to one customer may be dreadful service to another!

We can define a customer then as

> "a person or organisation who chooses to buy or use the services or goods we provide or offer"

Business Knowledge and Understanding

Types of Customer

Even though there are so many differences in our customers, we can break down all customers into two fundamental groups. These are – Internal and External Customers.

External Customers

External Customers are those from outside the organisation who use the goods and services that the organisation offers and are dealt with in a traditional Supplier - Customer role.

Below is a typical hierarchical structural for an hotel. Look at this and notice how few people have a direct customer facing role with hotel guests and yet every single person is required to provide the goods and services, to the standards required - by the customer. The role of those who are not customer facing are just as important in achieving customer satisfaction as those on the front line.

The customer facing staff will be trained to deliver high levels of customer service, so our customers are impressed with the service they receive and are likely to recommend us to their family and friends which in turn will generate more business with more satisfied customers and so on. That does not mean that non-customer facing staff do not need customer service training. It is vital that all staff are aware of their role in delivering exceptional levels of customer service.

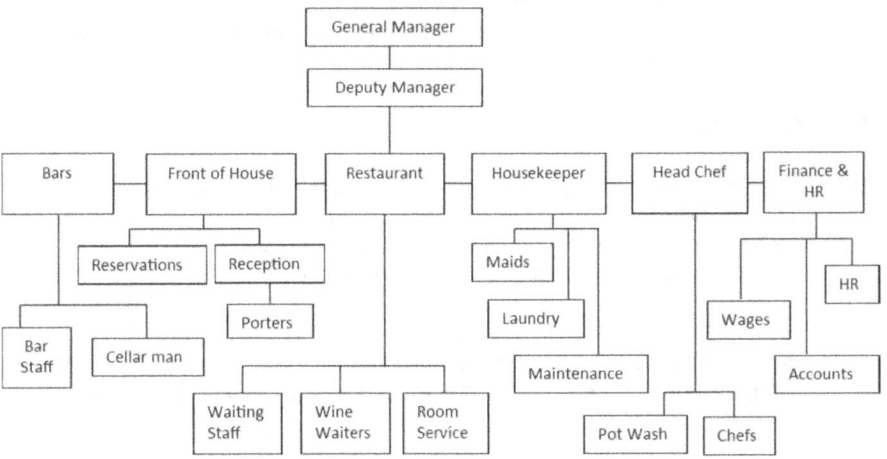

Internal Customers

Internal customers can be a more difficult concept to understand for some people. The notion that all departments are a customer of each other is difficult to grasp. It becomes easier though if we think of everyone being part of the same team. If all the members of a team work closely together, helping and supporting each other, that team will achieve far more than a team which works against each other.

Business Knowledge and Understanding

To win, a Tug o' War, the team must all pull at the same time and in the same direction. They would never win if half the team were pushing and the other half were pulling!!

To help understand this more, think about a situation where, in the structure above, the Pot washer's wages are incorrect - he will go to the Finance & HR departments to resolve it. Similarly, the Finance and HR department will go to the maintenance man when they need something repairing and so, they each become customers of the other.

In this case, the internal customers are using the goods and service from other departments. The restaurant is selling the food it gets from the kitchen. Room service delivers the food and drink it gets from the kitchen and bars. The chef obtains food from the stores and they obtain the food by arranging with the accounts department to buy it and so the relationships go on.

Although no money changes hands in internal customer transactions the transaction still takes place, and it can become frustrated, just as a sale to an external customer can cause complaints to arise. It is just as important that the relationship with internal customers is as good as the one we have with external customers. If not, our service standards will drop, the External customers will become dissatisfied and as a result, and the organisation's reputation will decline.

It is imperative that we do all we can to look after our internal customers just the same as we look after our external customers.

Other Customer Classifications

The range of customers and organisation you will be required to deal with, will represent all areas of society. They will come from different cultures, some will be customers who are returning, others will be new customers. They will approach the organisation through a whole range of different channels from face to face, to online digital channels.

All our customers will have different expectations as well as different requirements from the product or service they are buying. Some will be aggressive and demanding, others will be passive and may be reluctant to interact. Some may be affluent and others poor. The range and scope of customer types is limited only by imagination.

There will also be customers who will visit in groups rather than individually. The problem with groups is that they may all have the same basic need, but they will all have different expectations. You must try to meet all those expectations – all at the same time! This could be further complicated if they do not speak the same language or have special needs such as being deaf or blind. Their expectations will also change depending on their age, previous experiences and religion may affect expectations too.

Business Knowledge and Understanding

Needs and Expectations

Customer Needs

All customers will have needs. If they did not have a need for something, they would not be buying the services or products on offer.

Nothing is ever bought because we do not need it!

Once a need is identified, the customer will look to satisfy that need by purchasing the goods or services they have identified.

They will then begin to plan how they can make that purchase. They may look to a supplier they have used before; they may recall an advert in a magazine or the recommendation from a friend.

The needs of the customer may also affect their behaviour. A customer who rushes into a station shop to buy a sandwich before catching a train, has a need for food and wants to be able to grab the item, pay for it and still be in time to catch the train. We might expect that customer to be impatient and anxious. Conversely, a customer who is looking to buy an expensive piece of jewellery, will want to make sure they buy the perfect piece and therefore, may want to spend a considerable amount of time examining many different pieces of jewellery before deciding.

It is important that Customer Service staff look for clues as to the type, level, and standard of service the customer wants and then works to deliver it.

The problem is everyone is different! Customers all have different needs at different times, so satisfying customer needs is not always as easy as it sounds.

We all need to eat, but what we eat will be different depending on availability, price, time of day, or the time we have available – all these factors will affect, and be affected by, needs.

If we were abandoned on a desert island and we were thirsty, we could drink water from a spring in the ground – the moment we are given a choice though, some people may prefer mineral water, some people may prefer wine or beer and some champagne. In each case, the customer has an expectation, but in each case, the need is the same – they were thirsty!

If we only needed a mobile phone to make calls, we would only need one type of mobile phone. Because we want it to perform different functions, do certain tasks and look fashionably different to other phones – we now have thousands of different phones, all doing different things, in all shapes and sizes, all because, as customers, we all have different needs!

Business Knowledge and Understanding

Customer Expectations

Customers will form expectations about places they visit, things that they buy and the organisations they buy from.

These are formed by the things the customer hears and sees and having formulated those ideas, when they make the decision to buy the product or service, they will have formed an impression of what they think it may be like – in other words, they have formed an expectation.

How many times have you been disappointed by a product or service you have bought? If a film is advertised as a comedy, our expectation is it will make us laugh. If it does not – you will be disappointed and reluctant to follow advertising in future – your expectations have not been met.

If we buy the most expensive seats in a theatre, we have an expectation that they will be comfortable and have a good view of the stage.

If the customer does not get what they were expecting, they are disappointed, and the experience will not meet with their expectations.

This is not the fault of the venue or product they have bought; it is simply the expectation which the customer had formed is incorrect.

This is the challenge that is faced every day, with every customer when delivering customer service.

Customer service staff are expected to meet or exceed expectations – even though those expectations may be totally unrealistic.

It is clear that the amount of money involved in the purchase of goods or services will always influence a customers expectations. If they are paying, what they consider to be a substantial amount of money for a product or service, they will expect higher quality, closer attention to detail, etc. As a result, they will have higher expectations when they choose to buy it than perhaps someone who does not consider it to be expensive.

Price is not the only factor affecting expectation.

- *We can be told of a very nice restaurant which is not expensive and has good food*
- *We see a picture of a drink or cocktail in a glossy magazine*
- *We seem to notice most of our friends have the same mobile phone*

Business Knowledge and Understanding

In each of these cases, customer expectations are being set by others, whether they choose to believe them is a matter for them. How many times has someone recommended something to you which has turned out to be disappointing??

Customer expectations are not pre-set – they are formed through what they.....

- *see*
- *hear*
- *read*
- *the 'messages' an organisation sends i.e., via its reputation and brand*
- *what happens to them when dealing now and in the past with an organisation.*

  It is these expectations that are the basis of customer service.

While ever service levels continue to meet customer expectations, they will be happy with the service they receive, however, when the service or product falls below those expectations they will no longer be happy and they will begin to complain.

Customer expectations do not end at the point of purchase. Customer expectations will continue after the sale has been completed. Customers will have expectations of the product or service they have bought in the longer term too.

They will expect a service to be delivered in such a way that it meets their expectations and agreed timescales.

- *Any promises made during the buying process must be met.*
- *The customer will expect the purchase to represent value for money, they will expect quality and appropriate presentation.*
- *They will expect the item to be fit for purpose, they will expect it to be reliable, easy to use and to perform as specified*

These longer term expectations are the ones which, if met, will cause a customer to return and buy the same item or service again the next time they have a need for it. They will reflect on how their expectations were met, whether they have been met or exceeded and based on these new expectations, they will buy again!

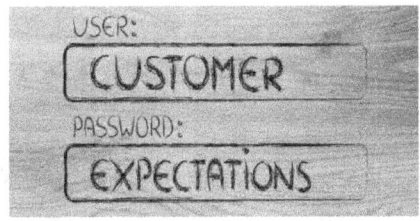

Business Knowledge and Understanding

Customer Satisfaction

Customer satisfaction is the measure of how well the expectations of the customer of a product or service provided by the organisation have been met.

Satisfied customers will spend more at a venue they are satisfied with. They will visit that venue more often. They will tell their friends and family about it and recommend that they visit too. As a result, the business becomes busier, attracts more customers, and will become more profitable over time than a business which does not satisfy its customers. Therefore, satisfying customers is very important.

Customer satisfaction is not a subject which can be easily quantified. It involves such factors as the quality of the product, the quality of the service provided, the atmosphere of the location where the product or service is delivered, and the price of the product or service.

Businesses often use customer satisfaction surveys to measure customer satisfaction. These surveys are used to gather information about customer satisfaction.

Typical areas addressed in the surveys include:

- *Quality of product*
- *Value of product relative to price - a function of quality and price*
- *Time issues, such as product availability, availability of sales assistance, time waiting at checkout, and delivery time*
- *Atmosphere of the venue, such as cleanliness, organisation, and the environment*
- *Service personnel issues, such as politeness, attentiveness, and helpfulness*
- *Convenience, such as location, parking, and hours of operation*

Customer Satisfaction should be thought of as a three-stage process.

Identify their needs
Provide for their needs
Meet their expectations

.... and they will be satisfied!

At its simplest level, this is true – the problem is, we may not always be able to satisfy their needs or meet their expectations. If their needs and expectations cannot be met, they must be offered an alternative and an explanation why it is better and how they will benefit from it.

This is the next level of customer service!

Business Knowledge and Understanding

Customer Experience

Customer experience is the impression customers have of your product or service as a whole throughout all aspects of the customer's journey.

An excellent customer experience is critical to the sustained growth of any business. An excellent customer experience promotes loyalty, helps you retain customers, and encourages brand advocacy.

Forty years ago, customers had little choice about where they bought goods or services, unless they were willing to undertake hours of laborious research. Today, they have access to a thousand sources of goods and services at their fingertips through the internet.

As a consequence, business have tried to compete on price – by being the cheapest supplier. Research, however, has shown customers are now far less price sensitive and are happy to pay more for goods and services when they are supplied on terms they demand.

The only way to gain competitive advantage today – through service excellence.

The key word here is Excellence. Good service is expected as the norm today, to stand out from the rest the level of service on offer must be the very best available for an organisation to stand out from the rest.

Good Service - is no longer good enough!

The customer today expects a seamless experience from the very first contact they have with the organisation through to the time they return to repeat the purchase.

This is known as the Customer Journey.

Service Delivery

Service delivery is a term used to describe how the customer experience is formed.

A customer may want to be served quickly; they do not want to be standing around in a queue.
They want to be served by polite staff, who know the products and services they sell and can answer technical questions, as well as routine ones and give advice to the customer when they need it.

There are four things which a customer requires from staff who serve them. If you always remember these four simple requirements, you will always be well on the way to keeping your customers happy

Business Knowledge and Understanding

- *Look at Me*
- *Smile at Me*
- *Talk to Me*
- *Thank Me*

Service delivery must also continue after the purchase has been completed. If the item proves to be faulty the customer will want a replacement or if they need technical help, they want to speak to someone who can help them.

The greater the focus placed on good service delivery, the easier it is to see that poor service delivery is all around us and the more we think about the higher standards we expect.

Think about fast food restaurants today:

- *The food is served in cardboard cartons or paper bags*
- *There is no cutlery involved*
- *There is no service in the restaurant area*
- *You clean your own tables.*
- *The food is often criticised*
- *The food never looks like it does in the picture*
- *It is not always hot, and the staff are sometimes rude and unhelpful*

Everything, in fact, we might expect would never meet customer expectations and therefore every customer would be dissatisfied. Yet fast food is one of the biggest sectors of the hospitality industry! Why is it so successful? Because it fulfils a need. The customer is usually hungry, and they do not have any expectations of the food or the visit experience.

In a survey about a major burger chain, customers said they expected the toilets to be clean and food to be served quickly. No mention of the quality of the food!

The burger chain experience is a good example of customer satisfaction. Because our expectations are so low, we are almost always satisfied, the food quality hardly matters and although we know our food will be served in cardboard box and may not be hot and served by some rude member of staff – we keep going back for more, time after, time after time.

The burger chain relies on this low expectation to keep customers satisfied but it also keeps the customers coming back!

Only when we begin to spend larger amounts of money on food do we begin to have higher expectations of the food we are served, the atmosphere and the level of service provided at the venue. Sometimes, we may have to deal with people who are buying things they do not know much about and they need advice and guidance. Some people may have a limited budget and may not be able to buy the best performing product or service and will require an alternative recommendation.

Business Knowledge and Understanding

Expectations of Internal Customers

Having considered the needs and expectations of external customers, it is also sensible to consider those of our Internal Customers.

- *We expect the wages department to their job and pay our wages every month.*
- *We expect the chef to supply the waiters with food promptly.*
- *We expect the pot wash team to wash the pots quickly so we can reuse them.*
- *We expect stores to have the components needed on demand.*
- *We expect our managers to perform effectively to ensure we are always busy, and our job is safe.*

……. and so, it goes on. Everyone has expectations of ourselves, our colleagues, our customers, and our suppliers.

Everything service interaction is based on expectations.

Failure to Meet Expectations

When expectations are not met, for whatever reason, we are not satisfied and a complaint should be expected. We can therefore state that:

If a customer's expectations are not met – they will complain

or

Customers will only be satisfied when we meet or exceed their expectations

It is vital that we know our customer's needs and expectations, so well; that we can anticipate what they are going to need and provide it in the manner they expect as far as customer service is concerned.

Some will need fast service, some will want a slow and relaxed service. The actual process of buying something can be pleasurable, especially if it is something important or expensive and people want to enjoy the experience.

Delivering Customer Service

The importance of customer service, in today's business environment, can never be underestimated.

Business Knowledge and Understanding

Constantly attracting new customers can be expensive, particularly for small businesses. Making customers feel valued and happy can be the difference between long-term success or liquidation.

85% of customers would rather spend more money with a company who consistently delivers an excellent level of customer care.

Organisations who continually treat their customers poorly, face a constant struggle to grow their business. Repeat business can only be achieved if a customer is willing to return to the organisation and is satisfied with the level of service they experience.

"It takes 20 years to build a reputation and five minutes to ruin it. If you think about that, you'll do things differently." - Warren Buffet

Ultimately, great customer service drives a brilliant customer experience, particularly when your staff exceed customer expectations by going above and beyond the call of duty.

Why do companies fail to deliver great service?

Corporate greed is a common cause. Owners setting up a business when their sole intention is only to make a profit. A recipe for failure!

On the other hand, if the primary goal is to add genuine value to customers, then the chances of growing a more profitable business becomes immensely stronger.

Customer retention is a popular and highly effective way to increase company revenue

Business Knowledge and Understanding

The Importance of Customer Service

Customer service is importance to any business because it retains customers and extracts more value from them.

By providing high levels of customer service, businesses can recover customer acquisition costs and cultivate a loyal following that refers customers, serves as case studies, and provides testimonials and reviews.

Investing in customer service helps the organisation maintain the growth momentum. Loyal customers help the organisation acquire new customers, free of charge, by convincing others to interact with the brand. Their positive testimonials will be more effective than any marketing efforts -- and cheaper, too.

89% of consumers begin doing business with a competitor following a poor customer experience.

Aside from that, there are a few more reasons why investment should be made in the customer service team.

1. Customer retention is cheaper than customer acquisition.

An increase in customer retention of just 5% can equate to an increase in profit of 25%. This is because repeat customers are more likely to spend more - 67% more, to be exact - which results in the organisation having to spend less on operating costs.

2. Customer service represents the brand image, mission, and values.

The organisation may have an idea of what the brand represents. However, the customers cannot share that idea, they will make assumptions about it based on the social media presence, advertisements, content, and other external marketing.

The customer service team is the bridge to the customers.

They have the responsibility of representing the brand to them. Without a customer service team, there is no means of direct communication.

The customer service team is essential in relaying to customers what the organisation wants the brand image to be. They can help influence customers and convince them of the organisation's strengths over competitors.

Level 3: Customer Service Specialist ver 2.0

Business Knowledge and Understanding

3. *Happy customer service employees will create happy customers.*

No employee is going to enjoy coming into work if they feel under-valued compared to employees on other teams. This applies to the customer service team as well.

87% of employees, who are happy with their jobs, are willing to work extremely hard for their business's customers.

Their reasoning behind serving customers, is less about wanting to provide quality service. Instead, it is about maintaining their professionalism and integrity, not wanting to get fired before quitting, being empathetic to customers, but getting recognition from them in the end.

A customer service team does its best work when they feel respected and appreciated. Only then will they find the motivation for doing a good job and serving their customers the right way, which will lead to your customers also feeling more respected and appreciated.

It is important to note that 55% of employees who are very unhappy with their jobs, still work especially hard for customers.

4. *Happy customers will refer others.*
When customers are happy, they are more likely to spread the goodness to friends, family, and co-workers. In fact, according to research, 77% of customers have shared positive brand experiences with others.

If a customer has a stunning experience with a brand, they are probably going to rave about it to their friends and family. It is quite natural for them to want people close to them to commit to a brand that they trust.

It is a chain reaction. If the customer service team is happy, they will work harder to satisfy and exceed the expectations of customers. Those customers will be extremely happy with the brand and refer others to it.

The customer can be the best and cheapest form of word-of-mouth advertising, - if they are given a reason to do so.

5. *Good customer service encourages customers to remain loyal.*
If a customer has a positive experience with the brand, there is no reason for them to look elsewhere. It is a lot cheaper to retain an old customer than to acquire a new one. In this sense, the higher a customer's lifetime value. This is the total revenue a company can expect

Business Knowledge and Understanding

a single customer to generate over the course of their relationship with that company - the higher the profit for the organisation.

In comparison to, possibly, hundreds of competitors with similar products and services, the organisation must do more than simply boast about the exciting features of its products.

Providing stellar customer service, can differentiate the organisation to customers.

Loyalty is rooted in trust, and customers can trust real-life humans more than the ideas and values of a brand. By interacting with the customer service team, those customers can build, hopefully, life-long relationships with the organisation.

6. Customers are willing to pay more to companies who offer better customer service.
50% of customers increase their purchasing with a brand after a positive customer service experience. In fact, 86% of customers would pay up to 25% more to get a better customer service experience. Clearly, customer service matters so much to customers that they will pay more to interact with a brand that does it well.

86% will pay more for better customer support

These are statistics that cannot be ignored. In an era where companies are learning to prioritise customer service, any organisation that does not do so will crash and burn.

Customers are influenced by even a single experience; one positive experience could be the deciding factor for them to stick to a brand, whereas one negative one could send them running to a competitor.

7. Customer service employees can offer important insights about customer experiences.
It does not matter how the organisation perceives its brand. What matters is how the customer perceives it.

If you work for a sportswear company, the organisation might associate the brand with fitness, health and wellness and people who play sports. However, the customers may purchase the brand because they associate the brand with leisure, comfort, and attractiveness. Marketing should be aligned with those values as well.

The customer service team can answer a lot of these probing questions.

Business Knowledge and Understanding

Rather than having to spend time and money on constantly surveying customers, the customer service team can simply ask questions while interacting with customers. Their response can give a great deal of insight into improving the products, marketing, goals, and employee training.

Without a solid customer service team, the brand may fall behind on shifting customer trends.

8. Customer service grows customer lifetime value.
Customer lifetime value (CLV) is a very important metric for every organisation. It represents the total revenue you it can expect from a single customer account. Growing this value means customers are shopping more frequently and/or spending more money with the organisation.

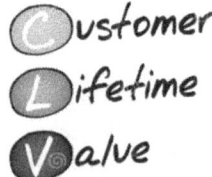

Investing in the customer service offer is an excellent way to improve customer lifetime value. If customers have a great experience with the service and support teams, they will be more likely to buy again from the organisation. Furthermore, they will share their positive experience with others, which builds rapport with the customer base.

This makes new customers more trusting of the organisation and allows sales teams to upsell and cross-sell additional products with less friction. New users will trust that the sales team is recommending products that truly fit their needs which will create a smoother buying experience for both the customer and the employees.

9. Proactive customer service creates marketing opportunities.
An organisation looking for a cost-effective way to invest in the business, should consider adopting proactive customer service.

Rather than waiting for customers to report issues, this approach reaches out to them before they even know they exist. That way, customers know the organisation is constantly working to remove roadblocks from their user experience.

Proactive customer service isn't just used for customer delight. It is also an effective marketing tool for introducing and promoting new products and services.

If an organisation creates a new feature that solves a common problem with a product, the customer service team can refer it to the customers. They can use a CRM or ticketing system to identify customers who have had this problem previously, reach out to them and

Business Knowledge and Understanding

introduce the new feature as well as its benefits. This can sometimes be more effective than a sales pitch because customers feel like the customer service representative truly understands their issue after troubleshooting their problem.

10. Excellent customer service is a competitive advantage.
No matter what industry an organisation is in, it wants its brand to stand out.

No one strives to be the "second-best" at something.

The organisation wants to be better than every other organisation they are competing with and want the customers to know it, too. This is the key to keeping customers loyal and getting them to continuously interact with the brand.

Customer service can be an excellent differentiator for your company. In fact, 60% of customers stop doing business with a brand after one poor service experience. 67% of this turnover is preventable if the customer's problem is resolved during their first interaction. That means an organisation which provides excellent customer service will not only retain customers but acquire competitors' customers as well.

Business Knowledge and Understanding

Benefits of Retaining Customers

It is undeniable that a well-trained, positive customer service team can make the organisation the best version of itself. However, it is their ability to communicate directly with customers that can totally revolutionise the organisation and grow the customer base.

Depending on the industry, it can cost up to 5 times more to attract a new customer than it costs to retain an existing customer.

On average, customers who experience poor service tell 20 other people the bad news. Do not risk losing a customer due to heated arguments or customer conflict.

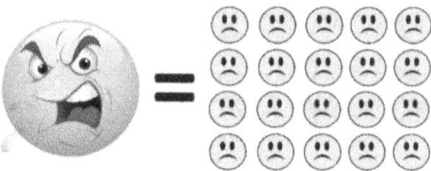

The benefit of customer retention is customers are more likely to stay loyal even if product prices increase. New customers are more price conscious whereas long serving customer value the organisation over the competitors.

Great Service Reduces Customer Conflict

All businesses experience customer complaints from time to time, it is how they are handled that separates it from its competitors.

Customers appreciate honesty, own up to the mistake and put it right immediately. Do not react in a personal manner to complaining customers, even if they become aggressive.

React and behave with a professional mind-set and avoid complaints from escalating.

Excellent Customer Service Helps Convert Interest into Sales

The customer service team can be the main difference between a prospect converting into a valuable customer or leaving the premises before they even reach the checkout. Treating customers well and creating positive interactions will help increase sales revenue due to repeat business.

On average, one happy customer can lead up to 9 referrals depending on your industry.

Business Knowledge and Understanding

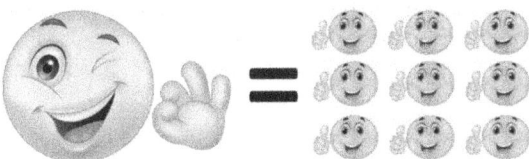

If the organisation does not take care of the customers, the competitors will.

Customer Service Excellence Reduces Staff Turnover

Employees will pay careful attention to how the organisation treats its customers.

When they see positive customer relationships, friendly communication and even banter, it makes employees feel proud to be part of a team that really cares about their roles and responsibility.

Employees are far likely to stay if respect is high on your company values.

Customer Service Excellence Raises the Brand Profile

Brand value increases through consistently delivery exceptional service to customers.

Word-of-mouth advertising is priceless. When considering why customer service is important, the reputation of the brand will trump everything else.

7 out of 10 people search for online business reviews before they make a purchase.

Before a customer contacts the organisation, they will consider or even research what other people have said before they are confident enough make a purchase. It is said that 90% of people will take the advice of friends or family when considering a purchase. Do not chase quick sales, focus on building a brand that has integrity.

Whilst businesses talk a great deal about the importance of customer service, there is a surprising amount of confusion about just how important it really is to business success. After all, some companies with notoriously bad customer service continue to prosper.

When customer service gets done properly, it can significantly boost a company's profitability. So, there is a strong, positive, relationship between customer service and business success, irrespective of how one defines "success."

Business Knowledge and Understanding

This positive correlation is not inevitable or unlimited. Some organisations have poured too many resources into improving customer service – and ended up paying the price. The key is for organisations to build customer service operations that succeed without vastly expanding the budget.

Customers Reward Good Service

Surveys drilling down on this question have found that building a strong customer service operation can increase sales, revenue, and profits.

> *70% of consumers say they have spent more money to do business with a company that delivers great service*

The value of customer service is increasing, as consumers say they are willing to spend 17% more on those businesses, up from 14% a few years ago. Part of this change is driven by millennials, who are the most willing to spend more for greater care.

A group of researchers also examined this question by digging into more than 400,000 customer service-related tweets and following up with shoppers months later. The researchers announced their finding that:

> *Customers remember good and bad customer service experiences, and they are willing to reward companies that treat them well.*

Customer Service on a Budget

The good news is that excellent customer service does not have to cost a great deal.

Many of the most important steps a business can take are free.

Organisations should help their customer service teams learn to use a personal touch, maintain a positive tone, respond promptly to queries and be proactive about resolving concerns. Providing self-service options online that are easy to navigate and actually help customers can also save time and money, removing some of the burden from customer service personnel.

Building online communities, in which users of the product post questions and offer each other ideas and advice, can also boost the experience for everyone involved.

Repeatedly, surveys are finding that shoppers believe customer service is improving. But they are also finding that customer service is becoming even more important.

Microsoft reported:

Business Knowledge and Understanding

"54% of respondents say they have higher expectations for customer service today than they had one year ago. This number jumps to 66% for the 18–34-year-olds surveyed."

Defining Business Success

The relationship between customer service and business success depends on the definition of "business success."

Business leaders, from famous ones like Bill Gates, to entrepreneurs and consultants, give different descriptions of what success means to them. More and more are focusing on social impact.

Some business leaders are now gauging customer satisfaction as a measure of business success in and of itself.

Praise from satisfied customers provides a feeling of accomplishment that, for some business owners, is as important as the financial rewards they earn.

When an organisation is on a low budget, there are probably several functions that are considered higher priority when allocating funds and it may seem like a waste to invest money in a customer service team. After all, how can it really improve?

Contrary to popular belief, the customer service team should be just as important - if not more important than the other teams. It is the direct connection between customers and the organisation.

Customer service is not just about being courteous to your customers – it is a vital element of business operations that can impact on the bottom line and affect how the organisation is viewed in the public eye. Several high-profile companies have been in the news of late because of poor customer service policies. The good news is it is relatively simple to implement a customer service improvement plan that keeps your business on top.

Customer service consists of a collective set of policies that define and govern every way in which you and your employees interact with your customers. It encompasses everything from how much parking you have available, to how you greet customers, handle service complaints, and back up your product or service. At its core, quality customer service is about making sure your customers feel they are valued, treated fairly, and appreciated by your business.

Business Knowledge and Understanding

The Impact of Negativity

Customers frequently share their opinions of businesses online and through social media, which means even one wrong move or perceived slight – especially one caught on camera – can spread quickly and damage an organisation. In addition to providing high-quality service, monitoring what is being said about an organisation online can allow the issue to be quickly addressed and resolve complaints as they arise.

Many businesses are competing for the same customer pound and customer loyalty. Chances are good that an organisation is investing in marketing and advertising to bring consumers through the doors. The key part of customer service is keeping the customers once they have passed through the door.

It costs significantly more to attract new customers than it does to take care of the ones already held.

Customer service is also important to reducing staff turnover. Employees who deal with unhappy customers are unlikely to enjoy their jobs for long and will leave to search for more hospitable working environments.

Business Knowledge and Understanding

Providing Exceptional Service

Good service starts with organisational values and employee training. Good service starts at the top and permeates downwards. Employees who are specifically trained in the delivery of quality customer service are far more likely to represent an organisation in a way that ensures satisfaction and repeat business.

Develop customer service policies: Implement service policies that address every conceivable aspect of the customer experience. This includes how quickly the phone is answered or website or email questions are responded to, how many help desk operators you have on busy days, how generous the return or exchange policy is, and how irate customers are handled.

Consider situations from a customer's perspective and brainstorm every potential scenario the organisation could encounter, and then develop customer-friendly ways to address them. Involve all staff in the process – it will provide fresh ideas as well as buy-in to the customer service concept.

Recruit well: When you interview candidates, ask them what quality customer service means to them. Pose sticky customer scenarios and ask them how they would respond to the situation. This gives you an idea of whether the people you hire for your front lines will represent your business in a way you find acceptable.

Provide customer service training: Train employees on customer service policies. Make customer service training an ongoing part of an organisation's professional development program so that staff are continually urged to up their games.

Business Knowledge and Understanding

The Importance of Consistency in Customer Service

It is one thing to deliver good service to a customer, but quite another to achieve this with regular consistency. However, it is exactly this kind of consistency that today's customer demands.

A customer focussed organisation will always be aware of the important role excellent customer service plays in its success.

It is critical to understand that winning customers and building loyalty takes time and to build good customer relationships, an organisation needs to deliver consistent service if it is to retain customer's hard-won loyalty.

It is also important to understand just how fragile customer relationships can be. It is far easier to lose a customer due to poor service and issues not quickly resolved to the customer's satisfaction, than it is to obtain loyalty in the first place.

Customers value consistency from their service providers because they base their expectations on previous positive experiences. Therefore, it is crucial to not only deliver good customer service at the first meeting, but to keep on delivering service at the same level, every time, if you are to continue ensuring customer satisfaction.

This means an organisation will need to focus on making sure its interactions with customers are consistent and quality based. It is only logical that a consumer's confidence in an organisation will increase if it delivers a consistent level of quality in its service – achieving this ensures that the customer feels valued by the organisation.

No enterprise is perfect, and customers understand that. However, they are more likely to forgive an occasional mishap, provided the problem is handled quickly and with care. What customers will not tolerate is any kind of rudeness, neglect, or failure to deliver on promises.

This is why consistency is so important. Customers need to know that an organisation will deliver on its promises every time, rather than only when it may be convenient for it to do so. This is brought into perspective by the fact that customers, on average, will tell fewer than 10 other people about good service they have received, whereas the number is closer to 20 when it comes to letting people know about a bad experience.

Business Knowledge and Understanding

Creating Consistency in Customer Service

It is necessary for employees across the organisation, from salespeople to customer service staff, to meet regularly to share problems and possible solutions to customer service-related issues.

A critical element of consistency lies in breaking down silos between departments. Furthermore, an organisation can conduct online surveys and invite customers to provide feedback on their experiences with the organisation, to learn what is most important to them.

Once aware of what the key issues are, they can be fixed immediately. In addition, monitor customers on all their social streams to catch praise or dissatisfaction, both of which can be learned from.

Always provide customers with a time frame for expecting a response and consider setting up automated responses to incoming client emails, to ensure nothing falls through the cracks.

When it comes to demonstrating an organisation's consistency in customer service, there are three key areas of focus. Naturally, there needs to be focus on delivering customer journey consistency. This means having clear policies, rules, and supporting mechanisms to ensure consistency during every interaction with a customer.

Since the customer journey usually involves different parts of the organisation, an organisation may need to specifically create internal teams that are responsible for the end-to-end customer journey across these functions.

Organisations operate in a multi-channel world, and it is crucial to ensure that whatever channel, or even multiple channels, the customer chooses to use, they receive the same level of service across each one. The greater the variance in their experience, the less likely it is that the customer will ultimately being happy with the service received – variability is, after all, the very opposite of consistency.

The second area of focus needs to be emotional consistency. An organisation always needs to create a positive customer emotion. This builds trust and helps forge a deeper and more meaningful relationship with clients. The greater the emotional connection between the customer and an organisation, the higher the customer loyalty. Nothing is more trustworthy than consistency.

Finally, the organisation should focus on delivering communication consistency. The brand is driven by more than simply promises made and promises kept. It is also about ensuring that customers recognise when an organisation has delivered on those promises. This means an organisation should proactively shape key messages and customer communications to consistently highlight such delivery.

Business Knowledge and Understanding

Focus on Continuous Improvement

Achieving excellence in customer service will mean an organisation must constantly track progress, effectiveness and predict opportunities, which may require it to rethink both its metrics and analytics, to properly report on the customer journey, rather than individual touchpoints.

Furthermore, it is critical to immediately fix those areas where negative experiences have been identified as being a common occurrence. Reducing bad experiences, even when service is not necessarily at an exceptional level yet, will help to give the customer a stronger feeling of consistency.

Perhaps most importantly of all, an organisation must bear in mind that the overall customer journey includes much more than just the customer service aspect. Everything from pre-sale engagement through to after-sales service forms part of this journey. True consistency will encompass every single aspect of the organisation.

Customers today have far more control than they did in the past. They are also increasingly perceptive and pay attention to every little detail. Therefore, an organisation simply cannot afford to compromise on any component of the customer journey. Customers expect the same level of service quality across every stage of the customer journey. The only road to true success is to pay attention to detail, offer the highest quality service possible and ensure that every member of the team stays focused on maintaining the high standards set for the organisation. There is little doubt that customers today expect that – as an absolute minimum.

Continuous Improvement

Have you ever corrected a spelling mistake in one of your organisation's documents or manuals? Have you ever added a new step to a process that that was not included before? What about updating how you do things to take advantage of better tools or software?

All of these and more are examples of continuous improvement.

Business Knowledge and Understanding

Continuous improvement is used to make sure that processes, methods, and practices are as efficient, accurate, and effective as possible by routinely examining and improving your processes to eliminate bottlenecks in processes, use the best software for the tasks, and take advantage of the most efficient methods.

Areas such as sales, quoting for new business, running credit checks in accounts, effective customer service practices and engineering flexibility to configure specific customer requests are all areas for continuous improvement focus. Improvements in these areas can impress new customers and elevate your business above your competitors.

Continuous improvement has become an integral part of every successful organisation, regardless of the industry involved. It is true to say that continuous improvement was born in automotive production, the Japanese company Toyota leading the way.

> *"Being satisfied with the status quo means you are not making progress"*
> - Katsuaki Watanabe, CEO of Toyota Motor Corporation

Toyota recognised that processes, products and services are never perfect, and they must be constantly and relentlessly improved on a never-ending basis. This continuous improvement also based on developing and continuously improving people's capabilities.

Business Knowledge and Understanding

The Concept of Continuous Improvement

The concept of continuous improvement started in the car factories of Japan. Continuous improvement strives to identify opportunities for ensuring the organisation is continuously, as efficient as it can be.

This involves the continual reassessment of processes, products, and services to ensure that output is maximised, and waste is minimised. The key here being the word continual – the challenge never stops – it never reaches an end. It must also be embedded into the culture of the organisation – it must become part of the working routine.

Continuous improvement must become part of the way the business operates, everyone must be on board. Creating a culture of improvement must be a priority to make it work. This can be done by empowering everyone within an organisation to understand that they can point out places for development to spark positive change.

Continuous improvement means to constantly strive to improve the products or service to achieve the highest standards.

It is a process which, in the long term, achieves:

- *Customer focus*
- *Enhanced quality of service delivery*
- *Simplified processes and procedures*
- *Attitudinal change*
- *Recognition of customers, both internal and external*

Continuous improvement today, is a necessity. As companies compete for survival and for market dominance, they must consider:

- *Ever higher productivity*
- **That customer loyalty is decreasing;** customers now look for what product or service best meets their needs, not who is offering it
- *Product life cycles are decreasing*
- *Aiming for zero defects*
- *The effect of technology on business and customers*
- *That those who cannot maintain improvement are falling behind*

Through the continuous assessment and enhancement of products, processes, procedures and attitudes, an environment can be developed where all team members strive for greater levels of quality and customer service.

Business Knowledge and Understanding

Improving Quality

'Quality' is normally defined in terms of what the customer needs or expects. This includes:

Timeliness: how long a customer must wait for service, and if it is completed on time; and whether a product is available when it is required
Completeness: providing everything the customer asked for or expected.
Courtesy: behaviour of the service-provider toward customers
Consistency: expectation that the service will be provided the same way each time
Accessibility and convenience: ease of obtaining the service
Accuracy: correctness of the service performed, or information provided (particularly important for professional services, like accounting, physician, and lawyer services)
Responsiveness: reaction of service-provider to unusual or unexpected customer requests
Cost: associated with the product or service and whether it is perceived 'value for money'

Because customers always expect high quality, the cost of poor-quality goods or services can be far greater than the cost of 'doing it right the first time'.

There are different approaches to quality:

Quality Control
Standards are set which determine the acceptable quality of the product or service:

- *Products and services are measured against the standard*
- *Non-conforming products and services are scrapped, reworked, or changed until the standards are met*

Quality Assurance
Quality controls and methods are fully documented to ensure that products and services:

- *Are fit for their designated purpose*
- *Will meet the customer's needs and expectations every time*

Total Quality Management
Commitment to excellence by all levels of the organisation:

- *Incorporates all aspects of control and assurance measures*
- *Continuous improvement is the cornerstone of the business*
- *There is no endpoint to continuous improvement*

Business Knowledge and Understanding

Customer Focus is Key

The success of any business is based on the customers.

No customers, No business!

It is therefore, primarily, on the customers that continuous improvement efforts should be focused.

We often get caught up in telling everyone how great our products and services are in relation to the competition, but we tend to forget that the organisation exists because customers want a solution to their particular problem, not just a product or service. The continuous improvement effort must be focused on delivering that solution.

There are many areas in every organisation where improvements can be made that will help to solve customer problems, and most of these are not on the factory floor. Whether it is reducing the response time on customer enquiries or quote requests, customising products to exactly what customers need to solve their problems, reducing delivery lead times or ensuring that products and services are defect-free, the continuous improvement process needs to be focused on what the customer actually requires, not the organisation's perception of what is required.

Many companies are reporting that existing customers are not buying more products or services than they have before, so the only way a business can grow is by finding new customers for their products and services and making sure they are as accessible as they can be. The organisation must identify, satisfy and deliver against that customer need faster than the competition or the business will be lost.

Many of the customer-facing functions of the organisation that contribute to fast, flexible, and efficient delivery of products and services to new customers are in the administrative, R&D and engineering areas, not on the factory floor. It is in those areas that continuous improvement efforts will deliver the greatest returns.

Business Knowledge and Understanding

The Continuous Improvement Model

One of the more common process improvement tools is the "Plan Do Check Act" cycle (PDCA). This cycle is credited to Dr. William Edwards Deming and Walter Shewhart. This four-step model is often shown as a circle because continuous improvement is a process that should be repeated.

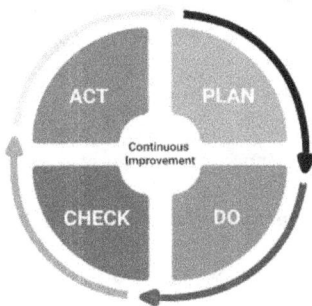

Here is a closer look at each of the steps of the PDCA Cycle and what they involve:

Plan
In this first part of the cycle, you will identify the opportunity present and create a plan for improvement. You can begin by defining the problem, outlining the opportunity present, brainstorming ideas, and developing a plan. You should also state what your desired outcome is once your problem is resolved.

Do
Now that you have identified a possible solution you need to implement this plan on a smaller scale. This will allow you to test your solution and figure out whether your changes achieved your desired outcome. Testing your solution in this way will be a good way to see if it works or not without making any major disruptions.

Check
During this stage, you will compare your results to the expected outcome you outlined in the planning phase. If your expected outcome was not achieved, you should start the cycle over again. If it does work, you can continue to the fourth stage of the cycle.

Act
During the final stage, you will implement your solution on a wider scale. However, keep in mind that PDCA is not a one-time initiative. Whenever there is an opportunity for improvement within the company, you will need to repeat the process.

Business Knowledge and Understanding

Types of Process Improvement

There are other, widely used, methods of continuous improvement, such as Six Sigma, Lean, and Total Quality Management. Each one emphasises employee involvement and teamwork, work to measure and standardise processes, reduce variation, defects, and process times. These are explained briefly below.

LEAN Technology: *Created by Toyota to optimise its production cycle, LEAN improvement is customer focused. It defines what customers value from the process most to determine what can be eliminated from the production of a product to decrease waste and cut costs.*

Six Sigma: *Six Sigma is a method that focuses on improving the quality of business processes. It is aimed at limiting the variation in processes to ensure consistency and increase performance. It uses statistics to measure deviations from a defined centre line on a control chart.*

Total Quality Management: *With some similarity to Six Sigma, Total Quality Management (TCM) holds all involved parties responsible for producing quality outputs. It looks to standardise processes to reduce errors.*

Getting Started with Continuous Improvement

It is important that the implementation of Continuous improvement is done is such a way that it becomes embedded into the culture of the organisation. If not, it will become a five-minute wonder which will be forgotten and ignored. Below are some ideas how the concept can begin to be implemented into the organisation and its culture.

Think Tanks
Setting up regular think tanks and brain storming sessions can benefit the organisation enormously. They can be run with a specific outcome in mind or simply to engage key personnel so that valuable ideas are discussed. During these sessions, you can explain how processes are currently being run to see if there are places that need to be improved and changes made.

Surveys and Suggestions
The people who work within the organisation are the most informed and know where improvements can be made. It is not only important to gain feedback from customers and vendors, but important and often overlooked is employee feedback. By asking the team, you can find out their points of issue and identify places for improvement.

Monthly Training
In large organisations it is common that employees work within a silo or prescribed activity. Cross-training and process documentation can contribute to process improvement. For example, if you train employees how to do multiple jobs, if someone is absent because of sickness or holiday, the process will be unaffected by the absence.

Business Knowledge and Understanding

Furthermore, if the process has been documented, the process can be run by virtually anyone with access.

Time Audits
One of the most significant resources wasted within a business is time. Being able to accurately measure how much time a process takes can offer insight into where it can be optimised. It can be as simple as using a stopwatch to time a process. Then analyse how long processes takes and find ways to eliminate wasted time. This could be in the form of automating some stages and/or reducing touchpoints, thereby preventing potential bottlenecks and delays from occurring.

Catch ball
Within organisations, a process is rarely started and completed by one person. Every process needs to have someone who can be held responsible for its completion, but the process itself still requires the input and assistance of multiple people. "Catch ball" is a method of continuous improvement that requires the person who initiated a process to explain its purpose and concerns to the others involved clearly. In this way, they can then "throw" it out to the group for feedback and ideas for improvement, yet the single person remains responsible for its completion.

The above are just some ideas to get continuous improvement started within an organisation.

Business Knowledge and Understanding

Implementing Continuous Improvement

As mentioned above, continuous process improvement does not have a clear beginning and end. Instead, it is part of the organisational culture and involves everyone within it.

Below are some suggestions how to integrate continuous improvement into an organisation:

1. **Manageable improvements**
   Set reasonable goals. When setting out for improvement, you want to break down larger projects into smaller, measurable pieces. This will help to reduce the scale of the task, as well as keep everyone involved on the right track to succeed.

2. **Seek Feedback**
   You should continuously seek feedback from customers, stakeholders, and employees throughout your operations. This feedback will not only help locate opportunities for improvement, but it can also offer new perspectives and breed new ideas.

3. **Motivate employees**
   Not only should you breed a culture where each employee feels empowered to notice inefficiencies and offer solutions, but you should also develop a rewarding culture to be motivational. For example, you can create rewards or develop an accessible system for employees to share feedback continuously.

Benefits of Continuous Improvement

Your business may be doing well now, but that is not going to last forever.

A changing economy, new technology, budgetary concerns, and staff shortages are all factors that will eventually force the organisation to make changes. An organisation that embraces continuous improvements will be able to act on these changes and stay on course. A rigid, authoritarian, inflexible company, on the other hand, will not.

Continuous improvement allows businesses to uncover problems and find ways to fix them. Small, positive changes made over time can dramatically impact a business's overall process. Continuous improvement can significantly benefit the organisation over time by:

Increased Productivity & Profitability
The incremental improvement of processes will lead to increases in production, reduction in time allocation leading to greater efficiency, which ultimately translates into higher profits.

Employee Morale and Accountability
Employees already know how to improve processes or products. A rigid organisational structure, however, can silence them and destroy their motivation.

Business Knowledge and Understanding

An organisation with a culture of continuous improvement, will ensure every employee is a key factor to organisational growth. Allowing employees to demonstrate their knowledge and go the extra mile by contributing to improving the process, makes them feel valued, increasing overall morale and accountability.

Greater Agility
An organisation must evolve all the time to stay ahead of the competition. If employees are used to things changing on a regular basis, they will not be phased during times of crisis and change.

They will embrace change and pro-actively support it rather than working against it, leading to an organisation which is agile and able to adapt to ever changing needs at will.

Business Knowledge and Understanding

Models of Continuous Improvement

We know that Continuous Improvement is an active, intentional practice, which should, cover the whole organisation. This continuous process of improvement can be very difficult to both set up and maintain unless there is structure applied to it. This structure is put in place by frameworks or models and most organisations with a commitment to continuous improvement, will adopt a model to manage the process.

The models vary in their rigidity of structure, but generally all aim to eliminate waste and improve quality and efficiency of work processes.

There are many models available which have evolved into what they are today, from a small number of original models.

These were commonly founded in the automotive industry and subsequently further developed for use by software development houses. More recently these models have been developed and refined to suit many different and diverse industries, but they all have their roots in the original models. Some examples of these are shown below

Route Cause Analysis Model (RCA)

Root cause analysis (RCA) is a systematic process for identifying the "root causes" of problems or events and an approach for responding to them.

RCA is based on the basic idea that effective management requires more than simply "putting out fires" for problems which arise, but rather finding a way to prevent them altogether.

RCA helps pinpoint the factors which cause or contribute to a problem or event

RCA helps organisations avoid the tendency to single out one factor to arrive at the easiest (but generally incomplete) solution. It also helps to avoid treating the symptoms rather than true, underlying problems that cause the problem or event.

Most RCA experts believe that achievement of total prevention by a single intervention is not always possible and see RCA as an ongoing process that strives for continuous improvement.

The primary goal of using RCA is to analyse problems or events to identify:

- *What happened*
- *How it happened*
- *Why it happened...so that*
- *Actions for preventing reoccurrence are developed*

Implementing RCA will help:

- *Identify barriers and the causes of problems, so that permanent solutions can be found.*

Business Knowledge and Understanding

- *Develop a logical approach to problem-solving, using data that already exists in the agency.*
- *Identify current and future needs for organisational improvement.*
- *Establish repeatable, step-by-step processes, in which one process can confirm the results of another.*

Principles of Root Cause Analysis

- *Focusing on corrective measures of root causes is more effective than simply treating the symptoms of a problem or event.*
- *RCA is performed most effectively when accomplished through a systematic process with conclusions backed up by evidence.*
- *There is usually more than one root cause for a problem or event.*
- *The focus of investigation and analysis through problem identification is WHY the event occurred, and not who made the error.*

Origins of RCA

Root cause analysis is not a one-size-fits-all methodology. There are many different tools, processes, and philosophies of accomplishing RCA. In fact, it was born out of a need to analyse various enterprise activities such as:

- *Accident analysis and occupational safety and health*
- *Quality control*
- *Efficient business process*
- *Engineering and maintenance failure analysis*
- *Various systems-based processes, including change management and risk management*

Applying RCA

Examples of events where RCA is used to solve problems and provide preventive actions include:

- *Major accidents*
- *Everyday incidents*
- *Minor near-misses*
- *Human errors*
- *Maintenance problems*
- *Medical mistakes*

Business Knowledge and Understanding

- Productivity issues
- Manufacturing mistakes
- Environmental releases
- Risk analysis, risk mapping

Basic method to use

- Define the problem.
- Gather information, data, and evidence.
- Identify all issues and events that contributed to the problem.
- Determine root causes.
- Identify recommendations for eliminating or mitigating the reoccurrence of problems or events.
- Implement the identified solutions.

RCA methods

The nature of RCA is to identify all and multiple contributing factors to a problem or event. This is most effectively accomplished through an analysis method. Some methods used in RCA include:

- **The "5-Whys" Analysis** — A simple problem-solving technique that helps users get to the root of the problem quickly. It was made popular in the 1970's by the Toyota Production System. This strategy involves looking at a problem and asking "why" and "what caused this problem". Often the answer to the first "why" prompts a second "why" and so on—providing the basis for the "5-why" analysis.

- **Barrier Analysis** — Investigation or design method that involves the tracing of pathways by which a target is adversely affected by a hazard, including the identification of any failed or missing countermeasures that could or should have prevented the undesired effect(s).

- **Change Analysis** — Looks systematically for possible risk impacts and appropriate risk management strategies in situations where change is occurring. This includes situations in which system configurations are changed, operating practices or policies are revised, new or different activities will be performed, etc.

- **Causal Factor Tree Analysis** — An investigation and analysis technique used to record and display, in a logical, tree-structured hierarchy, all the actions and conditions that were necessary and sufficient for a given consequence to have occurred.

Business Knowledge and Understanding

- **Failure Mode and Effects Analysis** — A "system engineering" process that examines failures in products or processes.

- **Fish-Bone Diagram or Ishikawa Diagram** — Derived from the quality management process, it is an analysis tool that provides a systematic way of looking at effects and the causes that create or contribute to those effects. Because of the function of the fishbone diagram, it may be referred to as a cause-and-effect diagram.

- **Pareto Analysis** — A statistical technique in decision making that is used for analysis of selected and a limited number of tasks that produce significant overall effect. The premise is that 80% of problems are produced by a few critical causes (20%).

- **Fault Tree Analysis** — The event is placed at the root (top event) of a "tree of logic". Each situation causing effect is added to the tree as a series of logic expressions.

Total Quality Management Model (TQM)

TQM was developed by William Deming, a management consultant whose work had a great impact on Japanese manufacturing. While TQM has much in common with the Six Sigma quality process, it is not the same as Six Sigma. TQM focuses on ensuring that internal guidelines and process standards reduce errors, while Six Sigma looks to reduce defects.

Total quality management (TQM) is a structured approach to organisational management. The purpose of the process is to improve the quality of the organisation's outputs, including goods and services, through the continual improvement of internal practices. The standards set as part of the TQM approach can reflect both internal priorities and any industry standards currently in place.

TQM places emphasis on fact-based decision making, using performance metrics to monitor progress; high levels of inter-organisational communication are encouraged to maintain employee involvement and morale.

- *Total quality management (TQM) is an ongoing process of detecting and reducing or eliminating errors.*
- *It is used to streamline supply chain management, improve customer service, and ensure that employees are trained.*
- *The focus is to improve the quality of an organisation's outputs, including goods and services, through continual improvement of internal practices.*
- *Total quality management aims to hold all parties involved in the production process accountable for the overall quality of the final product or service.*

Business Knowledge and Understanding

While TQM originated in the manufacturing sector, its principles can be applied to a variety of industries. TQM focusses on long-term change rather than short-term goals. Because the change affects the whole of the organisation, TQM is used in many industries, especially in manufacturing, banking and finance, and medicine.

Primary elements of TQM

TQM is simply a management system for a customer-focused organisation which involves all employees in a cycle of continuous improvement. It uses strategy, data, and effective communications to integrate the quality discipline into the culture and activities of the organisation. Here are the 8 principles of total quality management:

1. **Customer-focused:** *The customer ultimately determines the level of quality. No matter what an organisation does to foster quality improvement—training employees, integrating quality into the design process, or upgrading computers or software—the customer determines whether the efforts were worthwhile.*

2. **Total employee involvement:** *All employees participate in working toward the common goals. Employees will only commit to a quality regime when fear has been driven from the workplace, when empowerment has occurred, and when management has provided the proper environment. High-performance systems of work integrate continuous improvement efforts into normal business operations.*

3. **Process-centred:** *A process is a series of steps that take inputs from suppliers (internal or external) and transforms them into outputs that are delivered to customers (internal or external). The steps required to carry out the process are defined, and performance measures are continuously monitored to detect unexpected variation.*

4. **Integrated system:** *An organisation will consist of many different functional specialisms usually organised into vertically structured departments, but it is the horizontal processes interconnecting these functions that are the focus of TQM.*

    - Micro-processes add up to larger processes, and these larger processes combine into the business processes necessary to meet the organisational strategy. Everyone must understand the vision, mission, and guiding principles as well as the quality policies, objectives, and critical processes of the organisation. Business performance must be monitored and communicated continuously.
    - An integrated business system may be modelled on the ISO 9000 standards. Every organisation has a unique work culture, and it is virtually impossible to achieve excellence in its products and services unless a good quality culture has been created.

5. **Strategic and systematic approach:** *A critical part of the management of quality is the strategic and systematic approach to achieving an organisation's vision, mission, and goals. This process, called strategic planning or strategic management, includes the*

Business Knowledge and Understanding

formulation of a strategic plan that integrates quality as a core component.

6. **Continual improvement:** *TQM drive is continuous process of improvement. In turn, this drives an organisation to be both analytical and creative in finding ways to become more competitive and more effective at meeting stakeholder expectations.*

7. **Fact-based decision-making** *TQM requires that an organisation continually collects and analyses data to improve decision making accuracy, achieve consensus, and allow prediction based on history*

8. **Communications:** *Whether in times of change or day to day operation, during times of organisational change, as well as part of day-to-day operation, effective communications plays a large part in maintaining morale and in motivating employees at all levels. Communications must include strategies, method, and timeliness.*

These elements are considered so essential to TQM that many organisations use them as a set of core values and principles on which the organisation operates. The methods for implementing this approach come from the teachings of such quality leaders as Philip B. Crosby, W. Edwards Deming, Armand V. Feigenbaum, Kaoru Ishikawa, and Joseph M. Juran.

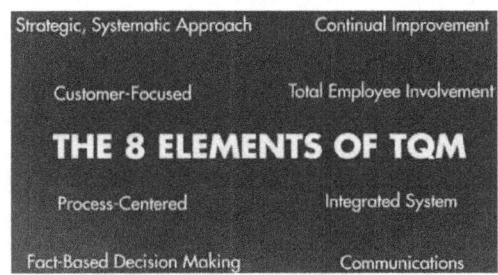

Business Knowledge and Understanding

Six Sigma

Six Sigma is simply a set of management tools and techniques designed to improve business by reducing the likelihood of error.

It is a data-driven approach that uses a statistical methodology for eliminating defects. This increase in performance and decrease in process variation helps lead to defect reduction and improvement in profits, employee morale, and quality of products or services.

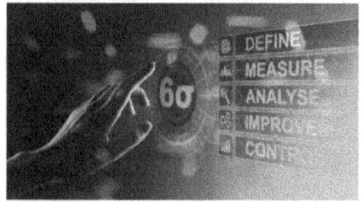

The American company Motorola developed a new concept of quality management process in 1986. Over the years, it has been refined and polished into a sound theory of principles and methods, aimed at business transformation through a clearly defined process. This finished product is Six Sigma

Sigma, besides being a Greek letter, is also a statistical term which is used to measure the deviation from a mean or target. There is a curve in statistics which is called a bell curve which symbolises the deviation from the mean. One Sigma symbolises a single standard deviation from the mean and if the process has six sigmas – three above the mean and three below, it means that the defect rate is extremely low.

The graph of the normal distribution below underscores the statistical assumptions of the Six Sigma model. The higher the standard deviation, the higher is the spread of values encountered. So, processes, where the mean is minimum 6σ away from the closest specification limit, are aimed at Six Sigma.

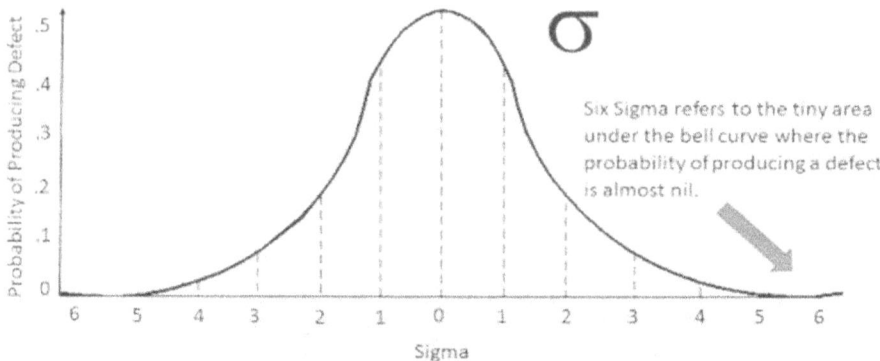

Six Sigma refers to the tiny area under the bell curve where the probability of producing a defect is almost nil.

Business Knowledge and Understanding

The 5 Key Principles of Six Sigma

The concept of Six Sigma has a simple goal – delivering near-perfect goods and services for business transformation for optimal customer satisfaction.

Goals are achieved through a two-pronged approach:

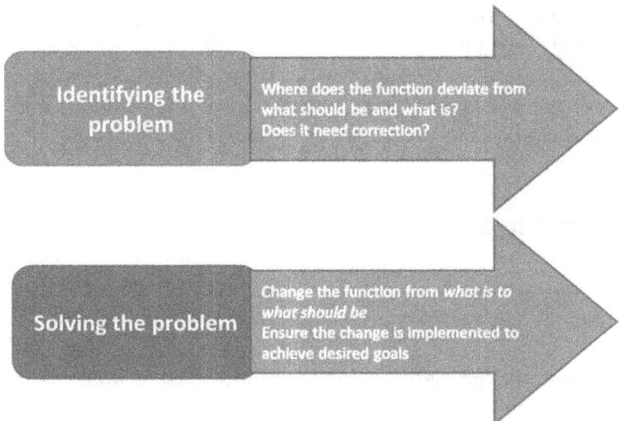

Six Sigma has its foundations in five key principles:

Be Customer-centric
This is based on the popular belief that the "customer is the king." The primary goal is to bring maximum benefit to the customer. For this, a business must understand its customers, their needs, and what drives sales or loyalty. This is necessary to define the standard of quality by what the customer or market demands.

Identify the Problem
Map the steps in each process to determine areas of waste. Collect data to identify the problem that is to be addressed or transformed. Define the overview to be achieved from the data collected, define the accuracy of measurements to be used, and create a standardised data collection system. Ascertain if the data is helping to identify the problem, whether the data needs to be refined, or additional information collected. Identify the problem. Ask questions and find the root cause.

Eliminate Waste
Once the root cause is identified, make changes to the process to eliminate variation, thus removing the defect. Remove activities in the process that do not add to the customer value. If the value stream does not reveal where the problem lies, tools are used to help discover the problem areas. Streamline functions to achieve quality control and efficiency. By removing bottlenecks in the process, waste is removed.

Maintain Involvement
Involve all stakeholders. Adopt a structured process where your team contributes and collaborates their varied expertise for problem-solving. Six Sigma processes can have a

Business Knowledge and Understanding

great impact on an organisation, so the team must be proficient in the principles and methodologies used. Hence, specialised training and knowledge are required to reduce the risk of project or re-design failures and ensure that the process performs optimally.

Ensure a Flexible and Responsive Ecosystem

The essence of Six Sigma is business transformation and change. When a faulty or inefficient process is removed, it calls for a change in work practice and employee approach. A robust culture of flexibility and responsiveness to change in procedures can ensure streamlined project implementation. Stakeholders involved should be able to adapt to change with ease. To facilitate this, processes should be designed for a quick and seamless adoption. The organisation that focusses on the data examines the bottom line periodically and adjusts its processes where necessary, will gain a competitive edge.

The Six Sigma Methodology

The two main Six Sigma methodologies are DMAIC and DMADV. Each has its own set of recommended procedures to be implemented for business transformation.

>   *DMAIC* - is a data-driven method used to improve existing products or services for better customer satisfaction. It is the acronym for the five phases: D – Define, M – Measure, A – Analyse, I – Improve, C – Control.
>   DMAIC is applied in the manufacturing of a product or delivery of a service.

>   *DMADV* - is a part of the Design for Six Sigma (DFSS) process used to design or re-design different processes of product manufacturing or service delivery. The five phases of DMADV are: D – Define, M – Measure, A – Analyse, D – Design, V – Validate.

DMADV is employed when existing processes do not meet customer conditions, even after optimisation, or when it is required to develop new methods.

The Six Sigma Process of Business Transformation

Although Six Sigma uses various methods to discover deviations and solve problems, the DMAIC is the standard methodology used by Six Sigma practitioners.

Six Sigma uses a data-driven management process used for optimising and improving business processes. The underlying framework is a strong customer focus and robust use of data and statistics.

Business Knowledge and Understanding

The Six Sigma Process of the DMAIC method has five phases:

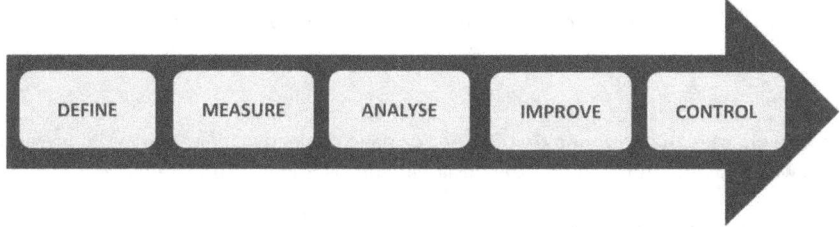

Each of the above phases of business transformation has several steps:

Define
The Six Sigma process begins with a customer-centric approach.

Step 1: The business problem is defined from the customer perspective.
Step 2: Goals are set. What do you want to achieve? What are the resources you will use to achieve the goals?
Step 3: Map the process. Verify with the stakeholders that you are on the right track.

Measure
The second phase is focused on the metrics of the project and the tools used in the measurement. How can you improve? How can you quantify this?

Step 1: Measure your problem in numbers or with supporting data.
Step 2: Define the measure for acceptable performance
Step 3: Evaluate the measurement system to be used. Can it help you achieve your outcome?

Analyse
The third phase analyses the process to discover the influencing variables.

Step 1: Determine if your process is efficient and effective. Does the process help achieve what you need?
Step 2: Quantify your goals in numbers. For instance, reduce defective goods by 20%
Step 3: Identify variations using historical data.

Improve
This process investigates how the changes impact. This phase is where you identify how you can improve the process implementation.

Step 1: Identify possible reasons. Identify the variable which is causing the problem
Step 2: Discover relationships between the variables

Business Knowledge and Understanding

Step 3: Establish process tolerance, defined as the precise values that certain variables can have, and still fall within acceptable boundaries, for instance, the quality of any given product. What operating conditions can impact the outcome?

Control

In this final phase, you determine that the performance objective identified in the previous phase is well implemented and that the designed improvements are sustainable.

Step 1: Validate the measurement system to be used.
Step 2: Establish process capability. Is the goal being met? For instance, will the goal of reducing defective goods by 20 percent be achieved?
Step 3: Once the previous step is satisfied, implement the process.

Crosby's 14 Steps

Quality, Crosby emphasised, is neither intangible nor immeasurable. It is a strategic imperative that can be quantified and put back to work to improve the bottom line.

Acceptable quality or defect levels and traditional quality control measures represent evidence of failure rather than assurance of success.

The emphasis, for Crosby, is on prevention, not inspection and cure. The goal is to meet requirements on time, first time and every time. He believes that the prime responsibility for poor quality lies with management, and that management sets the tone for the quality initiative from the top.

Crosby's approach to quality is clear. In his view, good, bad, high and low quality are meaningless concepts, and the meaning of quality is conformance to requirements.

Non-conforming products are ones that management has failed to specify or control. The cost of non-conformance equals the cost of not doing it right first time, and not rooting out any defects in processes.

Zero defects does not mean that people never make mistakes, but that companies should not begin with allowances or sub-standard targets with mistakes as a contingent expectation. Instead, work should be a series of activities or processes, defined by clear requirements, carried out to produce identified outcomes.

Crosby asserts that systems that allow things to go wrong - so things must be done again - can cost organisations between 20% and 35% of their revenues.

The 14 Steps to Quality Improvement are Crosby's recipe for long-term process improvement. His opinion was that these steps were the responsibility of management but

Business Knowledge and Understanding

involved the people who did the work. These steps provided guidelines as well as a method for communicating his Four Absolutes.

The 14 Steps

1. **Management commitment:** The need for quality improvement must be recognised and adopted by management, with an emphasis on the need for defect prevention. Quality improvement equates with profit improvement. A quality policy is needed which states that '... each individual is expected to perform exactly like the requirement or cause the requirement to be officially changed to what we and the customer really need.'

2. **Quality improvement team:** Representatives from each department or function should be brought together to form a quality improvement team. These should be people who have sufficient authority to commit the area they represent to action

3. **Quality measurement:** The status of quality should be determined throughout the company. This means establishing quality measures for each area of activity that are recorded to show where improvement is possible, and where corrective action is necessary. Crosby advocates delegation of this task to the people who do the job, so setting the stage for defect prevention on the job, where it really counts.

4. **Cost of quality evaluation:** The cost of quality is not an absolute performance measurement, but an indication of where the action necessary to correct a defect will result in greater profitability.

5. **Quality awareness:** This involves, through training and the provision of visible evidence of the concern for quality improvement, making employees aware of the cost to the company of defects. Crosby stresses that this sharing process is a - or even **the** - key step in his view of quality.

6. **Corrective action:** Discussion about problems will bring solutions to light and raise other elements for improvement. People need to see that problems are being resolved on a regular basis. Corrective action should then become a habit.

7. **Establish an ad-hoc committee for the Zero Defects Programme:** Zero Defects is not a motivation programme - its purpose is to communicate and instil the notion that everyone should do things right first time.

8. **Supervisor training:** All managers should undergo formal training on the 14 steps before they are implemented. A manager should understand each of the 14 steps well enough to be able to explain them to his or her people.

9. **Zero Defects Day:** It is important that the commitment to Zero Defects as the performance standard of the company makes an impact, and that everyone gets the same message in the same way. Zero Defects Day, when supervisors explain the

Business Knowledge and Understanding

programme to their people, should make a lasting impression as a 'new attitude' day.

10. **Goal setting:** Each supervisor gets his or her people to establish specific, measurable goals to strive for. Usually, these comprise 30-, 60-, and 90-day goals.

11. **Error cause removal:** Employees are asked to describe, on a simple, one-page form, any problems that prevent them from carrying out error-free work. Problems should be acknowledged within twenty-four hours by the function or unit to which the problem is addressed. This constitutes a key step in building up trust, as people will begin to grow more confident that their problems will be addressed and dealt with.

12. **Recognition:** It is important to recognise those who meet their goals or perform outstanding acts with a prize or award, although this should not be in financial form. The act of recognition is what is important.

13. **Quality Councils:** The quality professionals and team-leaders should meet regularly to discuss improvements and upgrades to the quality programme.

14. **Do it over again:** During a typical programme, lasting from 12 to 18 months, turnover and change will dissipate much of the educational process. It is important to set up a new team of representatives and begin the programme over again, starting with a new Zero Defects Day. This 'starting over again' helps quality to become ingrained in the organisation.

Business Knowledge and Understanding

Crosby's Four Absolutes

Cosby's Four Absolutes of Quality were developed to promote the idea increased quality did not mean increased cost. Quality and cost are not in competition.

First absolute: Quality is defined as conformance to requirements
Quality is not about how good something is, but it is about meeting requirements. The management needs to respond on it. They need to decide what the requirement is. If they do not, the operators should do. In addition, management must provide adequate tools to achieve the requirements.

So, the management has the following three tasks to perform:

1. **Establish the requirements to be met and communicate them to the employees**
2. **Provide the appropriate tools and techniques and the necessary training in them.**
3. **Provide continuous support and encouragement.**

Second Absolute: The system for causing quality is prevention, not appraisal
Prevention is better than correction, detection or appraisal. In the whole process you need to analysis what can goes wrong and then take preventive action. By that, it can minimise the error, damage and problem.

Third Absolute: The Performance Standard must be Zero Defects
Crosby states that nothing less than perfect quality must be the aim. Setting targets below 100% is the start of the downward trend.

Fourth Absolute: The Measurement of Quality is the Price of Non-Conformance
Quality must be measured as a cost to attract the attention of management. Like Juran, Crosby also believes in costing the quality as a powerful motivator for management. It was classified into two types.

- **The Price of Non-Conformance:** *all the cost of not getting products right.*
- **The Price of Conformance:** *what it costs to do things right.*

Business Knowledge and Understanding

Lean Production

Lean production is an approach to management that focuses on cutting out waste, whilst ensuring quality. This approach can be applied to all aspects of a business – from design, through production to distribution.

Lean production aims to cut costs by making the business more efficient and responsive to market needs.

The Lean approach sets out to cut out or minimise activities that do not add value to the production process, such as holding stock, repairing or correcting faulty product and unnecessary movement of people and product around the business.

Lean production originated in the manufacturing plants of Japan but has now been adopted well beyond in large and sophisticated manufacturing activities.

The lean approach to managing operations is about:

- *Doing the simple things well*
- *Doing things better*
- *Involving employees in the continuous process of improvement*
  ...and as a result, avoiding waste

The concept of lean production is an incredibly powerful one for any business that wants to become and/or remain competitive.

Why? Because waste = Cost

Less waste therefore means lower costs, which is an essential part of any business being competitive.

> **Over-production:** *making more than is needed – leads to excess stocks*
> **Waiting time:** *equipment and people standing idle waiting for a production process to be completed or resources to arrive*
> **Transport:** *moving resources (people, materials) around unnecessarily*
> **Stocks:** *often held as an acceptable buffer, but should not be excessive*
> **Motion:** *a worker who appears busy but is not actually adding any value*
> **Defects:** *output that does not reach the required quality standard – often a significant cost to an uncompetitive business*

Business Knowledge and Understanding

The pioneering work of Toyota (a leader in lean production) identified different kinds of waste which can be applied to any business operation. These are:

- *Time based management*
- *Simultaneous engineering*
- *Just in time production (JIT)*
- *Cell production*
- *Kaizen (Continuous improvement)*
- *Quality improvement and management*

Kaizen

Kaizen is a Japanese term meaning "change for the better" or "continuous improvement." It is a Japanese business philosophy regarding the processes that continuously improve operations and involve all employees. Kaizen sees improvement in productivity as a gradual and methodical process.

The concept of Kaizen encompasses a wide range of ideas. It involves making the work environment more efficient and effective by creating a team atmosphere, improving everyday procedures, ensuring employee engagement, and making a job more fulfilling, less tiring, and safer.

- *Kaizen is a Japanese business philosophy that focuses on gradually improving productivity by involving all employees and by making the work environment more efficient.*
- *Kaizen translates to "change for the better" or "continuous improvement."*
- *The small changes used in Kaizen can involve quality control, just-in-time delivery, standardised work, the use of efficient equipment, and the elimination of waste.*
- *Changes can come from any employee anytime and do not have to happen slowly, although Kaizen recognises that small changes now can have big future impacts.*

Some of the key objectives of the Kaizen philosophy include quality control, just-in-time delivery, standardised work, the use of efficient equipment, and the elimination of waste. The overall goal of Kaizen is to make small changes over time to create improvements within a company. That does not mean alterations happen slowly; it simply recognises that small changes now can have huge impacts in the future. Improvements can come from any employee at any time. The idea is that everyone has a stake in the company's success, and everyone should strive, always, to help make the business model better.

Business Knowledge and Understanding

Many companies have adopted the Kaizen concept. Most notably, Toyota employs the Kaizen philosophy within its organisation and has included it as one of its core values. Within its production system, Toyota encourages and empowers all employees to identify areas of potential improvement and create viable solutions.

> *Toyota's process of identifying solutions is called "Kaizen blitz."*

Requirements for Kaizen

Traditional Japanese ideas of Kaizen follow five basic tenets:

- *teamwork,*
- *personal discipline,*
- *improved morale,*
- *quality,*
- *suggestions for improvement.*

These five tenets lead to three major outcomes: elimination of waste (also referred to as economic efficiency), good housekeeping, and standardisation. Ideally, Kaizen becomes so ingrained in a company's culture that it eventually becomes natural to employees.

> *The Kaizen concept posits that there is no perfect end and that everything can be improved upon.*

People must strive to evolve and innovate constantly. The basic principle of Kaizen is that people who perform certain tasks and activities are the most knowledgeable about that task/activity; including them to effect change is the best strategy for improvement.

Teamwork is core to Kaizen, where regular team meetings are held involving discussions about improvements, changes, and projects.

Kaizen and the PDCA Cycle

Improvements generally follow the PDCA cycle format, which stands for "plan-do-check-act." The "plan" portion includes mapping out the changes so that everyone knows what to expect when teams try to solve a problem. The "do" means implementing the best solution to the problem. The "check" step involves evaluating the solution to the problem to see if it worked.

When a company performs the "act" stage, it determines whether the solution should become a company standard or if it needs further changes. If managers decide to implement more changes, Kaizen goes back to the plan step and the process starts over.

Business Knowledge and Understanding

Just-in-Time Inventory Strategy

One of the key goals of Kaizen is to reduce waste and increase efficiency in the production cycle. A just-in-time (JIT) inventory strategy allows management to minimise excess inventory by matching the delivery of raw materials from suppliers with production schedules. Also known as the Toyota Production System (TPS), for the company that popularised the strategy, JIT helps companies cut costs because manufacturers do not have to pay inventory carrying costs. It also reduces waste because companies are not left with extra inventory should a customer cancel or postpone an order.

Kanban is an inventory control system used in conjunction with a JIT strategy. It provides employees with visual cues that tell them it is time to order parts and materials as they run out.

The system relies on coloured cards that track production and alert employees that it is time to replenish a needed part or material. It enables employees to quickly order the correct number of parts from the supplier and have them delivered to where they are needed in the factory.

The summary goal of Kanban is to ensure the efficient running of the factory assembly line and to prevent bottlenecks from occurring.

Business Knowledge and Understanding

Organisational Mission, Vision and Value Statements

In the latter part of the 20th century organisations began to introduce Statements or Charters which were aimed at telling people why the organisation existed, what it did and how it did it. Today, successful businesses have moved on from issuing lengthy, wordy, statements that no employee can understand, never mind remember.

Today it is common to have three concise company statements:

The Vision Statement

A vision statement is a statement of an organisation's overarching aspirations of what it hopes to achieve or to become. Here are some examples of vision statements:

> **Disney:** *To make people happy*
> **IKEA:** *To create a better everyday life for the many people*
> **British Broadcasting Company (BBC):** *To be the most creative organisation in the world*
> **Avon:** *To be the company that best understands and satisfies the product, service and self-fulfilment needs of women—globally*
> **Sony Corporation:** *To be a company that inspires and fulfils your curiosity*

The vision statement does not provide specific targets. Notice that each of the above examples could apply to many different organisations. Instead, the vision is a broad description of the value an organisation provides. It is a visual image of what the organisation is trying to produce or become. It should inspire people and motivate them to want to be part of and contribute to the organisation.

Vision statements should be clear and concise, usually not longer than a short paragraph.

Business Knowledge and Understanding

The Mission Statement

The vision statement and mission statement are often confused, and many companies use the terms interchangeably. However, they each have a different purpose. The vision statement describes where the organisation wants to be in the future – the dream! the mission statement describes what the organisation needs to do now to achieve the vision – the how!

The vision and mission statements must support each other, but the mission statement is more specific. It defines how the organisation will be different from other organisations in its industry. Here are examples of mission statements from successful businesses:

> **Adidas:** We strive to be the global leader in the sporting goods industry with brands built on a passion for sports and a sporting lifestyle.
> **Amazon:** We seek to be Earth is most customer-centric company for four primary customer sets: consumers, sellers, enterprises, and content creators.
> **Google:** To organise the world's information and make it universally accessible and useful
> **The New York Times:** To enhance society by creating, collecting and distributing high-quality news and information

Each of these examples indicates where the organisation will compete (what industry it is in) and how it will compete (what it will do to be different from other organisations). The mission statement conveys to stakeholders why the organisation exists. It explains how it creates value for the market or the larger community.

Because it is more specific, the mission statement is more actionable than the vision statement. By describing why, the organisation exists, and where and how it will compete, the mission statement allows leaders to define a coherent set of goals that fit together to support the mission. The mission statement leads to the creation of strategic goals. Strategic goals are the broad goals the organisation will try to achieve.

Today, most businesses have a Mission Statement – whether it is a formal statement emblazoned on publicity materials, websites, etc or an informal statement which is used in house as a reference.

It is important for every organisation to have its mission and vision statements as it serves as a guide when it comes to decision making and alignment.

Business Knowledge and Understanding

The Values Statement

The values statement, also called the code of ethics, differs from both the vision and mission statements.

The vision and mission statements define where the organisation is going (vision) and what it will do to get there (mission). They direct the efforts of people in the organisation toward common goals. The values statement defines what the organisation believes in and how people in the organisation are expected to behave—with each other, with customers and suppliers, and with other stakeholders. It provides a moral direction for the organisation that guides decision making and establishes a standard for assessing actions. It also provides a standard for employees to judge exceptions.

Managers cannot just create a values statement and expect it to be followed. For a values statement to be effective, it must be reinforced at all levels of the organisation and must be used to guide attitudes and actions. Organisations with strong values follow their values even when it may be easier not to. Levi Strauss & Co is an excellent example of a company that is driven by its values.

> When Levi Strauss began to outsource its manufacturing overseas, the company developed a set of principles for overseas operations and suppliers called the Global Sourcing and Operating Guidelines. One of the principles covered the use of child labour:
>
>> Use of child labour is not permissible. Workers can be no less than 15 years of age and not younger than the compulsory age to be in school. We will not utilise partners who use child labour in any of their facilities. We support the development of legitimate workplace apprenticeship programs for the educational benefit of younger people.
>
> Levi Strauss found that one of its contractors was employing children under 15 in a factory in Bangladesh. The easy solution would be to replace the contractor, but in Bangladesh, the children's wages may have supported an entire family. If they lost their jobs, they may have had to resort to begging on the streets.
>
> Levi Strauss came up with a different solution, one that supported its values of empathy, originality, integrity, and courage: it paid the children to go to school. Levi Strauss continued to pay salaries and benefits to the children and paid for tuition, books, and supplies. Even though it would have been easier to just fire the child laborers and consider the problem settled, Levi Strauss was driven by its values to find a better solution.

Together, the vision, mission, and values statements provide direction for everything that happens in an organisation. They keep everyone focused on where the organisation is going

Business Knowledge and Understanding

and what it is trying to achieve. And they define the core values of the organisation and how people are expected to behave. They are not intended to be a straitjacket that restricts or inhibits initiative and innovation, but they are intended to guide decisions and behaviours to achieve common ends.

Customer Service Statement

In the 21st century, competition has never been greater, customer choice has never been wider and the needs and demands of customers is constantly changing. As a result, these three statements are no longer enough – today a business must also address Customer Service with a clear statement about Customer Service within the organisation.

In some instances, this may be included in the Mission Statement, but increasingly organisations are producing separate statements which detail exactly what type of customer service you want your company to provide to its customers.

Think of a mission statement for a football team – it may be "to win the Premier League title". However, that is not what the defenders or midfielders will say to each other at the start of the match!

Winning the Premier League is a result, not the action. The Customer Service Statement would be how the game would be played. This one statement is the one every employee in the organisation must be able to understand and know it backwards and forwards.

The Customer Service Statement is what each and every employee, regardless of department, level, or wage, must deliver to every Customer, every time. It provides a meaningful purpose for the employees.

The Customer Service Statement is never shared with the outside public, i.e., Customers. It is only used by the employees.

The Disney vision: – To make people happy – is just that - a vision. It is the Customer Service Statement which will define how the employees can achieve that.

Contents of a Customer Service Statement

There are certain criteria which must be met to ensure the statement is effective. These are:

It must be actionable
The statement must be easily understood so that it can be translated into actions by everyone across the organisation. It is the basic principle that tells how to deliver customer service. If necessary, it can outline the process using specific steps.

Business Knowledge and Understanding

It is measurable
When customer service ground rules are implemented, the statement should help the organisation evaluate its performance and quality of service. It is the guideline on how to measure customer service success. It must ask what can we improve in the way we deal with customers? Which of our service strategies work well? What should we continue doing?

It is observable
This means that you can watch an employee interact with a customer face-to-face, read their email, or listen to them on a call and be able to say, "Yes, they did achieve our vision for Customer service or No! There are areas for improvement".

It is trainable
It should be practical and actionable so it can be learned within the company. Can everyone in the organisation learn this? A customer service statement should be realistic.

Aside from laying the basics that must be mastered, there should also be space for innovation. This means that it must be able to keep up with changing times, technologies, and customer trends.

Benefits of a Customer Service Statement

An organisation can derive huge benefits from having a great customer service vision statement. Some of those are:

- *It helps the organisation stand out from the rest.*
- *It provides direction for the organisation.*
- *It shapes the relationship with customers.*
- *Loyal customers are derived repeat business.*
- *It increases sales.*
- *It engages partners and stakeholders.*
- *It creates a positive work culture; employees will feel recognised for providing excellent service.*
- *More satisfied customers means more referrals.*

Business Knowledge and Understanding

Organisational Strategy

An organisational strategy is the sum of the actions a company intends to take to achieve long-term goals. Together, these actions make up a company's strategic plan. Strategic plans take at least a year to complete, requiring involvement from all company levels. Top management creates the larger organisational strategy, while middle and lower management adopt goals and plans to fulfil the overall strategy step by step.

This unified effort can be likened to a journey. The journey starts at the point we are at today and ends at the ultimate destination. The route to get there will be formulated and the road conditions encountered on the journey are the challenges which need to be overcome to complete each stage of the journey, which will eventually lead to the ultimate destination.

The Purpose of Strategic Planning

Strategic planning is a systematic process that helps you set an ambition for your business' future and determine how best to achieve it. Its primary purpose is to connect three key areas:

- *your mission* - *defining your business' purpose*
- *your vision* - *describing what you want to achieve*
- *your plan* - *outlining how you want to achieve your ultimate goals*

Importance of strategic planning

Strategic planning is necessary to determine the direction for your organisation. It focuses your efforts and ensures that everyone in the business is working towards a common goal. It also helps you:

- *agree actions that will contribute to business growth*
- *align resources for optimal results*
- *prioritise financial needs*
- *build competitive advantage*
- *engage with your staff and communicate what needs to be done*

Another significant purpose of strategic planning is to help you manage and reduce business risks. Growing a business is inherently risky. Detailed planning may help you to:

- *remove uncertainty*
- *analyse potential risks*
- *implement risk control measures*
- *consider how to minimise the impact of risks, should they occur*

Business Knowledge and Understanding

Strategic Plans

Effective planning usually results in a written strategic plan. This is a formalised document that describes the business' goals, and the actions needed to achieve them.

There are a variety of models and approaches which can be beneficial in strategic planning. Many businesses include a SWOT analysis or a PESTLE analysis as key elements of their strategic plan.

SWOT Analysis

Managers can produce these quickly and simply to help to clarify their thinking and focus their attention on all aspects of the problem. A SWOT analysis is particularly useful for gathering, interpreting and analysing information. For each realistic possible solution, managers can analyse it using a SWOT analysis.

If your car has been breaking down and causing you problems, a SWOT analysis could show, for example:

	Option A – have it fixed every time to keep it going for as long as possible – maybe a year	**Option B** – replace the car with a brand-new, up-to-date version that should last ten years	**Option C** – replace it with a second hand, model that should last five years
Strengths	Not too expensive to run The problems are well-known and familiar	Good reliability Up-to-date technology Good warranty support	Reasonable cost Its service history should indicate reliability Know how to operate it
Weaknesses	Cost of repairs Frequent disruption of your life that cannot be planned Drop in your efficiency and performance	Very expensive May have to make sacrifices Will be difficult to look after properly	Does not benefit from the most up-to-date technology and design Only a short warranty Could develop problems at any time
Opportunities	Easy to arrange with garage for repairs	Three possible suppliers Available in about two months	Plenty available if researched online Could be bought quickly as changes to storage arrangements not needed
Threats to success	Garage staff may refuse to repair it when it breaks again. Repair costs are high. Wages could be lost due to delays	Cost and budget constraints Might be outdated after a few years Personal benefits may not justify the cost	Cost might not be justifiable if planning to keep it for less than five years

Although a SWOT analysis does not give a magic answer to the problem, it does help to identify the pros and cons of each option. Once they know their budget constraints and the

Business Knowledge and Understanding

long-term targets, the decision makers would be able to identify the best solution to the problem.

PESTLE Analysis

Another system that could be used when making well-informed decisions is a PESTLE analysis. This can be particularly useful when there are areas of concern, outside of the control of the organisation, and for gathering, interpreting and analysing information.

P	E	S	T	L	E
Political	Economic	Social Cultural	Technology	Legal	Environmental
Stability of government Potential changes to legislation Global influences	Economic growth Employment rates Inflation rates Monetary policy Consumer confidence	Income distribution Demographic influences Lifestyle factors	International influences Changes in information technology Take up rates	Taxation policies Employment laws Industrial regulations Health and safety	Regulations and restrictions Attitudes of customers

For example, if the problem is that the company has outgrown its present site and is considering solutions to the problem, it will have to consider many things that are outside its control. When doing a PESTLE analysis, managers would look at these areas:

P	Political	e.g., government funding for expanding in the same area or setting up in a different location
E	Economic	e.g., the overall economic climate and whether stakeholders would support investment and expansion if the economy is slow or in recession
S	Social	e.g., the effect on the local population if the company moves away/stays put and expands
T	Technological	e.g., the scope for using new technology as part of the expansion plans
L	Legal	e.g., legal requirements about redundancies or relocation of staff
E	Environmental	e.g., the regulations on emissions and waste management in the current area and the potential new area

You may also want to include an implementation schedule, key performance indicators (KPIs) and other accountability measures.

Business Knowledge and Understanding

A Customer-Focused Business Strategy

It is an acknowledged fact that customers are the most important part of any business. It is their feedback, interest and needs that drive sales, promote products and expand the reach of the brand. If you provide poor customer experiences and do not match audience expectations, it will be almost impossible to build a loyal, repeat customer base.

Some 86% of organisations choose to take a product-first approach, which neglects customers and puts the focus on sales.

Building a customer-focused strategy means the customer and their needs come first as a means to reach sales targets and grow the business. Important decisions begin and end with the customer, based on how it benefits them and offers them value. Rather than making decisions based on sales or growth, the focus is on customer satisfaction.

To create a customer-centric business strategy, there are a few ways below to get started.

Make it part of your company culture.

If customer-centricity is not a fundamental aspect spread across all areas of the organisation, then it is not a customer-focused business. Even if it is implemented in one or two areas, that still is not enough to provide for customers to its full potential. Customer-focused practices should permeate through every department and employee and starts with orientation and onboarding.

Create a customer-centred culture by implementing it from the beginning. When the whole team adopts these values and uses actions to show what the company values, it is easier to carry out this strategy and do so authentically. Each member of the team impacts the type of culture the organisation adopts, so everyone must be on the same page.

Include these values in the onboarding process. Even better, write in the job adverts that the organisation is seeking employees who will embrace a customer-focused culture. This will weed out applicants who are more sales-driven and prefer to take that approach.

Track customer-focused metrics.

How can an organisation determine how well its strategy caters to customers if it has nothing to measure it by? It is crucial to track specific metrics so the strategy can be refined as needed and continue implementing those values into the organisation.

Without measurable data to analyse, it will prove difficult to maintain a customer-centric culture.

Consider what metrics need to be tracked. These may include:

> **Customer lifetime value (CLV):** This measure how much a person will spend on your business as long as they are a paying customer. Since it costs more to

Business Knowledge and Understanding

acquire new customers than retain them, it helps you increase the value of existing customers.

Customer equity: This is the total value of all of the new customer relationships created in a specific period.

CLV by channel: This tracks customer lifetime value through various channels, such as social media or paid advertising since each result will differ. It is essential to analyse how each channel affects your growth based on what type of customers it attracts to your brand.

Net promoter score: This measures customer loyalty over time by gauging how willing they are to recommend your brand to others. It helps businesses indicate overall customer satisfaction to see where they stand with their audience.

View customers as the solution.

Many businesses view their customers as part of the problem rather than the solution. However, if an organisation is not meeting your goals and key performance indicators (KPIs), it means something is lacking in the strategy. It also means the brand fails to meet customer expectations. So, how exactly are they the problem?

Customers should be viewed as the solution to your problems rather than the problem itself. Make them part of the solution in the strategy to get the results required.

Collect customer feedback to tackle existing issues and determine pain points the organisation can solve. Consistent communication is vital to get to the root of their problems and present action-based solutions. This shows that the organisation is proactive about solving customer issues and cares about their satisfaction.

Business Knowledge and Understanding

Feedback

Feedback provides that insight into what is working well about the product or service and what should be done to make experience better.

An organisation may have the best expertise in the industry in which the organisation operates, but professional knowledge will never be more valuable to organisational performance than customer feedback. Their opinions help ensure that the end product meets their expectations, solves their problems and fulfils their needs.

Customer feedback also helps measure customer satisfaction. Customer satisfaction and loyalty is a crucial factor that determines an organisations financial performance. It is directly linked to many benefits, such as increased market share, lower costs, or higher revenues. The best way to find out if the product or service satisfies their expectation is to ask them!

There are 5 main reasons why feedback is collected:

- *Customer engagement*
- *Understand your customers*
- *Product improvement*
- *Obtain testimonials, reviews, referrals*
- *Evaluate and get better at things*

To identify areas for improvement, it is vital that the customer voice is heard. Internal systems and processes can be developed to ensure the delivery of Customer Service is smooth and defect free, but we can never know where service delivery is failing for the customer, unless we ask them.

This is done by seeking customer feedback. Customer feedback is information provided by customers about their satisfaction or dissatisfaction with a product or service and about the general experience they had in their interaction with an organisation. Their opinion is a resource for identifying areas for continuous improvement and adjusting processes and procedures to eliminate the defects and satisfy their needs. This data is collected proactively by polling and surveying customers, interviewing them, or by asking for reviews. Teams can also passively collect feedback by providing users a place where they can share comments, complaints, or compliments. Both sources are important to get a full picture of how the customer perceives the brand.

High performing organisations understand the important role that customer feedback plays in business. They continuously listen to the voice of the customer. They not only search the opinions their clients publish on social media and reviews they provide on websites designed for gathering feedback (e.g., TripAdvisor), but they also deliberately ask for feedback using distinct kinds of surveys. To stay ahead of competition, you should never stop listening to customer feedback whether it is positive or negative, prompted or unprompted.

Business Knowledge and Understanding

Without customer feedback, an organisation will never know if customers are getting value out of their product and are satisfied with the benefits it provides. Without knowing if they are getting value, the product and market teams will not know if they are nurturing loyal customers not to mention being able to measure customer retention and customer health.

Importance of customer feedback

When a new product, brand or service is introduced to the market, research will have already been done to ensure it meets the customer's needs. The market research conducted before bringing it to market will have established potential customers would be willing to buy it, however, it is only after the customers have used the product or service that the advantages, flaws and their actual experience can be identified. Furthermore, their needs and expectations evolve further with time so the product or service must do the same.

One of the most accurate methodologies that has helped many organisations measure, manage and improve customer satisfaction is NPS (Net Promoter Score). The metric is based on one simple question that investigates how likely it is that a customer would recommend a brand to a friend. Response options for the loyalty questions are based on a 0–10-point rating scale, with 0 representing extremely negative and 10 representing extremely positive. This methodology is both simple and universal, so every organisation can apply it in customer satisfaction management.

By asking clients for feedback the organisation is also communicating that customer opinion is important. By involving customers in shaping the organisation, they feel more attached to it.

Listening to the customer voice helps create stronger relationships with them.

By increasing customer engagement, it allows an organisation to gain valuable brand ambassadors who will spread positive messages for it. Recommendation is probably the most effective and the cheapest way to acquire new customers and become more trustworthy in the eyes of both current and potential customers.

Today, marketing is heavily based on the experience's customers have with products, services and brands. They do not buy Apple products just because they are good. They want to demonstrate their status and affiliation to a particular group. They do not buy Nike clothes because they are durable.

If an organisation focusses on providing the best customer experience at every touchpoint, customers will stay loyal to the brand. The most effective way to give them an amazing experience is asking them what they like about your service and what should be improved.

The increased levels of customer satisfaction mean customers will remain loyal to the organisation. Unhappy customer will find a better alternative to your organisation and leave.

Business Knowledge and Understanding

Customer feedback helps determine if customers are satisfied with the service provision and identify areas for improvement.

In the age of social media, customers do not trust commercials or expert advice as much as before. Opinions provided by other customers who have already used a product or service are considered a more reliable source for information. If a customer wishes to book accommodation or find a new restaurant to visit with friends, they will read reviews beforehand or ask for opinions on Facebook.

Many organisations today incorporate review system in their services and products. Think of Uber, or Airbnb. They do their best to ensure that poor service will be detected and excluded from their business.

Customer feedback is as important to the organisation as it is to other customers, make sure that both parties have easy access to opinions and reviews.

> *"Feedback is the breakfast of champions."* - Brian Halligan CEO of HubSpot

Using Customer Feedback

Organisations cannot succeed in today's markets by making decisions based on loose guesses.

Successful organisations gather and manage distinct data that helps them develop future strategies. It is only by doing this they can adjust their products and services to perfectly fit customer needs.

Customer feedback is one of the most reliable sources for tangible data that can be used in making business decisions. The customer insights feedback provides will help an organisation understand clients and their needs. By taking their suggestions into consideration it allows the organisation to find out where money should be allocated to get the highest return on investment. It may reveal that further product development is not necessary but instead, focus should be switched to promoting the brand to get bigger exposure.

Customer feedback is valuable source of data, but organisations must learn how to listen to it and how to translate it into an actionable response.

Customer feedback should be used at all corporate levels and across all departments in the organisation. The insights customer feedback provides will develop products, improve customer service, and manage customer satisfaction. Listening and responding to customer feedback will make sure that clients will stay with the organisation, be loyal to the brand and will spread positive word-of-mouth messages.

Customer feedback is everywhere

Business Knowledge and Understanding

Gathering Customer Feedback

Websites are a vital tool for capturing Customer feedback. Web analytics can provide a huge amount of data about how customers interact with the website. What do they search for? How long do they engage with the site for? What click throughs are taking place? This can be critical information for an organisation provided it is interpreted and analysed correctly

Collecting feedback on a website also helps engage visitors and discover problems they might be facing while browsing the website. To collect feedback on a website, use website surveys. They allow feedback to be collected from all users who visit the website. Smart widgets do not disturb visitors and provide you with lots of actionable feedback. You will easily find out what stops users from buying, how they assess your design or what their crucial characteristics are.

Live chat can be used to talk to website visitors and collect their feedback during conversations.
When it comes to collecting feedback on different channels, sending questionnaires via email is the most popular. But this technique can be used only to collect opinions of customers and you must know their email addresses. Response rates also tend to be poor – a better solution is to use one-click email surveys to collect more responses.

Social listening is another way of collecting customer feedback and its popularity is growing. Not all users want to talk to you. Many prefer to share their thoughts on social media. Sometimes they share positive news, sometimes pure frustration or anger. Social media monitoring will help you collect feedback from customers and react to their opinions.

Listening to your customers and applying those insights is the best way to move a business forward.

Collecting Customer Feedback

Collecting feedback is not difficult but there are some rules that apply to all feedback channels. Following best practices of collecting feedback will maximize not only the amount of feedback collected but also its usefulness.

Define a goal before starting to collect feedback
Some people make the mistake of jumping into collecting feedback with no clear goal. They just set tools up and see what they can find out. It is not the best choice. Define a goal first. It will lead to choosing the right technique and then the right tool. To find out how people assess a new website, website surveys may be the best method. But if interest centres on what people are saying about competitors on social media, social media monitoring is the best choice.

Choose the right technique
The goal of collecting feedback influences the choice of a technique. Consider the resources. If all members of the team are already working overtime, then choose a tool

Business Knowledge and Understanding

that requires as little effort to set up and handle as possible. If this is the case and feedback is to be collected from a website, choose a website survey tool rather than live chat which requires constant attention and spare capacity.

Make analysing feedback a routine
Feedback tools provide the most value when the results are regularly assessed, look for improvements, create new surveys, etc. Depending on the size of the organisation and the amount of feedback to be collected, trends might be evident in a matter of days after launching the survey. Making analysing results a part of a weekly routine will help make the most of collecting feedback.

Experiment
Do not be afraid to experiment. When using social media monitoring, try changing keywords from time to time. When using website surveys, try different questions, and targeting options. When using live chat try different targeting settings and pre-defined messages. Experimenting will help improve achieved results and help research different issues.

Turn conclusions into actions
Analysing feedback is only the first stage. Draw conclusions and respond to them. Then analyse feedback again to track how people have responded to the change and then start the process once again.

Collecting and acting upon customer feedback is a must for any business looking to provide users with the products they need.

Business Knowledge and Understanding

Feedback Channels

When collecting customer feedback, it is easy to get overwhelmed by the sheer volume of possibilities. With so many customers — and so many ways to connect with their feedback — it is hard to know where to start.

Below is the list of the most useful channels for receiving customer feedback and explanations how to get the most of each of them.

- *Social Media Listening*
- *Surveys & Polls*
- *Customer Feedback Communities*
- *Website Feedback Widgets*
- *Feedback from Support*
- *Feedback via Chatbots*
- *Emails & Customer Contact Forms*
- *Internal Team Feedback*
- *User Sessions*
- *Customer Interviews*
- *In-App Feedback*

1. Social Media Listening
The great thing about social media is that users are authentic and genuinely express themselves through comments, mentions, and hashtags.

47% of customers with a product or service complaint will voice it on social media

One of the ways you can gain valuable customer feedback is by monitoring mentions of your brand. When you see your company's name being talked about on social media, you can reach out to the people who mentioned it and ask about their experience. This allows you to develop a proactive approach that clients love because they feel that they are genuinely being taken care of.

Another great strategy to collect customer feedback is to **monitor your competitors** when they are mentioned. You can learn about the things their customers are unhappy with and see if you can provide a better solution. Not only will this help you to stand out from competitors, but also nurture their unsatisfied customers into leads.

Business Knowledge and Understanding

2. Customer Feedback Surveys and Polls

Not all customers will be open to leaving public and detailed feedback via comments or mentions on social media. Some people prefer to keep their opinions **anonymous**. Therefore, surveys have an important role.

> **Short surveys** can be used to ask one or two questions or conduct a brief poll, with the purpose of getting responses from active customers directly from a website or app and in the organisation's responses to customers (along with the request for direct feedback)
>
> **Longer surveys can also** be sent out via email, social media, or web. Lots of survey tool providers offer templates on which to base a survey depending on the case and purpose.

To make up a survey that the customers will actually complete, follow these guidelines:

- *ask open-ended questions that lead to the end goal.*
- *ask only the questions that will give useful insights.*
- *keep it short (up to 5 questions).*

3. Customer Feedback Communities

A customer community feedback channel is an effective way to collect useful insights from customers when they have something to say is by creating **Customer Feedback Community**. With the help of such a tool a specialised feedback forum can be created where customers share their ideas, feature requests, report bugs and organically create a self-service knowledge base by posting questions. This is a valuable source to get useful insights on what customers really want. It allows organisations to stop playing the guessing game by obtaining quantitative and qualitative data and reduce wasted hours on the development of the things that will not be used.

Compared to using surveys this can save money compared to collecting, processing, and analysing the information. With feedback forums or communities, you get all the relevant insights right at your fingertips.

When adding a customer feedback community portal to a website, it must be easy to reach and invite customers to visit the portal at certain stages of the customer journey. In most instances, customers will be happy to provide feedback, all they need is a convenient platform to enhance the process.

Too often it is hard enough for customers to reach out and give their honest opinion, so if you create extra barriers, they will not give you their insights at all.

4. Feedback Widgets

Feedback widgets make it easy for users to report when they stumble upon something they do not like.

Business Knowledge and Understanding

As customers use the productor service, they are constantly spotting things they like, dislike, or would love to change. Having feedback widgets, makes it easier for them to reach out and give their honest opinion.

Keep the feedback form short – a simple title and description box should work. Once feedback is received, ensure it is followed up as soon as possible.

5. Feedback from Support
Quite often customers leave feedback regarding the product to customer service agents. In many organisations there is a gap between Customer Support and Product Development teams, and most of this valuable feedback gets lost among the numerous requests.

When a customer service agent receives some feedback, they need a process to keep it and subsequently refer it on. Spreadsheets can be used for these purposes, and in many cases, it works to some point. But when there are lots of requests and feedback, it is easy to get duplicates and loose information.

Specialised customer feedback software in combination with customer support tools helps to ensure that the voice of the customers is heard.

6. Feedback via Chatbots
Chatbots have been widely recently used thanks to the improvements in artificial intelligence and machine learning. This new generation of tools transforms the feedback-giving experience differently and in a more interactive manner.

7. Email and Customer Contact Forms
This channel allows customers to contact the organisation directly and privately. It is a more personal approach, and it will allow the organisation to engage with the customer directly. By choosing this route, the conversation can be developed, and the customers turned into loyal fans, simply because they have been taken care of.

When communicating with customers, remember to follow these *tips*:

1. **Make sure your customers get responses quickly.** In today's fast-paced world, customers expect to be responded as soon as possible. Therefore, try to reply to them immediately.

2. **Get organised.** With so much feedback coming in, it can be hard to keep track of it. Make sure you have a system that can handle this for you.

3. **Always follow up.** Always thank customers for completing your surveys. Send out surveys based on certain actions or over periods of time but try not to be spammy. Ask about customer experience, send satisfaction surveys after they interact with the support, etc.

Business Knowledge and Understanding

8. Feedback from Internal Team
Each department can provide their own unique perspective on what they think about the products or services, and what can be improved. The support department communicates with clients directly and know exactly what the customers are experiencing better than anyone else because every day they are dealing with their challenges and problems and can spot common patterns that need to be fixed. This first-hand knowledge of problems and issues is invaluable and should be regularly analysed and responded to as this information is critical to business growth.

Create a survey with some open questions and send it out to the team members with the option to fill it out anonymously.

9. User Sessions
When customers are using a website to research or use your products or services, their activities can be observed as they interact.

A user session monitoring service is added onto the website or app and when a user enters the site or app, the service records the whole session from a user perspective.

The goal is to analyse how users behave throughout the process and strive to make their experience better. Identify the things that caught their attention and what was challenging for them.

This source is ideal for start-ups launching new products to analyse the customer's behaviour, as it identifies the maximum number of insights from every user. As a result, they highlight the weak parts of your product and can be corrected to avoid future problems.

10. Customer Interviews
While most data extraction methods still revolve around technology, face-to-face interviews are still one of the best customer feedback methods. They allow the analysis of verbal and non-verbal cues, give the interviewer control over the process, and allows the capture of the emotions and behaviours that a technology channel could not.

When conducting these interviews be sure to focus on:

- **Identify the root problem.** When you ask users what your design should look like, that will not get you very far. However, when you understand their underlying motives ("your web page is hard to use"), then you can get a clear picture of what the real problem is and fix it.
- **If they experienced a problem.** Ask them to remember a specific time when they faced this challenge. It may reveal a pattern that happens only on certain occasions.
- **Understanding user habits.** When asking customers how they use the products or services it allows the discovery of problems they were unaware of. For example, they can be going through various steps of a process when they could achieve their desired task within just one step. This will allow identification of ways to improve workflow and create a better user experience.

Business Knowledge and Understanding

11. In-App Feedback
Mobile customer interactions are naturally app-based. In-app feedback allows organisations to embed key feedback forms in the app in a seamless way. Feedback can be asked after certain action criteria, or at a certain period to find the best moment possible when the customer will be loyal to give feedback.

- **Make it noticeable but do not interrupt:** *Do not hide a feedback button or link in a menu, instead, place it in a noticeable place with clear incentive to provide feedback like "We want your feedback on how to improve our App".*
- **Make it transparent.** *Let users see the feedback of others for greater inspiration. Show that the feedback workflow is transparent, and users are kept updated on the status of their requests and ideas.*
- **Always update.** *Quite often companies receive feedback, implement it, but do not bother to update the customer, and as a result they think that their voice was not heard. Always update on the status of the idea, either it was declined or implemented.*

The best results come when both data and customer feedback are combined and analysed. By taking this approach, it gives a clear picture of customer's true behaviour as well as the information needed to make decisions on where focus should be directed and the things which need improving.

Today, there are dozens of tools that provide data and analytics to help understand what customers value the most in an organisation and identify areas for improvement. However, no matter how much insights are available at your fingertips, the most important thing is to *analyse* and use them appropriately.

If the results do not align with the current product development strategy, change the strategy. It may well require lots of resources and efforts, but to be customer-centric - you will have to do it. Otherwise, all the work on gathering customer feedback is just a waste of time and money.

Customers can transform every aspect of an organisation for the better if they are listened to. Think about the most pressing goals and start with one clear, simple method for collecting customer feedback before expanding out to more complex tactics like usability testing and analytics.

Customer support channels are the ideal place to begin — a support team brings more value when they approach every interaction as an opportunity to collect quantitative and qualitative feedback on real experiences with the organisation.

Business Knowledge and Understanding

The world's most successful businessmen agree:

Your most unhappy customers are your greatest source of learning.

BILL GATES
Founder Microsoft

We see our customers as invited guest to a party, and we are the hosts. It is our job every day to make every important aspect of the customer experience a little better.

JEFF BEZOS
CEO Amazon

Chapter 3: The Customer Journey

The Customer Journey

The Customer Journey

The customer journey can be defined as

"the complete sum of experiences and touchpoints that customers go through when interacting with an organisation and its brand".

Touch points can be defined as:

A touchpoint is any time a potential customer or customer comes in contact with your organisation – before, during, or after they purchase something from you.

The customer journey documents the full experience of being a customer. This would include all touchpoints or interactions via all available channels (telephone, digital, in-branch, mail, broadcast media, face to face and so on). This is known as the Customer Journey Map.

This should not be confused with the Customer Lifecycle which is defined as:

"The customer lifecycle is a term that describes the different steps a customer goes through when they are considering, buying, using, and remaining loyal to a particular product or service".

The Customer lifecycle is a more holistic view of the customer relationship.

The Customer Journey concerns itself with what people do, what they experience, what they expect and how they feel about those interactions and the organisation as a result of those interactions.

It can focus on a specific task (say buying a product or service) or the entire customer lifecycle.

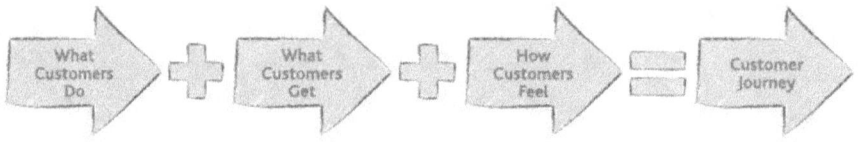

To analyse the Customer Journey requires a profound understanding the customers' behaviour, experiences and emotions at each stage of the journey. By better understanding the Journey the customer takes, a more profitable customer relationship can be created.

The Customer Journey

Customers

Before any customer journey can be mapped, more needs to be known about the people we call customers.

In a small, local, shop, we know that Mrs Smith will pop in on Friday for a loaf and a bottle of milk and Mr Green will buy two cans of beer everyday around 6.00pm and so on.

Unfortunately, with a global economy, the potential customer base for some organisations is the World. That means we need to begin to break down the potential customer base into smaller groups so we can begin to identify exactly who our customers are.

There would be little point trying to sell a pair of roller skates to an eighty-year-old and likewise, someone living on the 23rd floor of a tower block would have little use for a lawnmower.

We need to be able to spot our customer in the middle of a crowd – as if they were wearing a very tall hat!

It is therefore important that we know who our products and services are for.

The first pre-requisite for our lawnmower is that the potential customer has some grass to cut. However, as noted above, that does not mean we can contact everyone with an address. We need to identify people who have and address and a lawn. We can therefore discount everyone who lives in a flat or in serviced accommodation. That does not mean that we disregard these people completely, we may have someone who lives in a tower block, with no garden, but who wishes to buy a lawnmower as a gift for a friend.

Whilst this person may not be a primary customer target, they are a secondary target that we could look for in the longer term.

We need to classify potential customers into groups so we can start the Customer Journey by making sure we are telling the most appropriate people about the products or services we offer.

The more we know about our customers and our potential customers – the more targeted our market and sales endeavour will become.

50% of a marketing budget is wasted on unqualified traffic and leads

The Customer Journey

Customer Profiles

A customer profile is made up of certain characteristics held by our customers or potential customers which include likes and dislikes, what and how they buy goods and services, demographic classifications and behaviours which they display. Like fingerprints, no two people have exactly the same customer profile.

Typical criteria for profiling include:

- *Lifestyle*
- *Age*
- *Location*
- *Income*
- *Interests*
- *Buying patterns*
- *Purchasing preferences*
- *Stage of life*

What we wish to do with the information, will direct what the profile contains. It would be impossible to fully profile every person on every criterion. As a result, selected characteristics are used to create a profile which best suits the product or service we offer.

Gender is one of the primary classifications used. If our target market is men, we can halve the potential customer base by simply classifying people based on their gender.

Age is also a primary way to classify customers. We have, essentially, limitless choices as to the way we classify by age. We could classify people into the following groups:

Classification				
0 - 18	19 - 50	51 -		
0 - 10	11 - 20	21 - 30	31 - 40	Etc.
0 - 18	18 - 65	65 -		
18 - 25	25 - 40	40 - 65	65 -	

Each classification is used for a specific reason. The third one in the list classifies people into groups to differentiate those in education, working and retired. The fourth one classifies people into life stage and so on.

Employment status could be used if we wanted to contact people who are in full time employment.

The Customer Journey

Using a Customer Profile

Once you have collected relevant information about your current and potential customers, creating consumer profiles that describe specific segments allow you to envision a person interested in your product. This gives you an in-depth understanding of:

- *What will motivate them to find your business.*
- *The benefits they are looking for.*
- *Where they are most likely to interact with your advertising.*
- *The messaging that will best appeal to their needs and wants.*

Once you have a clear picture of the type of customers your business should be targeting, you can create an appropriate marketing strategy. Your ideal customer profile will help you pinpoint the who, where, and how to reach potential consumers interested in what your business has to offer

Creating a Customer Profile

The process of creating a customer profile is straightforward but can be time consuming. The more time invested in planning and preparation the easier it will be to obtain the information needed and the more effective and beneficial it will be.

1. Identify your primary customers
The first step is to find and analyse people who love your products or services.

Identify five to ten customers by asking yourself:

The Customer Journey

- Which customers have been with the organisation the longest?
- Who has been recommending the organisation to others?
- Who would benefit the most from the products and services the organisation offers?

If you produce office chairs, computer users could be one of your best customers.

2. List their notable attributes

Once you have compiled a list of your best customers, write down all their important attributes. The main attributes usually relate to:

Demographics

Demographic attributes reveal the age, gender, race, ethnicity, and religion of your ideal customers. With this information at your fingertips, it becomes easy to target advertising at these people or build products or services that they would find useful.

For instance, a chic female clothing store may choose to only market its products to young female audiences who have an interest in buying stylish apparel.

Psychographics

Psychographics offer a deeper understanding of your customers' beliefs and values. They include things like:

- **Activities :** Netflix, exercise, baking, etc.
- **Lifestyle:** Extrovert, stay indoors, socialise three times a week, etc.
- **Values:** No alcohol, moderate views, etc.
- **Aspirations:** Work-life balance, grow following on Instagram, etc.
- **Pain points and fears:** Low-quality product, hidden charges, etc.

The psychographic part of a customer profile helps to create and market products that speak to the way people think, their pain points, and their emotional triggers.

Socio-economics

Most ideal customer profiles also feature attributes related to education, income, neighbourhood, and household size. But you can even research what socio-economic class the best customers fall into.

The main socio-economic classes are:

- *Upper class*
- *Middle class*
- *Lower middle class*
- *Skilled worker class*
- *Unemployed class*

The Customer Journey

Your chances of meeting your customers' expectations should significantly improve when you have a clear picture of their socio-economic attributes.

Geographic segmentation
Geographic segmentation helps answer questions related to the location of the customers.

- *Do your customers live in a temperate climate?*
- *Do the customers live in an area with Internet access?*
- *Are there any cultural or ethical limitations?*

This information can be particularly valuable if you sell items that are subject to differences in accessibility to technology, population, or climate.

A car company, for instance, would be able to use geographic segmentation to determine the type of vehicles they should produce in greater quantities. If most of its best customers reside in rural areas, it would make sense for the company to make cars with thick and heavy tires that allow customers to navigate bumpy roads with ease.

3. Survey them

When you begin to profile customers, you will find that you have more information about some customers than others. That is where surveys can help fill the gaps.

Tools like SurveyMonkey or Google Forms can be used to create surveys on specific customer traits. Below are some ideas for the type of questions to include in your survey:

Demographic-related questions
Keep in mind that these can be personal and sensitive questions. Pay particular attention to the way they are structured. One method is to give multiple answers to choose from.

What is your nationality?

In what year were you born?
From 1944 to 1964
From 1965 to 1979
From 1980 to 1994
From 1995 onward

What is your gender?
Male
Female

What is your relationship status?

The Customer Journey

Socio-economic related questions
Below are some examples of questions to gain socioeconomic data:

What is your employment status?
Employed full-time
Employed part-time
Self-employed
Retired
Unemployed

What is your highest educational qualification?

What is your household's annual income?
£14,999 or less
£15,000 to £34,999
£35,000 to £49,999
£50,000 to £74,999
£75,000 to £99,999
£100,000 or more

Psychographic-related questions
Since there are so many potential answers to these types of questions, you can ask open-ended questions like the ones below:

What hobbies do you enjoy?

What do you value most in life?

What factors affect your decision to buy a product or service?

Geographic-related questions
These are generally easy-to-answer questions about a consumer's geographical location, such as:

In what region are you situated?

How would you describe the weather in your area?

Are you exempt from paying taxes in your region?

4. Create the customer profile
Once the key customers have been profiled, the results need to be documented. When creating a customer profile, the level of detail recorded is entirely up to you. However, try to keep it simple to avoid analysis paralysis with too many insights.

List the information in the following order:

- *Give your ideal customer a name*

The Customer Journey

- *Put a face to their profile*
- *Add their demographic information*
- *List their psychographic and socioeconomic attributes*
- *Include a quote from the customer*
- *Add their goals, pain points, and motivators*
- *Add the type of communication channels they would prefer to use*

While you can create a customer profile document from scratch, it is always easier to use a template. Many different customer profile templates are available to help you in creating powerful profiles. Remove or add fields based on the data available.

Multiple Customer Profiles

It is unlikely that any organisation will have only one customer type and therefore more than one profile will be required to correctly identify all of the primary customers.

Think about Ford Motor Company. They produce a range of vehicles to meet the needs of a variety of customer profiles. They will produce vehicles for commercial use to support business clients. They will produce vehicles which are cheap to insure for new drivers, large crossover vehicles for families, sports cars and more sedate, refined vehicles for the more mature driver. Each of the vehicles produced will have at least one profile for the primary customer for each vehicle.
Consideration should be given following factors when planning profiling activities:

> *Your customers might all be the same age but live in different geographic regions. You offer products at different price points to allow you to reach customers at different income levels.*
> *You offer one product that can appeal to customers with different interests. Some of your customers watch satellite TV, while others are more likely to see advertising on social media.*

Creating multiple consumer profiles allows organisations to classify customers based on these differences. This classification can then be used to ensure marketing, advertising, product development and most importantly – the customer service we provide, meets their needs and expectations!

The Customer Journey

Brands and Branding

The word "brand" is one of those words that is widely used but seldom fully understood.

A brand is the way a company, organisation, or individual is perceived by those who experience it. More than simply a name, term, design, or symbol, a brand is the recognisable feeling a product or business evokes.

A long-standing definition of the word brand is when farmers would "*brand*" their animals with initials or a symbol to indicate which animals are theirs, so when they were brought down from high ground or rounded up following an escape, the brand would identify who they belonged to.

In the 19th century, goods started to be packaged and producers started to put their name or mark on the packaging to differentiate their products from those of other producers. This was the start of the development of branding. Bass, the brewers from Burton on Trent branded their beer in 1882 with the first known trademark.

Coca-Cola Company was getting started around the same time and wishing to differentiate their product from others, the Coca Cola brand was born. The early success of the Coca-Cola product meant that there were countless attempts to copy it and despite developing unique labels and stylised writing, the copies continued until they came up with the idea of changing the packaging and so the globally recognised bottle was designed and patented. The bottle itself became a registered trademark in 1961.

These two early brands have become iconic over the years and the products are recognised simply by a symbol or the shape of a bottle.

In the latter part of the 20th century, it became clear that the **brand** of the product was more than just a name and a logo. Marketeers realised that it is possible to create a specific perception in people's minds regarding the qualities and attributes of the product or service.

Consumer perception became known as "the brand."

The power of the brand is enormous and this is clearly evidenced in everyday life when customers begin to refer to products by their brand identity or generic term, rather than the actual name of the product.

Some examples are:

The Customer Journey

Generic Term	Product
Astroturf	Artificial grass
iPod	MP3 player
Biro	Ball point pen
Britvic Orange	Orange Juice
Cashpoint	ATM machine
Coke	Cola soft drink
Filofax	Personal organiser
Frisbee	Arial Toy
Hoover	Vacuum Cleaner
Jacuzzi	Hot tub
JCB	Excavator
Jeep	Four-wheel drive vehicle
Kleenex	Tissues
Onesie	Leisurewear
Post-it	Self-adhesive notelet
Pritt Stick	Glue stick
Scalextric	Slot car racing
Sellotape	Adhesive tape
Stanley Knife	Craft knife
Super glue	Cyanoacrylate adhesive
Swarfega	Degreaser
Tupperware	Plastic storage containers
Vaseline	Petroleum Jelly
Velcro	Hook and loop fastener

The process cannot be stopped!

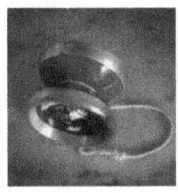

The Yo-Yo is a toy first launched in 1929 which became an overnight success and remained so for many years to come. The name Yo-Yo was deemed to be a generic term in 1965, despite the trademark owner, Duncan Toys, doing everything possible to make the company name the generic name with the slogan

'if it's not a Duncan, it's not a yo-yo'.

Many manufacturers used the term yo-yo to describe their product, not realising it is a branded name and that they should be calling their own version a toy on a string!

The Customer Journey

Brands become embedded in our minds. They exist in the minds of everyone who experiences them: employees, investors, the media, and, perhaps most importantly, customers.

Simply put, brands are perceptions.

Brands are an Asset

The Brand is the organisations most valuable asset. Despite their intangible nature, brands are business tools that drive commercial value.

Think about Apple.

> *The brand does not suggest phones, computers, watches, etc – they are the products that Apple manufacture.*
>
> *The Apple brand is not slick advertising or heavily stylised shop windows – that is just marketing and advertising.*
>
> *Even the Apple logo has no association, whatsoever, to what is meant when the organisation and its products are discussed.*

In fact, the Apple Brand isn't anything! You cannot hold it, hear it or touch it. But that does not mean the Apple Brand is not the single, most valuable thing that Apple owns.

It is the strength of the Apple brand that means loyal Apple customers would never contemplate using any other product.

The implied philosophy of the Apple brand has become embedded in the identities of its devoted followers.

This is the reason that, it is the brand that gives Apple its ultimate competitive advantage. Nothing else even comes close.

A strong brand increases the chances of customers choosing your product or service over your competitors. It attracts more customers, at a lower cost per sale, who are happy to pay a little more and will buy a little more often.

The Customer Journey

Think of a brand -

Brand	Logo
Apple	(Apple logo)
Coca-Cola	(Coca-Cola logo)
Porsche	(Porsche logo)
McDonalds	(McDonald's logo)

None of these brand names or logos actually identify the product it represents.

The Customer Journey

The Five Stages of a Customer's Journey

The customer Journey can be broken down into five stages which reflect the customers experience during this part of their journey.

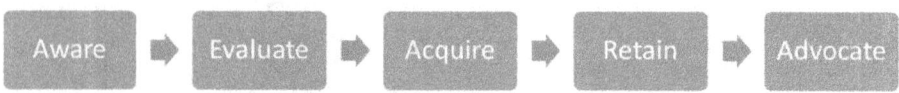

1. Awareness
The prospective customer will only become aware of the organisation if they need or want something it provides. They can identify the organisation by a variety of ways, through a search engine, word-of-mouth, website, testimonial, or even a social or blog post. They may have found a voucher or coupon through a marketing email or a physical mailing. At this stage, the prospective customer will have formed an impression of the organisation based on the interaction which has taken place so far. Remember- this interaction may be exclusively via a website or the internet – no human interaction may have taken place at this point.

Method	Effect
Visual symbols	Seeing a visual symbol such as a brand or logo
Brand Name	Hearing or seeing a brand named such as attending an event sponsored by a brand where a brand name is mentioned several times
Environments	Stepping into a physical environment such as a shop or visiting a website. At this stage, the visit is curiosity driven because the customer knows little about the brand.
Product Sightings	A customer sees someone with the product, e.g., you notice someone wearing some interesting shoes and wonder where they bought them from
Word of Mouth	Hearing about a brand product or person from friends
Media	Media mentions or coverage of a brand product or service which could also be negative
Promotion	Promotions such as viewing an advertisement or a product placement in the film
Search	And countering the brand or product in a search. At the awareness stage, customers are not searching for the brand directly.
Networking	Networking suggests talking to an employee or salesman from a firm at an exhibition

2. Evaluate/Deliberate
The organisation and others (who supply similar products or services) have now made it to this second stage of the customer journey. At this stage, prospective customer investigates, they will do their research and read content (instruction manuals, product

The Customer Journey

descriptions/specs, Q&As, product reviews, etc.) This will assess what is on offer against their needs and expectations.

Activity	Results
Visits	Visiting a digital or physical location. Visit is now purpose driven
Reviews	Reading product reviews
Social Media	Reading community posted content about the brand and product
Media	Viewing media related to the brand such as promotional videos brochures etc.
Information	Reading information such as product specifications
Examination	Viewing visuals of the product such as an online brochure
Contact	Contacting the organisation with an enquiry
Conversion	Taking positive action as the result of a marketing effort
Meetings	Meetings with sales or other representatives of the organisation
Questions	Asking questions about the product of staff or friends
Statement of Need	Providing sales department with information about your needs

3. Acquisition

Having deliberated and evaluated the options available, the customer is about to make the decision to buy. It is vital to ensure this step is as easy and smooth as possible. Frustration at this point could lead to the customer changing their mind. For some organisations, this may

The Customer Journey

seem like the ultimate goal, but in fact, it is only the beginning. The next step after the sale, is to keep the organisation and its brand at the forefront of their mind and get them to interact further with the organisation (e.g., to "like" or comment on the company's social posts/pages, make repeat purchases, etc.)

Frustrations	Impact
Information Overload	Too much information can be detrimental
Ambiguity	Customer does not really understand the product so will buy one that they do
Decision Fatigue	Customer may choose not to buy if the decision has been too difficult
Relationship Building	Issues building relationship with sales staff - a member of staff was rude
Samples and Trials	Obtaining a free sample or a trial of the product or brand
Price Comparison	Comparing prices between two or more options
Customization	The ability to customise the product or brand will increase commitment
Quality Comparison	Comparing the quality between two or more products
Features and Functions	Comparing the features and functions of different products
Quotes	Ask for a quotation if the price is negotiable
Negotiation	Negotiation of price and terms of the agreement
Coupons	Looking for discounts or coupons or waiting until sale time
Decision Justification	Customer needs to be satisfied but the by indecision is justifiable
Product Selection	Finding the correct product e.g., size, colour
Shopping Cart	Adding or removing items from the shopping cart when more favourable options are available
Closing	Saying yes to close the deal
Purchase	Making a purchase that does not involve negotiation such as online
Purchase Confirmation	Reviewing the confirmation of the purchase to satisfy that it is correct
Buyer Remorse	Regretting the purchase. This often happens after an impulse by indecision
Rebuy	A routine purchase when no consideration is given prior to the decision
Re Evaluate	Re-evaluating the product to see if there are more beneficial alternatives

The Customer Journey

4. Retention

One the sale has been made the next step is to retain the customer by providing a strong after sale service (such as emails or ads offering coupons, discounts or free shipping). By retaining the customer at this stage, there is less need for the customer to pass through steps one and two again in future if they are happy with the experience they have had. The aim is now to develop the customer further into an advocate for the brand and the organisation.

Factors	Effect
Service Delivery	The delivery of the product or service is as agreed or promised
Unpacking	The ease with which the purchase can be unpacked
Adoptability	How easy is the product to put into service?
Stability	How consistent the performance of the product is
Usability	The ease with which the user can interact with the product or service
Performance	The performance of the project such as its speed or economy
Safety	The way in which the product or service performs
Look and feel	The presentation and the feel of the product is satisfying
Environments	The environment in which the product or service is experienced should be appropriate
Sensory Experience	The impact the product or service has on the human senses
Customer Service	The interactions which take place between the customer and customer service
Convenience	The ease of use or convenience derived from using the product or service
Comfort	The sense of wellbeing to be derived from using the product
Special Experience	The customer derives and experience which they feel is particularly meaningful to them
Billing	The ease with which the total price can be established including any extras or surcharges
Problems	Any instances which the customer considered to be a problem and cause them unnecessary hindrance
Problem Resolution	The expediency with which the problem was resolved

The Customer Journey

5. Advocacy
If the journey has been smooth and trouble free, the customer would be more than happy to share the positive experience they had with the organisation/brand/product or service, whether it be by word-of-mouth, on a review page or on social media. A recent study showed that 71% of buyers were more likely to buy after reading a recommendation on social media. This is how valuable the customer journey can be.

Method	Activity
Reviews	Posting reviews of the product, services or brands
Recommendations	Recommendation by word of mouth or on social media
Media Mentions	Talking about the product in the media, social media, etc.
Answering Questions	Answering questions posed by other users on blogs community pages, etc.
Solving Problems	Users who identify solutions or work arounds to problems other users may find annoying
Media Creation	Creating media which supports the use of the product or service
Feedback	Providing feedback to the organisation on issues which have been identified such as bugs, faults, failures, etc
Product Extensions	Extending the functionality of the product to expand its use or performance
Design	Supporting the organisation as part of the research and development team in a non-executive capacity

This summary of the customer journey above, barely scratches the surface of the full detail of the actual customer journey. It is abundantly clear that this process is far from straightforward and needs a great deal of analysis to fully understand the complexities of the customer journey. To begin to fully understand this, the customer journey should be mapped.

The Customer Journey

Customer Journey Map

A customer journey map is a visualisation that display the story of the customer's experience starting from initial contact, through the process of engagement and getting converted into a long-term relationship. This exercise helps organisations step into their customer's shoes and see their organisation from the customer's perspective. It allows the organisation to gain insights into the points where customer's experience difficulty or challenges and how to improve them.

The customer journey is not only affected by the interactions which take place with the sales team, many other departments will have an involvement too. To deliver the very best customer journey and fully satisfy customers there must be a common understanding and cooperation across all teams.

69% of consumers want to talk with a company in real-time

Every customer journey will be different depending on the organisation specifics, industry characteristics, and preferences of the customers in any given sector. Therefore, a dedicated customer journey map should be produced designed especially for each individual brand.

There are software tools available to help map the journey, but it can be done simply with pen and paper and plenty of blue-sky thinking.

Benefits of a customer journey map

> *Enhanced Customer Experience*
> Allowing you to optimise the customer onboarding process. Customer experience is the number one determining factor of whether customers are willing to continue doing business with an organisation or not. Currently, 89% of organisations compete primarily on the criteria of customer experience – growing from just 36% in 2010.
>
> Organisations can build the prosperity of their brand through satisfied customers. Satisfaction instinctively rises as customers are provided with the experiences they like to see.
>
> *Better Understanding of the Customer*
> Understanding the customer is essential for any organisation. Successful entrepreneurs know what their customers want and how they can make the product or service available, effectively and efficiently.
> A customer journey map will help to gain that in-depth knowledge of customers. As the customer goes from touchpoint to touchpoint, a map will show how easily they can do that.

The Customer Journey

Identify areas of issue

A customer journey map helps uncover where customer service lapses may arise. Staff shortages may lead to customer frustration. A badly written website with inconsistent layouts can be annoying. All these factors will be identified and highlighted in a customer service journey map.

Contents of a Customer Journey Map

A journey map developed from the perspective of the customer would use the experience of the customer as the basis of the journey map. The journey focuses on what the consumer does instead of mentioning the steps of the journey from a system or business process viewpoint.

The Customer Journey	
Awareness	Customer identifies the need to make a purchase and begins to seek a source of the supply for the purchase
Evaluate / Deliberate	Customer compares products, specifications, warranty, price, availability, service options, etc. Will take advice from family, friends, blogs, consumer reports, etc
Acquisition	Buying decision is made and product or service is purchased. Attention now switches to retention
Retention	Follow up emails can be sent where warranty is offered to seek feedback, upsell add on items or services, upgrades, etc
Advocacy	Customer shares positive feedback on the product or service to friends, via blogs, website, reviews, social media etc.

Concentrate on the thoughts and feelings of the customer because they experience various touchpoints as they interact with the brand at different stages.

Customer journey maps should be developed with particular customers in mind and primarily focused on a sound awareness of their background and information drawn from the experience of previous customers which has been captured in a Customer Profile.

The map should be constructed based on a true understanding of their behaviour, thoughts and feelings.

The Customer Journey

Performance indicators should also be included in the map as they will provide the framework for the assessment of journey maps. Most customer journey maps take advantage of analytical data to imagine the emotional ups and downs of customers.

Visual indicators show positive/neutral/negative or exceeds/meets/does not meet expectations so that areas of opportunity can be effectively assessed and responded to effectively. They become important and useful to evaluate customer experience improvement over time especially if quantitative metrics are used.

This will be beneficial if an improvement program is to be implemented, as the same metrics can then be collected to measure the effect of the improvement. The metrics you gather might typically consist of net promoter score or other customer loyalty measures, customer satisfaction measures, etc.

By adding other supplementary information on the map as well as the key features of the journey makes the visualisation of the map considerably more effective. By adding the essential performance metrics in your map, it becomes more attractive to people who may otherwise have taken less interest in the map.

80% of customers now consider their experience with a company to be as important as its products.

The map is a useful way to reframe the performance dashboards that are often used to enlighten senior management by incorporating touchpoints with real customer experience.

Other stakeholders may also gain significant advantages from data drawn from sources as diverse as the view of the people, processes, systems and "behind the scenes" activities related to providing customer experience at each touchpoint so that they can obtain clear visibility of how the areas they manage lead to either favourable or unfavourable customer experiences.

Producing a Customer Journey Map

Set Objectives
Establish the reason for producing the map in the first place. Why is time, effort and money being invested in producing it? What benefit is being strived for? Write down the expectations for the map.

Identify the specific target customer type to be mapped. This imaginary customer represents the average customer with all their demographics and psycho graphics. By having a specific customer type in mind will steer all aspects of the customer journey map to them.

Generate a customer profile
Generate a customer profile so it is clearly understood whose journey is being mapped. Base the profile on research from genuine customer feedback to create a more accurate profile. Questionnaires and surveys are effective ways to gain priceless customer feedback. Targeting only the current or potential customers is essential.

The Customer Journey

Here are some questions your buyer profiles should address:

- *What are your customers' job titles and responsibilities?*
- *Where are they located?*
- *What hobbies, activities, or organizations do they partake in?*
- *Are they the decision-maker for buying your product? If not, how do they connect with the decision-maker?*
- *What challenges are they facing?*
- *What solutions have they already tried to solve those challenges? Why did those solutions come up short?*
- *What are they interested in learning about from you?*
- *What are the most important factors when they are deciding to make a purchase?*

You also need retrospective feedback from people who have already purchased products and services and who have already communicated with the organisation or are intending to do so.

Identity the Touchpoints
By identifying all the touch points, this step gives you vital knowledge about what the customers do. By knowing the touchpoints and how people are likely to react will help acknowledge the customer journey's simplicity and goals.
Depending on the research, list all the touchpoints presently used by current and potential customers, and those who might also be used if there is no overlap.

Think about social channels, paid ads, email marketing, third-party review sites or mentions that the customer will use to find the organisation online. Perform a quick Google search to see all the websites that are associated with the brand and the competitor websites. Experience the competitor websites and record the experience so it can be compared.

Change and develop
Once the entire customer journey has been mapped, it becomes easier to envisage what the customer experiences as they make their purchase. The process should be as simple and streamlined as possible. If not, it needs fixing!

Follow each customer journey via their online activity, their emails, or via online searching. Try to identify where the process does not work as it should. Once the process is clear the necessary adjustments can be made to meet the objectives.

It maybe that it is not clear how to order or select goods or services. Perhaps the descriptions or specifications are weak or inadequate. It does not matter how minor the changes are, they will be powerful as they are directly related to what customers have cited as their problem areas.

The Customer Journey

Presenting the results

The results can be presented in any format, there are no hard and fast rules as to how this should be done, however, the results need to be displayed in a way in which they are easily understood and the issues that it raises are very clear to see.

When quantitative data has been captured, this can be displayed in graphical form if necessary and qualitative data can be RAG rated to highlight its importance and include it in the graphical representation.

Below are two examples of Journey maps and you will find hundreds more online.

A simple spreadsheet could be easily configured to display the information.

The Customer Journey

Customer Journey Map

Purpose of the map:	Review of service standards						
Objective:	To identify and remediate problem points in customer interaction with the organisation						
Customer Profile:	Young professionals 18 – 30 years of age						
	Initial Contact			Product Selection			
Touch Points:	Website	Telephone	Social Media	Face to face	Range	Information	Price
Positive:	Easy to navigate with informative resources for products.	Free phone Number easy to remember	Accessible on many platforms	Warm welcome Needs identified quickly and referred to product expert.			
Negative:	Can be very slow to use. Took 8 seconds for page to load	Took 3 attempts to contact – lines engaged	Carries lots of adverts and click bait links	Staff poorly presented. Shop floor dirty.			
Metric:	Time taken for page to load	Number of attempts to get a response	Ease of accessing information	Initial impression			
Assessment:	7/10	5/10	3/10	6/10			
Graph:							
Potential Solution:	Identify ways to improve speed and response times	Obtain more telephone lines Review call handling Recruit more staff	Try to remove unnecessary visual clutter	Regular public presentation checks to be carried out by floor manager. Consider introducing staff uniforms.			

Level 3: Customer Service Specialist

The Customer Journey

Customer Journey Map

	Awareness	Evaluate / Deliberate	Acquisition	Retention	Advocacy
Activities	Identifies a need / Sees it on TV or in a magazine / Knows a friend who owns it	Performs a search / Reads a review / Checks price / Reads specification	Negotiates price / Discuss with customer service / Places order	Receives feedback form / Receives survey / Is offered up sell deals	Provides online review / Provides feedback / Recommends to friends / Buys again
Motivation	Views an advert / Sees a logo / Recommendation / Receives a free sample	Seeks value for money / Needs to feel part of trend / Meets needs / Latest and greatest	Justifies the purchase / Has a discount voucher / Identifies the benefits	Maintain product / Future proof item / Positive experience	Customer satisfaction / Supports the brand
Customer Journey					
Questions	Asks what it is/does / Asks a friend / How much? / Is it an improvement	Compare quality / Compares features / Compares price / Can I afford it?	Does it meet the need? / Is it affordable? / Will it satisfy the need? / Do I want it?	Benefit to them? / Want to be associated with / Asked to reflect on experience	Asks to be kept informed of updates / Asks for further information
Barriers		Questions integrity of a review / Price / Availability	Too expensive / Does not meet needs / Too complicated / Coupon / voucher rejected	Bad journey experience / Product not as described / Strong attraction from competition	Identifies a flaw with product / Not given the opportunity / Issues not dealt with

The Customer Journey

Customer Journey Analysis

Once the customer Journey has been mapped, it needs to be further analysed. The example above provides an insight into the overarching journey, but further analysis is needed at some stages to really understand the customer experience in detail. This is best explained by using an example. The second biggest purchase a person makes in their lives after a house, is a car.

This is not something which is bought impulsively like a packet of biscuits or a bar of chocolate at the checkout of a supermarket. A great deal of time is spent thinking about and planning this purchase and although it should ultimately be a pleasurable experience, many people find it challenging and very stressful as well. This becomes clearer when it broken down into greater detail. This process can be an emotional roller coaster for the customer, and it is important that these emotions are anticipated and are addressed accordingly to avoid issues arising during the customer journey.

As is shown in the table below, the customer will experience a range of emotions when they make a purchase. Anything which affects those emotions during the buying process will affect the perception of the customer about the organisation, the brand, the product or the service on offer.

Think about the choice of vehicle first. A suitable car to one person, will not be suitable to another, therefore there is little point in trying to convince someone who wants to buy a small electric hatchback that a large diesel powered 4x4 is an appropriate alternative. They will simply become annoyed and walk away.

A customer who is planning to spend £20,000, £30,000 to buy a new car is entitled to expect the dealership to roll out the red carpet, provide good quality coffee and nice chocolate biscuits. The customer buying a second-hand car for £1,000, on the other hand, may not have similar expectations, however, it is still a major purchase for them and warrants them being treated as a valued and worthy customer as well.

When researching the vehicles, information should be readily available a slow, difficult to navigate website will frustrate customers and they will go elsewhere. It is important to remember that people seldom buy out of need - they will buy for benefit. A person may need a new coat, but they will not buy any garment which can be called a coat, they will buy one which is waterproof or one which is warm, in a particular style or made from a particular material. It is important these benefits are highlighted to the customer at every opportunity. The fitting of the infamous cup holders in cars became something of a joke but nonetheless the addition of cup holders to vehicles used by travelling salesmen sold many more cars than an economical engine or nice fabric trim!

By breaking down the journey into its smallest steps, it becomes possible identify where issues can arise in the relationship with the customer. The "what if" question should be used at every step to identify what could go wrong. These must all be identified, and practices, policies or procedures should be put into place to prevent there being any form of conflict or irritation arising for the customer. By eliminating these points of possible conflict, the relationship between the customer and the organisation will be mutually beneficial and the transition from customer to advocate will be smooth and problem free.

The Customer Journey

Activity	Customer feeling / Emotion
Notices an attractive car on the road	Catches attention and begins to think about the car – *no need for a new vehicle at this stage.*
Sees the car in an advert and notes the brand and model name	Has created a mental note to research the vehicle – *begins to find reasons to justify change of car*
Navigates to manufacturer website whilst browsing the internet	Researches detail and specification of the vehicle – *begins to identify with the features and benefits of the new vehicle*
Notices a similar vehicle which also fits the perceived need	Questions initial choice of car and researches alternative model – *has some doubts about initial choice of car – enthusiasm wanes*
Adds second vehicle to list of choices	Completes online review of both cars – *books a test drive with local dealer*
Undertakes test drive	Reflects on the experience of driving cars – *identifies one model as being preferable to the other*
Asks for quotations for both models and part exchange valuation	Begins to consider buying decision – *decision will be influenced by cost benefit*
Makes buying decision based on price and research experience and reflection	Identifies source of funding for the purchase - *is funding available? Is it affordable?*
Obtains funding approval	Recalculates deal to identify where additional benefit can be gained – *added extras, inclusive servicing, extended warranty, etc*
Negotiates on price	Now in a dominant position – *Will try to negotiate the best deal possible – add uprated stereo, free fuel, etc*
Places the order and signs agreement	Euphoric, excited, keen to get the keys – *Sense of relief the decision is made, funding arranged, and agreement signed.*
Awaits delivery of the vehicle	Reflects on the process – continue or abort – *Is it the correct decision, has research been thorough? Is there an exit route out of the agreement?*
Car delivered	Sense of elation – excitement and happiness – *keen to show family, friends, peers, etc.*
Completes dealership review form	Reflects on the process and scores accordingly
Submits a review to Car magazine	Feedback on vehicle - *will be influenced by experience throughout the journey*
Car breaks down	Anger, Frustration, Embarrassment, etc

The Customer Journey

Customer Emotions

Emotion plays a key role in any customer journey, with customers going through a range of positive and negative emotional reactions. The measure of customer emotion will therefore indicate how customers feel about their experience with an organisation. To offer a good customer experience you need to ensure that positive emotions outweigh the negative ones. The challenge is how to identify what these emotions are and when they occur during the customer journey.

The dynamics behind customer emotion are surprisingly complex. The increasing importance of customer emotion in customer experience can be summed up by appropriating an old quote:

> *"Customers may not remember what the quality of your product was, but they will always remember how the experience made them feel."*

Those feelings can be the difference between good, and great, results for a business.

This is because customer emotions inspire decisions. Research has demonstrated that a customer's emotions are the best indicators of not just individual purchases, but of the likelihood to continue the customer journey, and inspire others to take that journey, as well.

> *customers with an emotional connection spent twice as much as customers who were merely satisfied with the product*

Businesses need to understand how emotion affects both individual decisions, and the customer's long-range journey. Determining these will help you figure out how to make customer emotion a key part of a customer experience strategy.

Understanding the customers' emotional engagement with the brand can help lead to loyal customers that are more likely to nurture a lucrative relationship with a brand.

Having invested time, effort and money into bringing the customer up to the point of making the buying decision, it would be unthinkable to lose the customer at that point because of their fears or anxiety about the decision they have made. It is vital to read the customer at every stage of the process and study the emotions and behaviours identified throughout the journey so the necessary precautions and safety nets can be put in place to ensure the journey is not frustrated by factors which can affects the customers emotions.

By maintaining open communication channels and passing information to the customer it will allay those fears and they will remain committed to the purchase. The customer who is ignored at this stage will reflect on the decision and could withdraw.

The Customer Journey

Why Emotions Matter

Customer experience is the battleground between competitors and emotion is a powerful weapon in that battle. Customer emotion will impact on customer loyalty, the value of the order and whether customers are spreading good or bad feedback about the organisation.

A study found that 74% of customers with positive emotions will recommend the organisation while only 8% of customers with negative emotions will.

When a customer is going through an experience they are not thinking about metrics, they are living the experience. They are thinking about how they feel. Excited about placing an order, frustrated at trying to find information, the anticipation of waiting for something to be delivered, anger while waiting in a phone queue to report an issue.

When that experience ends, and someone asks you to leave a rating between 1 and 10 does that include everything about the ups and downs of the experience?

Customer experience metrics like NPS are great for identifying overall trends but they cannot identify how the customer truly feels during the experience and uncover the negative emotional points that could decide if this customer will return or not.

Best-in-class brands average 17 emotionally positive experiences for every negative experience, while the lowest-performing brands provided only two emotionally positive experiences for each negative one.

Emotion is critical to a brand's bottom line.

Measuring Emotion in Customer Experience

Measuring emotions can be difficult but there are a few ways you can start to identify the common emotions that your customers feel.

A range of emotions could be offered, and the customer asked to choose the one that most closely matches how they feel.

Sentiments could be tracked from open text responses to not only identify how someone feels but the specific area they are talking about when they express that emotion.

There may be such a wide range of emotions which could be applicable that it would be difficult to categorise these in a way that makes sense to the organisation and its customers.

One of the most popular approaches to classifying emotional responses was created by Robert Plutchik in 1980. He believed there are eight primary emotions – anger, fear, sadness, disgust, surprise, anticipation, trust and joy.

The Customer Journey

His 'Wheel of Emotion' allows emotions to be expressed at different degrees of intensity or a combination of emotions to form different emotions. By allowing customers to choose from this range of emotions it will identify the intensity of how they feel and identify derived emotions that might be occurring subconsciously.

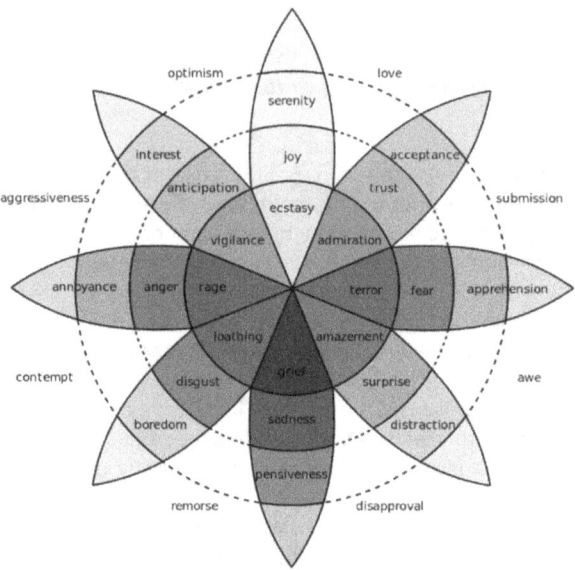

Map the Emotional Journey

Once a method of measuring emotions has been identified, the key is to identify where they occur in the customer journey. If someone expresses anger, the only way it can really be dealt with is to pinpoint where that anger occurred and try to eliminate it. There are a few ways you can try to achieve this.

Continuous Feedback
An 'Always On' feedback system allows customers to engage throughout the customer journey.

They can provide feedback at various stages in the experience rather than just express how they feel at the end of the journey. This will allow you to map the emotional journey throughout the experience and identify when the negative emotions are occurring.

Customer Journey Surveys
An alternative which is less reliant on the customer having to keep coming back to provide feedback, is to improve the post experience survey. This will take the customer back through the journey they have just completed, identify the key touch points in the journey and ask the customer to express how they felt at each stage. This allows a chart to be created that can track how they felt at each stage helping you identify both the positive and negative peaks.

The Customer Journey

Intelligent Text Analytics

Rather than separating out the customer journey it is possible to set up common topics and map these to touch points in the journey. This allows a customer to talk more openly about their experience and the areas they mention can be automatically assigned to key touch points.

If someone has been on a holiday there are key areas in the customer journey from booking the holiday, traveling there, checking in, the service during the holiday and the return journey etc. By mapping common terms to these areas of the journey it is possible to piece together the journey and overlay the emotions being expressed at each stage.

Summary

There are several ways you can begin to measure emotion in customer experience and start to map these to customer journey touch points. No matter how you approach this, but it is essential you start to track customer emotions as they can provide so much more insight than a rating will ever provide.

Metrics such as Net Promoter Score will always have a place in customer experience and allow a more universal view of performance. By starting to track the emotional journey of the customer and improve the negative peaks, it will allow an assessment of how this impacts on the overall NPS rating and how it impacts on the organisation's KPI's.

This ultimately will allow the calculation of a return on investment (ROI) based on emotions, which will evidence just how powerful delivering a positive emotional customer experience can be.

The Customer Journey

Types of Customer Journey

The customer journey can take different forms when it is analysed. In the car buying example above it is shown as a timeline or linear journey.

There is nothing wrong with a linear representation of the customer journey, however, it is no longer acceptable to regard the whole customer journey as being linear. This would mean that a customer would purchase a brand or service and never repeat the process again. After the purchase, there would be no further interaction with the organisation.

In the example above – the customer has progressed through the customer journey experience, however, at some point they will need to replace the car when it is passed its useful life. The manufacturer of the car and the dealership who sold it, will be anxious to ensure that the customer returns to the dealership to buy the same brand again bringing the customer journey through its full circle and repeating when a new model or style is brought to market. This is a cyclical customer journey and is far easier to conceive if a product such as groceries is being purchased. There is a tendency to buy the same product time after time because we consider it a trusted brand and a valued product or service. Provided the customer is not upset by the product, the consumer will continue to purchase it. Clearly, the place where they purchase it may upset the customer, but provided the alternative source supplies the same product, they will continue to purchase the brand from the alternative supplier, in fact, they are more likely to purchase the product from an alternative than they are to purchase an alternative product from the existing supplier!

Another type of customer journey are those driven by seasons. We buy certain items at specific times of year whether it is clothes for a summer holiday or festive products for Christmas. Once the purchase has been made, the organisation will look to keep the customer engaged with offers for other seasonal items at other times of year as in the case of clothes, or they will seek to remind the customer of their previous purchase when the season is approaching in the hope, they will recall their buying experience from the previous season and repeat it.

Customer Service Issues

Under ideal conditions, the Customer will experience a very smooth journey, without interruption, every expectation met and they are happy to recommend the organisation to others. On many occasions this will be the case, however, even with the best intentions, problems will arise. This immediately brings the prospect of completing the journey into question.

It has been shown that if the issue is dealt with promptly and emphatically, rather than reducing the customers perception of the business, it can actually increase it.

The problems which can arise can range from minor queries to deal breaking situations which need to be handled very carefully and closely managed until resolved.

Problems can start from a simple question.

The Customer Journey

Customer Questions

"NO, SIR, WE DON'T HAVE A BIG NOISE. WE HAVE A CHIEF LIBRARIAN."

A major part of the Customer Service function is dealing with routine enquiries and after a short time in a role you will know the answer to most of the common questions and will be able to respond positively.

Where IT systems are used to assist the Customer Support function, there will be guides and scripts as to how to deal with these routine issues so they can be quickly and effectively resolved.

These types of questions usually fall into two categories - Queries and Requests.

Queries are usually routine questions regarding opening times, stock availability, questions about offers and deals and how to return an item for refunds etc. These can be dealt with very quickly and an immediate resolution can be found.

Requests are more specific and usually relate to a specific piece of information. Brochure and specification requests are common. Details of websites, email addresses and requests for information about additional products or services are also common.

It is vital that these requests are dealt with correctly. When a customer request information, they have already passed the awareness stage in the customer journey and are at the evaluation stage. The request for information could make or break the decision to buy so it is critical it is handled correctly.

Customers will often make requests of Customer Service staff or query policies and practices because they are unsure. These questions will come from a variety of sources such as face to face at a customer service desk or by telephone. More recently there has been a significant increase in the use of social media as an information channel.

By listening carefully to the question, the customer service assistant can assess whether it is a routine query or whether the customer requires more detail.

If the customer can be seen, an experienced person would be able to tell from someone's body language whether they were happy or not. A customer on the telephone will use a different tone of voice depending on what they are asking. When the customer is on-line, we do not have any clues so service levels must be even higher.

At some point all customer service staff will be asked a question which they are unable to answer. How this

The Customer Journey

is dealt with is most important because the customer will want a prompt response and may not be able to hang around whilst you find the answer.

At this point you will need to refer the customer to someone else. Maybe if you are on the telephone, you could transfer the call or if you are face to face maybe take the customer to the person who can help.

When done promptly and efficiently this may well even exceed the customers' expectations, they will be able to discuss an issue in detail and receive an equally detailed response.

The decision on who to refer the person to depends on the question. It could be a colleague or a line manager or even the manager if the question is of a serious nature.

It is important that any customer question is dealt with positively.

Positively in this case means responding quickly, either answering the question directly or making the decision who to refer it to and how to refer it. If a customer is on the telephone never put them on hold unless there is no alternative. Similarly, do not refer the customer to another member of staff if that person is already busy. These are negative actions because we are not dealing with the question effectively.

Firstly, apologise to the customer and explain you are unsure of the correct answer, but you will find someone who can help them. If there is a procedure for dealing with the situation it should always be followed but be willing to bypass people if they are busy and go to the next level on the list. Customer service staff should always be polite to the customer.

Avoid resorting to small talk and ask the customer questions which they must answer with a sentence. These are called "open" questions. A closed question simply requires a yes or no answer. Always try and relate it to the question they have raised. This way you can find out more about the customers' needs and pass the information on to the person who will deal with it.

Sometimes a customer will have raised a question about a product or service which cannot be dealt with immediately as a third party may be involved. For example, a customer calls a garage to ask if their car has been fixed. The garage is waiting for a new part to be delivered before they can finish the car. This must be explained to the customer and tell them that the supplier will be called to find out when the part will be delivered.

The customer will be satisfied with this, but not for long. They will expect you to call the supplier and then call them back as quickly as possible. The customer may need to make travel arrangements and book appointments which he would be unable to do without his car. By keeping the customer informed they feel valued and that you as the garage, actually care about their expectations. Such positive communication will also encourage recommendations to their friends and repeat business from this customer.

The Customer Journey

Frequently Asked Questions

Many businesses today will use a FAQ to deal with customer questions and queries. This is a list of frequently asked questions which have been drawn together in one place with company approved answers. This means that the answers to the same question will always be the same and approved by the business.

This can be on-line so a customer can refer to it themselves via the website or it may be printed as a hardcopy which can be used by staff to answer customer questions on the telephone or face to face.

It is very important that a customer who telephones or visits the business must never be referred to the FAQ to get the answer to their question. It is quite acceptable to inform the customer about the FAQ for future reference, but on this occasion their enquiry should be dealt with immediately.

Dealing with routine customer service problems

There are a number of issues which regularly cause problems for customers and can very easily cause dissatisfaction and unhappy customers.

These are issues which are usually out of the business's control such as delays to deliveries caused by traffic problems or vehicle breakdowns, delays due to a third party failing to deliver in time, or problems due to strikes or availability of materials. Incidents such as incorrect deliveries or delivery errors are often caused by human error.

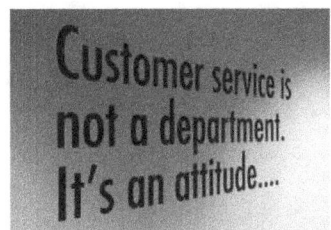

Regardless of the cause of the problem, there is still a very unhappy customer who feels as though they have been let down.

As a result of this, they will be angry and this will show in their tone of voice and if it is a face-to-face situation, it will show in their body language and facial expression. They may well be rude or impolite and they will speak abruptly.

The way in which this situation is dealt with is critical.

If it is dealt with effectively and positively, the customer will be satisfied and will return to the business. If it is not dealt with correctly, the customer will be lost to the business and tell everyone they know of their unhappiness.

Nobody makes mistakes on purpose, but they do happen. If you are working in a call centre, behind a counter or in any Customer Service role you are going to encounter an angry customer at some time.

The Customer Journey

The most common response is to evaluate the merit of the complaint whilst listening to it. Try to curb that natural reaction and replace it with the assumption that the customer has a right to be angry, even before you know the details.

The customer will feel let down because the product or services did not meet expectations. The customer may be angry because he or she made incorrect assumptions based on information given by staff.

It is very important not to get angry yourself. The customer may be rude or impolite, but they are not angry with you. Let them say all that they need to say, but make sure you are actively listening, so you fully understand what the problem is. You do not want to ask the customer to repeat it all again.

Stimulus and response

The way in which you react to a person or situation will directly affect how they react back to you. This is known as stimulus and response. When we provide a stimulus, it will prompt a response from the person receiving the stimulus – How they respond will directly affect behaviour.

If the response is positive - the situation will de-escalate, whereas, if the response is negative - the situation has the potential to escalate and become more serious.

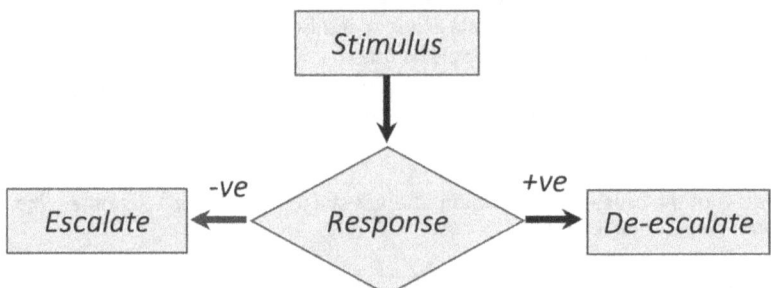

The Emotional versus the Rational Response

When customers find themselves in a situation where they feel they are being ignored or not being listened to, they will become angry and they may start to shout or become aggressive. This situation has the potential to become very dangerous, very quickly. It the customer is not handled correctly the situation could escalate to a point where the situation becomes dangerous.

Human beings have two ways of dealing with a situation – an Emotional response (responding to how we feel) and the Rational response (When we think about what we should do)

The Customer Journey

These two work together and we normally balance one against the other, making many emotional and rational decisions every day.

When we feel threatened or vulnerable our emotional mind takes over and we lose our ability to think and behave in a rational manner. This is a very animalistic behaviour trait –

Pull a dog's tail and it will bite you!

This is an automatic animal response from an emotional level.

Humans are different however, because we are usually able to make a choice about how we will react to any given situation. If we are afraid, we are inclined to run away – This is our emotional response – However if we spend a moment thinking about what is happening, we will rationalise the situation and probably realise we are not in danger and we will then relax.

Fight or Flight Response

If we feel seriously threatened, our body's natural reaction is to prepare us for this situation by releasing adrenaline. This causes the heart to pump more blood into the large muscles and reduce flow elsewhere. The eyes open wide to allow more information to be taken in and focus on the threat. Hearing becomes more heightened and thought processes become less rational and our ability to perform complex physical tasks is seriously reduced.

The body is geared for action whether that action is flight (run away) or fight.

This is a natural animal reaction. It is an instinctive reaction from prehistoric times and though the dangers we face today are very different – we still respond the same way – instinctively.

We can affect the way in which people react when they are afraid as they are more likely to fight if we:

- *invade their personal space*
- *continue to make them feel threatened*
- *block their exit route*

These apply to an irate customer as well. If we invade their personal space, if they feel they are not being listened to or if they feel threatened, there reaction and response may not be what we might normally expect.

It is vital that anyone dealing with customers who are displaying any form of irritation or anger should proceed with caution and do all they can to avoid doing anything which may further antagonise the customer.

The Customer Journey

The Escalation to Violence

The escalation from a state of simple frustration to anger, aggression or even violence, can happen in a split second. Whilst in most cases the escalation will be incremental, there is no guarantee of this and customers with metal health issues or under the influence of alcohol or drugs may leap form frustration directly to violence without warning.

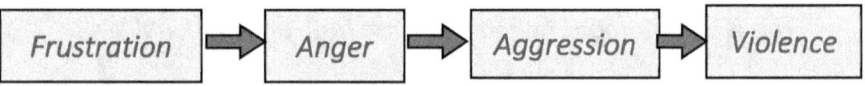

Triggers and Inhibitors

Triggers are very often small inconsequential issues which, when combined with other problems, spark aggression. They are often the last straw that breaks the camel's back.

A person who is already frustrated by long waits, poor service or other issues which are on their mind, can result in a trigger. You may never know what had pulled the trigger but if you do, you may be surprised that it is seemingly so insignificant.
People tend to be triggered into an anger reaction if they feel:

- *Embarrassed*
- *Humiliated*
- *Insulted*
- *Afraid*
- *Rejected*

They can feel this if they feel someone is talking down to them, ignoring them or not taking them seriously.

Any customer who is not always treated with respect, could react to a trigger you give them.

As a consequence, they will regard your actions as being the cause of their reaction, even though they may behave in a manner which is considerably worse than yours. The net result is they will claim you started it!

Inhibitors are things which prevent people from completely losing their temper. Not everyone gets violent when they become angry and this is due to our inhibitions or our inhibitors which include.

- *self-control*
- *personal values*

The Customer Journey

- *fear that the other party may fight back*
- *social or legal consequences*
- *experience*
- *training*

Your choice of response in these situations is vitally important. You may even have passed the fight or flight stage, but we can still choose to escalate or de-escalate the situation. If you react at an emotional level, you could easily make the situation worse.

Your response such as pointing a finger could be a trigger which leads to an escalation to violence.

You must consciously choose to respond to the incident in a way which we de-escalate the situation by thinking about every step you take.

The Attitude and Behaviour Cycle

It is extremely unlikely that you will have a positive attitude towards everyone you meet. Some people, for any number of reasons, will cause you to have negative feelings towards them. If you have these negative feelings, you will communicate this unconsciously to them and their reaction will be negative.

Once the person has become aware of your negative feeling, they will behave in a negative manner towards you. This will cause your negative feelings to cause you to behave in a negative manner. This will cause them to behave in a negative way which will, in turn,

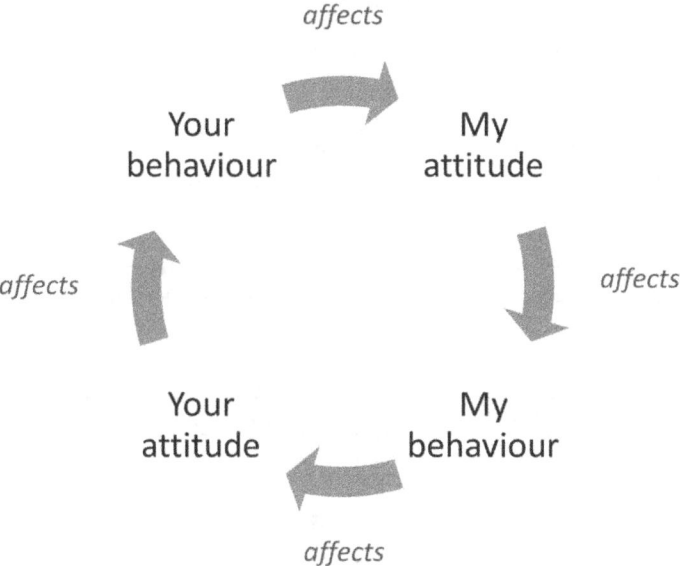

The Customer Journey

increase your negative feelings and behaviour. And so, the situation continues and deteriorates.

It is very difficult to change your attitude to someone. However, you can easily change your behaviour. You need to learn to behave so your negative feelings do not show, and your behaviour does not reveal and negative traits. This will break the cycle and stop it getting worse.

Communication Skills

It must be realised that you cannot expect to completely avoid conflict whilst fulfilling your job role, so it is vital that you understand how to deal with conflict and aggression when it happens.

Good communication skills are vital to diffusing conflict. Firstly, you will need to understand how we communicate.

Often there are situations where communication does not work and this is due to communication blocks, you will need to recognise these. We tend to think we communicate only through speech but in fact we use many other communication methods. Non- verbal communication is very important in emotional and threatening situations.

The basic elements of communication are:

When someone has something in his/her head to pass to you they create a coded message – usually made up of words, tone and non-verbal behaviour (body language)

You then decode this message and reply with one of your own

> We communicate with words, tone and body language

- **Words** - *the actual words spoken*
- **Tone** - *the way in which the words are spoken*
- **Non-Verbal** - *the stance, gestures and expressions which accompany the words*

Many studies have been done about communication and it is generally accepted that when we are in a face-to-face situation, the message is received by the receiver in the following proportions.

Method	Percentage
Words	*7%*
Tone	*38%*
Non-verbal or body language	*55%*

The Customer Journey

It is clear that words alone will not work unless the tone and body language are correct as well.

Effective communication influences behaviour. Good communication skills will allow you to take control of situations and people.

- *Your body language and tone of voice will make a big impact*
- *It is not so much what you say – but how you say it*
- *If you try to understand the other person's point of view it will ease understanding*

Some body language can make people feel threatened. Any gestures that could or might be regarded as aggressive – should be avoided.

These include:

Body language	Effect
Finger pointing/wagging	Associated with being told off and can be humiliating
Crossing your arms	Makes you look defensive
Sudden or quick movements	This could be misinterpreted as an attack
Rolling your eyes upwards	Indicates irritation and impatience
Looking down on people	Lowering your eyes rather than your head to look at someone is a sign of irritation
Frowning or Scowling	If you look unfriendly, fed up or miserable it will affect the people you are dealing with

A great deal of conflict can be avoided by using positive communication

You can go a long way towards preventing conflict by:

- *looking and sounding professional*
- *acting consistently and fairly*
- *working effectively as a team*

The Customer Journey

Blocks to Communication

Anything which stops, interrupts or prevents communication is called a block

There are three types of block to communication

- *Physical Blocks*
- *Psychological Blocks*

These can be further broken down:

Physical Blocks

Noise and physical distractions

This relates to anything in the environment or workplace which makes it difficult to hear or concentrate. Strobes and flashing lights, excessive heat or noise can all cause disruption to communication.

Alcohol and drugs

This can be the biggest block to communication. People's inhibitions are reduced and also their ability to comprehend what is being said to them. Alcohol has a depressive effect which reduces people's ability to understand what is being said to them and a slower reaction to normal stimuli.

In this state people can be unpredictable and unreasonable.

In this situation, you will need to:

- *adopt a non-aggressive stance*
- *maintain space between them and you*
- *talk slowly and calmly*
- *be prepared to repeat information*

Different cultures will communicate differently

In our multicultural society we have to deal with a variety of cultures and ethnic backgrounds. This means they may communicate differently, pronounce words differently, and structure sentences differently.
Their body language could be different, and, in some cultures, they may stand closer together and maintain eye contact for longer. It is therefore important that we do not misinterpret this behaviour as rude or threatening.

The Customer Journey

Psychological Blocks

Psychological barriers to communication
Psychological barriers can be much more difficult to spot and may not be obvious to either the sender or the receiver. The sender with a limited vocabulary may not be able to translate images or express themselves as they might wish (Encoding) as a consequence when you decode this information you may not understand what is being said

Psychological noise
People tend to hear what they want to hear. Receivers with inflated egos may filter out any parts of a message which do not agree with their own self-perception. They will simply not hear any criticism of themselves. They will also defend their opinion rather than listen to what is being said.

In highly charged and emotional situations there is a great deal of psychological noise. The receiver's ability to decode information is seriously compromised by what they have experienced and the images and emotions that have been involved.

Mental Illness
Mental illness can take many forms – you may be uncomfortable with this, but you are unlikely to face a physical threat as long as you behave sensitively and professionally. You should respond to aggressive behaviour rationally by understanding the possible cause

Fear	of noise or people. This leads to desperation and the only escape is fight
Paranoia	may be directed toward authority and probably caused by previous bad experiences
Anger	at provocation by others
Voices	this is rare but schizophrenics voices may tell them to injure others

All customer service staff must be sensitive to Mental Illness and whatever behaviour is exhibited you need to signal non-aggression and strive to defuse the situation

In order to control your own behaviour and manage the possibility of your personal situation escalating at the same time you must remember the four "A"'s

The Customer Journey

Do not get **A**ngry
Manage **A**buse
Maintain a positive **A**ttitude
Be **A**ssertive

Signalling Non-Aggression

If you are able to remember the four "A"'s and always apply it – you will already be beginning to signal non-aggression – there are, however, many other ways to emphasise it.

- *comfortable distance apart*
- *relaxed shoulders*
- *standing to the side*
- *calm voice*
- *open hands*
- *normal eye contact*

If these are the signs of non-aggression – it is clear that aggressive behaviour would be the opposite

- **close in** – *invading personal space*
- **standing square on** – *shoulders parallel*
- *excessive eye contact*
- *pointing or clenching of fists*
- *head and chin pushed forward*
- *clenched teeth*
- *raised voices*
- *swearing and abusive language*
- *abuse focussed on an individual*

If you understand the differences between aggressive and non-aggressive behaviour it will help you to assess situations and demonstrate nonaggressive behaviour through your own behaviour.

People are happy to communicate with others who are non-aggressive or threatening.

The Customer Journey

Dealing with angry customers

Do not assume you already know what people are going to say. The customer will respond to signs that you are listening and understanding his or her point of view. Use phrases like:

> *"I can see that this has made you very angry"*

> **or**

> *"I can understand why this has made you angry".*

In order to reassure the customer that you are really listening to what they are saying, it is important to:

- *Focus your attention on them*
- *Give non-verbal cues (e.g., nodding the head)*
- *Show that you have understood. Say things like: "OK let me see if I've understood you correctly..." and then summarise what they have said*
- *Let then finish speaking before you act. Never interrupt or cut across a person's speech*
- *Always let the customer say all they want to say trying to interrupt will not have the desired effect.*

When the customer has finished explaining their problem, speak softly and slower than you might normally speak. By speaking softly, the customer will have to listen to what you are saying, and they are less likely to interrupt you. It may seem that the customer does not care about what you have to say at first but remember that the customer approached you to solve their problem.

After you have listened carefully to the customer, repeat the issues that you believe that you heard from the customer perspective. This will assure them that you are focused on the appropriate issues and reassure them that you are concentrating on them as a priority.

At this point it does not matter who created the problem or what happened before the customer got to you. Tell the customer that you will resolve the problem.

By doing this the customer has a name, a face, a point of contact, who is dealing with their problem.

Because you are taking responsibility, the customer will calm down and no longer see you as the enemy, but as a friend.

The next thing is to record the details. Take their name and address and contact number and tell them your name and the telephone number of the business and any extension.

The Customer Journey

If you need to work with other departments, get manager approval or coordinate some other type of response, inform the customer that you will personally take the matter into your own hands and follow-up on the issues. It is important that you see the process through from start to finish. Getting other people involved in communication with the customer can lead to more complaints if they do not meet customer expectations.

Once you have a good idea of the problem and its cause, decide how long it will take to resolve. Can it be done immediately or are there other people who need to be contacted? The last thing you want to do is to detain the customer for a period of time only to find it still cannot be resolved. It is much better to explain how you will set about dealing with the problem and explain that you will call them at an agreed time to update them. You then need to set an alarm for that time to make sure you call the customer even if you have little to report. The customer will know you are working on their problem and will be pleased with your efforts.

You then need to work to find a solution to the problem. You may need to speak to other departments, the manufacturer your manager and so on. This is your job! You are responsible for delivering customer service.

Once you have a solution to the problem contact the customer and explain what you have resolved and agreed. Always ask if the customer is satisfied with that solution.

If a final resolution will take a few days to complete always make a follow up call to the customer to check they are now satisfied and happy with the outcome. Offer a final apology for the problem having arisen and assure the customer you will be available should any further issues arise.

By dealing with the problem this way the customer may still be angry with the initial problem but as far as your resolution is concerned, they cannot have any complaint. Because they see you as the representative of the business, they will have no issue in using the business again.

Complaints

Complaints should not be a common occurrence in an organisation which has a commitment to delivering quality products and services and has effectively mapped the customer journey and identified all touchpoints where issues could arise which led to the dissatisfaction of the customer. Nonetheless, there are always instances where these problems arise and need to be dealt with.

The policy should cover all forms of complaint, from minor moans through to major complaints which could have serious, adverse effects on the business. Every complaint will need to be managed on its own merits; however, a policy can be produced which deals with

The Customer Journey

issues on a varying scale. It is important to establish the nature of the complaint and identify the best and fastest way to resolve it, being always mindful of the customer.

There are standard complaint handling procedures which all staff should be trained to use, and the procedure should outline the alternative course of action to take if the standard procedures prove to be inadequate.

Customer Service Practices and Procedures

Inevitably there will be times when a customer is not satisfied, their expectations have not been met and they want solutions to their problem.

This is where practices and procedures come into effect. There will be practices set up to deal with the job role an individual has and who reports to whom. There will also need to be policies to deal with common occurrences such as when they will issue refunds, how they will deal with complaints and how they will deal with suspected criminal activity. The policy will state how the business deals with that issue. This way the same problem will be dealt with the same way each time. A returns policy for an item of clothing may say that a return will be accepted if the item is as new and unworn. This means if a customer brings back an item of clothing which smells of cigarette smoke, then a refund or exchange will not be granted.

Staff will need to know these policies or how to find out what they are should the need arise.

The procedures will detail how to deal with the situation. In the above example the customer may become angry when told they cannot have a refund. The procedure may then say the staff member should refer the problem to their line manager by first apologising to the customer and then escalating the problem to a line manager. There may also be procedures for financial transactions and reporting absences.

Working Within the Limits of Authority

It is vitally important that staff only operate within the limits of their authority. Any member of staff who operates outside this framework will be making decisions about things they do not understand, have not been trained for and do not have the authority to address.

It is therefore essential that staff dealing with customers always call-in senior staff when the limit of their authority has been reached. To ensure this, there will normally be a set procedure for handling complaints which should be complied with at all times

Typical customer complaint procedure

Handling customer complaints effectively will ensure that most dissatisfied customers' return as satisfied customers.

The Customer Journey

Only 4% of customers bother to complain, 96% just leave, unlikely to return.

One of the keys to successfully handling difficult situations is to try to see things from the customer's point of view.

Staff should be encouraged to receive feedback from the customer and then have a set procedure for dealing with a variety of common complaints.

It is well recognised that the quicker a complaint is dealt with and the least fuss made the more satisfied the customer becomes.

Consequently, effective managers, preceded by appropriate training, delegate responsibility to front line staff to deal with specific areas and levels of complaint.

It is important to determine what authority your staff should have in order to deal with complaints.

There will be occasions where the level of complaint needs to be handled by more senior members of staff. Such circumstances need to be clearly identified and set procedures agreed.

Handling Customer Complaints

Handling customer complaints effectively will ensure that most dissatisfied customers' return as satisfied customers. One of the keys to successfully handling difficult situations is to try to see things from the customer's point of view.

Staff should be encouraged to receive the feedback from the customer and then have a set procedure for dealing with a variety of common complaints. It is well recognised that the quicker a complaint is dealt with and the least fuss made the more satisfied the customer becomes. Consequently, effective managers, preceded by appropriate training, delegate responsibility to front line staff to deal with specific areas and levels of complaint.

It is important to determine what authority your staff should have to deal with complaints. There will be occasions where the level of complaint needs to be handled by more senior members of staff. Such circumstances need to be clearly identified and set procedures agreed.

General guidelines for a complaint procedure:

- **Ask the customer's name and use it** – *but be respectful*
- **Listen attentively** - *Find out what the customer is complaining about. Not all customers make it clear what their complaint is, particularly if they are upset*

The Customer Journey

- **Do not interrupt** - Let the customer have their say and then ask questions to clarify the situation. Deal with all complaints sensitively
- **Do not argue** - Even if it is thought the customer is wrong. Arguing will only inflame the situation.
- **Be polite and stay calm** - Let the customer explain, and do not blame others
- **Apologise sincerely** – The customer needs to see that the team member recognises they have been upset.
- **Thank the customer** - for bringing the complaint to the business's attention
- **Repeat the complaint** - Check understanding of exactly what the problem is by repeating it back to the customer - this will avoid any misunderstanding
- **Establish what the customer wants to happen** - if able, make a definite decision – avoid saying what cannot be done. Inform the customer what can be done and when it will happen
- **Be seen to immediately rectify the complaint** – this demonstrates the level of seriousness the business attaches to the situation
- **Check that the complainant is happy** - with how the complaint has been handled
- **Thank the customer again** - for bringing the complaint to the attention of the business
- **Record the complaint for a later review** – every complaint should be reviewed to understand what went wrong and why. Only then will it be possible to minimise the likelihood of it re-occurring.

If a disabled customer makes a complaint unrelated to their disability, then it must be dealt with as it would be for any other customer. If the complaint relates to their disability, the business must ensure that they make a reasonable adjustment but there is no obligation to go beyond what is reasonable.

REMEMBER: A business will be primarily judged on the quality of service that the customer receives.

A common procedure for dealing with customer complaints is H.E.A.T.

When a customer raises a complaint, they want it to be resolved. They see it as winning the outcome they want. Likewise, the organisation does not want to lose out as a result of the complaint either. The organisation wants to win too. It is this, elusive, Win : Win situation that should be sought when trying to resolve a customer complaint.

When dealing with a complaint it is not about having to be right, it is not about laying blame, justifying why something happened or making excuses. It is about resolving the situation quickly and amicably, ideally keeping the client in the process, but at the very least, limiting the damage that an unhappy customer can do. If you always remember the acronym HEAT, this will help to address all problems effectively, as they arise.

The Customer Journey

Acronym	Steps to deal with a problem
H	**Hear the customers complaint** – listen carefully to what they are telling you
E	**Empathise with the customer** – view the problem from their perspective
A	**Apologise** – Empathise with the customer and apologise for their experience
T	**Take Action** – Decide how to resolve the problem and explain your solution to the customer

A great deal of money is spent on attracting customers and training staff to be able to fulfil their needs. Unfortunately, some customers, for a variety of reasons, are unhappy and complain. Some employees tend to get defensive or lay blame elsewhere in order to 'get the complaint out the door as soon as possible' instead of taking steps to remedy the situation in a positive manner.

Next time you get a complaint remember the H.E.A.T acronym. It helps you focus on the positive steps needed to handle complaints and achieve a Win : Win outcome.

Service Breakdowns

Whilst it is the intention to ensure that every transaction with a customer is smooth and trouble free, there will be instances where the customer journey goes wrong, and customers become dissatisfied with the outcome.

By mapping the customer journey many of the common pitfalls can be anticipated and eliminated. At other times this will not be possible, however, it must be anticipated, and strategies identified to deal with it.

A common example is websites which, under normal trading conditions, are fast simple to use and have been streamlined to make the buying process as straightforward as possible.

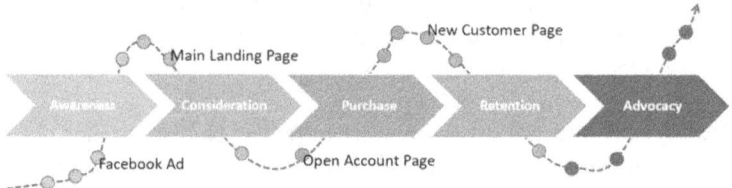

At times of high volume, this may not be the case. The website may slow down due to the volume of activity, Customers become frustrated and start making multiple clicks and the problem becomes even worse.

The Customer Journey

Ultimately, the website crashes and people pick up the telephone, so the customer service helpline becomes swamped and calls are not answered, and the customer becomes increasingly irate, abandoning the purchase and vowing never to use the organisation again.

In these extreme situations, there is very little that can realistically be done; however, it is vital that for all the issues identified in the customer journey map, a procedure is in place to deal with that situation. These usually take the form of organisational policies and procedures and in a retail environment might include:

- *Policies and procedures for issuing refunds*
- *Policies and procedures for paying compensation*
- *Policies and procedures for dealing with returns/exchanges*
- *Policies and procedures for dealing with complaints*
- *Internal/external service level agreement*

These may seem straightforward; however, different organisations will have different policies and what the customer may expect with one organisation may not be offered by another organisation. This, in itself, can cause problems with the customer, including their behaviour, attitude and emotions.

Refunds

The refunds process is used when a customer does not wish to use a product or service they have purchased previously. This could be due to many reasons and it is vital that there is a clear policy on issuing refunds.

A customer who buys a ticket for a sporting event does so in the expectation that the sale is made on the basis that the event will take place on planned date and time. If the event is subsequently cancelled by the organiser, the customer should have the right to a refund for the cost of the ticket and this is covered by legislation unless specifically excluded in the terms and conditions. If the customer decided not to attend the event because it was raining, there would be no right to a refund as the organiser had no control of the weather, regardless of whether the event went ahead or not. The customer made the decision not to attend in this case.

Decisions of this type, where the customer is disadvantaged, often cause an emotional response and tempers rise. It is at this point that customer service training should trigger and the customer must be dealt with correctly, with appropriate explanations being given and in line with the policies and procedures defined for handling this type of issue.

If these policies and procedures are not followed, it could lead to the customer becoming even more angry and aggressive or the organisation could become financially disadvantaged by refunds being issued without qualification.

The Customer Journey

At a more practical level it will also be defined how the refund is to be made. This will usually be made via the same method used to pay for the item in the first place. An item purchased by credit card will be refunded to the same credit card whilst goods purchased by cash would be refunded by the same method. This is used to eliminate fraud and prevent money laundering.

Compensation

There may be instances where a service or product does not perform as expected and may warrant the payment of a modest amount of compensation. A garage may accidently damage a car whilst working on it and may offer to pay compensation in the sum of the cost of the repairs necessary to bring the vehicle back to its original condition, or a hairdresser, who encounters a problem with the application of chemicals to a client's hair, may pay compensation for the person to visit another hairdresser to have the problem resolved.

There are many issues associated with the payment of compensation, not least that by paying compensation guilt is being accepted. This can be a very serious matter and, in many cases, will need to be resolved in court. It is very important that any policy relating to the payment of compensation is very clear about what, when and how much compensation is payable and under what circumstances. Furthermore, it should be very clearly defined who has the authority to authorise the payment of compensation.

Returns / Exchanges

Returns and exchanges are a common occurrence in the Retail sector. People buy items which are subsequently found to be the wrong size or colour and the customer seeks to exchange the item for the correct size or colour or request the money back in full.

This is a fairly straightforward process. The customer has become accustomed to having to prove the purchase by presenting a receipt for the item, although some organisations will also accept the item as a return, if the brand is unique to them.

This has been a policy for many organisations for many years, however, more recently some people have seen fit to steal the item and then take it to the service desk for a refund or have worn the item and the returned it claiming a variety of reasons why it is being returned. The process for this should be very carefully written and all staff should be aware of the procedure for handling transactions of this nature. Failure to do so could, once again affect, affect the financial status of the business if procedures and policies are not followed exactly as written.

The Customer Journey

Managing Customer Related Problems

It is very important to ensure that all customer issues are correctly and swiftly resolved to the satisfaction of both the customer and the organisation alike. However, it is also important that all such incidents are recorded, and accurate records kept of the problem itself, the likely cause, the consequences and the subsequent resolution. By maintaining such records, it allows the organisation to identify trends which are repeated occurrences of similar issues and will allow the problem to be highlighted for further investigation.

This could identify manufacturing faults, the need for further development or remediation of the design or construction of the product or it may highlight recurrent failings in service standards which may be traced back to the performance a particular employee or team or products used in a particular process.

It is important that these records are kept and periodically checked to ascertain any trend or regular recurrence which could save the organisation a substantial amount of money over an extended period.

Escalation

Sometimes customer issues do not fit into the standard framework of policies and procedures and need to be dealt with by other, more senior, staff. This is no reflection on the employee, but often leads to a quicker and more effective resolution.

It may be part of the policy and procedure that a customer who is seeking compensation should be referred automatically to senior staff. Similarly, it may also be a requirement that a refund or an exchange is handled by the customer service representative but must be authorised by a senior staff member to ensure that any applicable legislation or internal governance has been complied with.

The repeated issue of refunds and compensation payments can become a significant cost against the business, especially if it becomes common knowledge that refunds and compensation is paid without proper checks and authorisation.

This process of escalation is designed to ensure the person dealing with the problem has the appropriate level of authority, knowledge and training to be able to deal effectively with the problem and resolve the problem with as little fuss as possible.

Another example of escalation is when the same problem keeps coming up. This may warrant an escalation to the manufacturer for a remedial fix to be identified and put into place

The Customer Journey

Service Level Agreements

A Service Level Agreement (or SLA) is the part of a contract between supplier and customer which defines exactly what services a service provider will provide and the required level or standard for those services. The SLA is generally part of an outsourcing or managed services agreement or can be used in facilities management agreements and other agreements for the provision of services.

The service-level agreement (SLA) will define how the level of service is to be measured, as well as any remedies or penalties which will be applied should the agreed service levels not be achieved. This is a critical component of any formal contract to supply goods and services on a formal basis.

A broadband providers SLA, for example, may promise network availability of 99.999 percent which works out to about five and a quarter minutes of downtime per year. This can still be too long for some businesses! If they fail to meet this target the customer will be allowed to reduce their payment by a given percentage. usually on a sliding scale based on the scale and duration of the breach.

A properly drafted and well thought out SLA should have the following elements:

- *It will state the business objectives which will be achieved through the provision of the services.*
- *It will describe in detail what the service will provide.*
- *It will define the standard of performance expected in the provision of the services.*
- *It will provide an ongoing reporting mechanism for measuring the expected performance standards.*
- *It will provide a mechanism when problems occur and a compensation regime where performance standards are not achieved.*
- *It will provide a mechanism for review and change to the service levels over the course of the contract.*
- *It will define the customer's right to terminate the contract where performance standards fall consistently below an acceptable level.*

The Customer Journey

Legal Implications When Delivering Customer Service

Whenever goods or services are provided to customers there are expectations from both the supplier and the customer of the goods and/or services being provided.

There is a minimum expectation that the goods or services will be fit for purpose.

A window cleaner that does not leave clean windows will not have many happy customers nor will they be in business for long. The customer, however, will have paid to have their windows cleaned and if they are not clean, they have a right to demand a refund of the monies paid.

Similarly, promises made by suppliers must be met in full – A new sofa in your home before Christmas is a common message on TV advertising, they are making a promise that they will achieve the delivery deadline – if they do not, they will be in breach of contract and the purchaser can make a claim against them for failing to fulfil the contract.

All these rights are defined and covered by The Consumer Rights Act which came into force on 1 October 2015 and replaced a number of old laws which had become outdated.

The law is now clearer and easier to understand, meaning that consumers can buy with confidence and businesses can sell to them with similar confidence. On the rare occasions when problems arise, disputes can now be sorted out more quickly and cheaply.

Alternative Dispute Resolution, for example through an Ombudsman, offers a quicker and cheaper way of resolving disputes than going through the courts. The changes are relevant to all consumers and every business which sells directly to them.
UK consumers spend £90 billion a month across all sectors. This new, clear, statement of consumer rights helps them to make better choices when they buy and save both time and money.

The Consumer Rights Act came into force on 1 October 2015 which meant from that date new consumer rights became law covering:

- *what should happen when goods are faulty*
- *what should happen when digital content is faulty*
- *how services should match up to what has been agreed, and what should happen when they do not, or when they are not provided with reasonable care and skill*
- *unfair terms in a contract*
- *what happens when a business is acting in a way which is not competitive?*
- *written notice for routine inspections by public enforcers, such as Trading Standards*

The Customer Journey

- *greater flexibility for public enforcers, such as Trading Standards, to respond to breaches of consumer law, such as seeking redress for consumers who have suffered harm.*

Most of these changes were important updates to existing laws. But two new areas of law were also introduced.

- *For the first time, rights on digital content have been set out in legislation. The Act gives consumers a clear right to the repair or replacement of faulty digital content, such as online film and games, music downloads and e-books. The law here has been unclear, and this change has brought us up to date with how digital products have evolved.*

- *There are now also new, clear rules for what should happen if a service is not provided with reasonable care and skill, or as agreed. For example, the business that provided the service must bring it into line with what was agreed with the customer or, if this is not practical, must give some money back.*

In terms of what is covered by the new Act, the old standards remain, and these are as follows:

- **Claims about goods** - It is an offence for the business or any member of staff to issue false statements about services, accommodation and facilities, or to give misleading information about prices, discounts or special offers.
- **Description of goods** – Examples are labels such as 'home-made', 'made in France', 'fresh vegetables', etc. There is still a sale by description even where the customer selects the goods, for example, in a self-service restaurant, if he or she relied in some way on the description.
- **Satisfactory Quality** – Goods must be fit for the purpose for which they are usually bought
- **Fitness for a particular purpose** – Reasonable fitness for a purpose known to the seller
- **Samples** – Ensuring that goods when sold correspond with samples

Other Legal Considerations

There are many other industry specific pieces of legislation which will apply when delivering customer service and these are too diverse to address in this context.

There are, however, some others which do apply to all sectors, the principal one being the Health and Safety at Work Act and its associated regulations. The H&SWA covers all aspect of safety and imposes a legal duty to ensure the safety of everyone on the premises, including customers.

The Customer Journey

Employees must not compromise the safety of customers whilst they are on the premises including demonstrating the use of equipment in a manner which could compromise health and safety. Customers must comply with any safety requirements deemed necessary and staff must enforce them. No one should do anything which compromises Health and Safety anywhere at any time.

Another important piece of legislation is the Data Protection Act and the GDPR regulations it encompasses. Customer service employees have access to a great deal of customer information, and it is vital that this information is kept private and protected from being viewed by any person who is not authorised to do so. There are severe penalties for anyone who is found to have breached the GDPR Regulations.

The following are just a small sample of additional legislation which applies to every business in the UK.

- Health and Safety Act
- Financial Laws including Tax Laws
- Employment law
- Freedom of Information Act
- Privacy and Electronic Communications Regulations
- Copyrights, Design and Patents Act
- Human Rights Act
- Equality Act

In addition, there is also the legislation which defines how a business should conduct itself.

These can include:

The Customer Journey

Legislation	Purpose
Companies Act	Defines the duties of the Directors of all companies registered in the UK
Financial Services and Markets Act	Regulates shares and securities
Financial Services Act	Applies criminal offences for making false claims or misrepresentation and creating false impressions
Insolvency Act	Governs the winding up of companies including liquidation and bankruptcy
Consumer Credit Act	Protects credit cards, loans and hire purchase agreements
Consumer Rights Act	Protects and assigns rights to the consumer including the right to compensation
Misrepresentation Act	Protects consumers from false or fraudulent claims
Payment Services Regulations	Protects consumers who are victims of fraud
Unfair Terms in Consumer Regulations	Defines the terms which are considered unfair in consumer agreements
Consumer contracts Regulations	Protects customers when buying items online

Chapter 4: Teamwork and Leadership

Teamwork and Leadership

Teams

In the workplace people are very often expected to work in a team, but very few people who actually work in teams, have ever undertaken any training in how to work effectively in a team. In fact, very few people understand how a team should work and what actually constitutes effective team working.

Teamwork is summarised as the bringing together of people who each contribute complementary skills.
The assembled team has a collective competence which allows the team members to achieve far more, together, than they could achieve alone. The team may be required to research information, provide a service or design and develop a product. They can achieve this even more quickly and more effectively by working together in a bigger team which might include product suppliers and consultants.

The composition of the team will vary according to the task it will be required to address, with each member contributing a different set of skills and abilities.

Teamwork calls for sustained leadership and goal orientation

Teamwork improves performance

When a team is performing at its best, you will usually find that each team member has clear responsibilities. Just as importantly, you will see that every role needed to achieve the team's goal is being performed fully and well.

Often, despite clear roles and responsibilities, a team will fall short of its full potential. Some team members do not complete what they are expected to do. Perhaps others are not quite flexible enough, so things "fall between the cracks." Maybe someone who is valued for their expert input fails to see the wider picture, and so misses out tasks or steps that others would expect. Or, perhaps, one team member becomes frustrated because he or she disagrees with the approach of another team member.

Teamwork does not "just happen." Often, an organisation will place a group of well-qualified individuals together to work in a team and is surprised when it does not achieve the targets set. Despite the many benefits of teamwork and cooperation at work, teamwork does not occur automatically.

Teamwork and Leadership

Team Balance

Dr Meredith Belbin studied teamwork for many years, and he famously observed that people in teams tend to assume different "team roles." He defined a team role as "a tendency to behave, contribute and interrelate with others in a particular way" and named nine such team roles that underly team success.

Belbin suggests that, by team members understanding their role within a particular team, they can develop their strengths and manage their weaknesses as a team member, and so improve how they contribute to the team.

Teams can become unbalanced if all team members have similar styles of behaviour or team roles.

If team members have similar weaknesses, the team as a whole may tend to have that weakness. If team members have similar team-work strengths, they may tend to compete (rather than cooperate) for the team tasks and responsibilities that best suit their natural styles.

Belbin's Theory

Belbin's theory classifies the roles people play in a team as:

- *Chair/coordinator* – able to get others working to a shared aim; confident, mature; good at making decisions and delegating
    - *The coordinator clarifies group objectives, sets the agenda, establishes priorities, selects problems, sums up and is decisive, but does not dominate discussions.*

- *Shaper* – motivated, energetic, assertive and competitive; thrives under pressure; achievement-driven, keeping the team focused
    - *The shaper gives shape and energy to the team effort. They can 'steamroller' the team but can get results.*

- *Innovator/plant* – innovative, inventive, creative, original, imaginative, unorthodox
    - *The innovator/plant is the source of original ideas, suggestions and proposals.*

Teamwork and Leadership

- *Monitor evaluator* – serious, prudent, critical thinker, analytical, impartial and even-tempered
    - The monitor evaluator contributes a measured and dispassionate analysis and, through objectivity, stops the team committing itself to a misguided task.

- *Implementer/company worker* – systematic, loyal, structured, reliable, dependable, practical, disciplined, efficient; uses common sense but can be inflexible about change
    - The implementer turns decisions and strategies into defined and manageable tasks, sorting out objectives and pursuing them logically.

- *Resource investigator* – good communicator, enthusiastic, networker, outgoing, affable, seeks and finds options, negotiator
    - The resource investigator goes outside the team to bring back ideas, information and developments. This person is the team's salesperson, diplomat, liaison officer and explorer.

- *Team worker* – supportive, sociable, flexible, adaptable, perceptive, listener, calming influence, mediator, dislikes confrontation, hard working
    - The team worker operates against division and disruption in the team, maintaining harmony, particularly in times of stress and pressure.

- *Completer finisher* – attention to detail, accurate, high standards, quality orientated; delivers to schedule and specification; good at finding errors
    - The completer finisher maintains a permanent sense of urgency with relentless follow-through and attention to detail.

- *Specialist* – technical expert, highly focused capability and knowledge, driven by professional standards and dedication to personal subject area.

These classifications can help managers to work out who might be best for each activity or task when managing the team as a whole. Managers could allocate:

- *Research activities to team members who are classified as Resource investigator, Specialist or Innovator/plant*
- *Repetitive, everyday activities to members who are considered to be classified as Team worker, Implementer/company worker or Completer finisher*
- *Quality control tasks to members who are Completer finishers or Specialists*
- *Liaison and coordinating tasks to people who are seen as Resource investigators*

Teamwork and Leadership

Team Role		Contribution	Allowable Weakness
Plant		Creative, imaginative, free thinking. Generates ideas and solves difficult problems.	Ignores incidentals. Too preoccupied to communicate effectively
Resource Investigator		Outgoing, enthusiastic, communicative. Explores opportunities and develops contacts.	Overoptimistic. Loses interest once initial enthusiasm has passed.
Co-ordinator		Mature, confident, identifies talent. Clarifies goals. Delegates effectively.	Can be seen as manipulative. Offloads own share of the work.
Shaper		Challenging, dynamic, thrives on pressure. Has the drive and courage to overcome obstacles.	Prone to provocation. Offends people's feelings.
Monitor evaluator		Sober strategic and discerning. Sees all options and judges accurately.	Lacks drive and ability to inspire others. Can be overly critical.
Team worker		Cooperative, perceptive and diplomatic. Listens and averts friction.	Indecisive in crunch situations. Avoids confrontation.
Implementer		Practical, reliable, efficient. Turns ideas into actions and organises work that needs to be done	Somewhat inflexible. Slow to respond to new possibilities.
Completer Finisher		Painstaking, conscientious, anxious. Searches out errors. Polishes and perfects.	Inclined to worry unduly. Reluctant to delegate.
Specialist		Single minded, self-starting, dedicated. Provides knowledge and skills which are in rare supply	Contributes only on a narrow front. Dwells on technicalities.

Teamwork and Leadership

Managers use team role theory to help create balanced teams. If team members have similar styles of behaviour, they can have similar weaknesses that weaken the team as a whole. If members have similar strengths, they might compete rather than cooperate, unbalance the team and affect productivity.

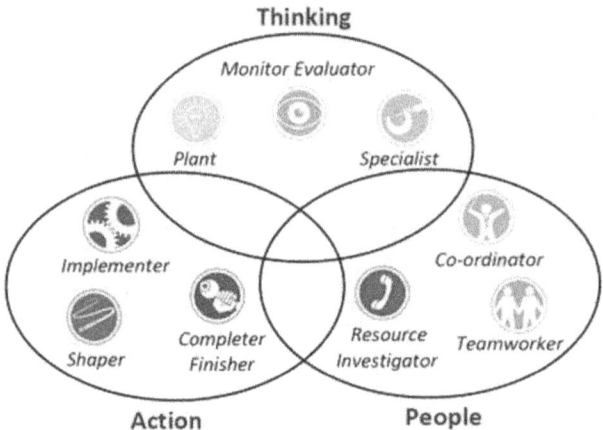

Teamwork

Whether a person is a jack-of-all-trades or the master of one, in today's world this will not bring about success unless you are able to work as part of a team. In the past, during the industrial era when most jobs involved people on a manufacturing line doing one thing all day – teamwork was not as important as it is today. The importance of teamwork cannot be emphasised enough. Teamwork is essential in today's multidisciplinary world.

Teamwork can be defined as:

> *the ability of team members to work together, communicate effectively, anticipate and meet each other's demands, and inspire confidence, resulting in a coordinated collective action.*

There are four key behavioural characteristics that combine in teamwork:

- *performance monitoring*
- *feedback*
- *closed-loop communication*
- *back-up behaviours*

Teamwork and Leadership

Performance Monitoring

The first requirement of teamwork is that team members monitor the performance of others, while carrying out their own task. This is the first difficulty that someone who does not understand teamwork is likely to encounter. The idea that they are being monitored by others could be disconcerting or it could even be considered to be spying!

However, monitoring ensures that team members are following procedures correctly and in a timely manner, while also ensuring that operationally they are working towards goals as planned.

Monitoring should be thought of as caring for each other rather than spying on each other. If someone is struggling, it is time to step in and help them, not report them for their failings.

The achievement of overall goals and targets by the team is the result of the efforts of the whole team anyone who fails to fulfil their role correctly, is not just letting themselves down, but is letting the whole team down.

Performance monitoring should be accepted as a norm in order to improve the performance of the team as a whole, in addition to establishing a trusting relationship between members.

Feedback

As a result of monitoring, there is a natural progression to feedback. This feedback should be based on the effectiveness or ineffectiveness of performance. Team members must feel at ease when providing feedback for teamwork to be effective. No obstacles (i.e., rank, role) should stand between team members who are giving and receiving this vital information.

> **Free-flowing, open, feedback is a critical element in the highest performing teams.**

Closed Loop Communication

Teamwork involves the effective communication between a sender and receiver. Closed-loop communication describes the information exchange that occurs in successful communication. There is a sequence of behaviours that are involved in closed-loop communication:

- *the message is initiated by the sender*
- *the message is accepted by the receiver and feedback is provided to indicate that it has been received*
- *the sender double-checks with the receiver to ensure that the intended message was received.*

Teamwork and Leadership

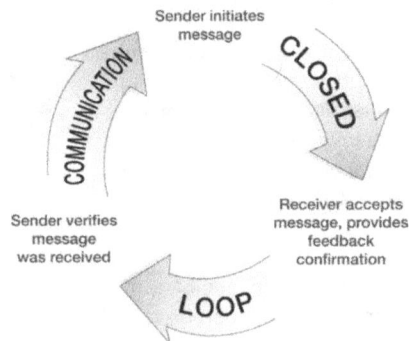

This type of communication is especially apparent in emergency situations.

Back-up Behaviours

Finally, back-up behaviours (i.e., the willingness, preparedness, and liking to support fellow team members during operations) are required for effective teamwork.

Team members must be willing to help when they are needed and must accept help when a need is identified without feeling they are being perceived as weak. This requires that members know the expectations of their jobs while also knowing the expectations of others with whom they are interacting.

These four behavioural characteristics—performance monitoring, feedback, closed-loop communication, and backing-up behaviours—are necessary for effective teamwork.

A failure in any one of these aspects, could result in ineffective team performance

Teamwork in Customer Service

Good customer service starts with the team that is behind it. If the team culture is healthy, other factors such as outstanding customer service and the building of a long-term brand will happen naturally.

A team brings people together from different backgrounds and levels of experience to work together in an homogenised unit. A team plagued by unhappiness and negativity will deliver unhappy customers and negative experiences, affecting the organisations performance and customer retention.

It is no secret that customer service has never been so important to customers as it is today. Exactly how important cannot be overstated.

Teamwork and Leadership

80% of buyers today agree that the experience a company offers is as important as their products or services.

Good customer service teams should be proactive and productive when it comes to building relationships with customers—proactive, so that they can resolve problems and issues before customers get annoyed, and productive, so that they can handle every customer query efficiently and reduce holding times for other customers. In order to achieve this, all customer service staff need to know how to work as a team.

Normal thinking tells us that customer service is basically a one-on-one relationship.

Customer contacts customer service (or vice versa)

Communication takes place

Problem identified

Problem is resolved

Repeat

This is a simple overview of a straightforward customer query. However, what happens when the person who first picks up the enquiry cannot deal with it? In order to resolve the problem, the customer must be referred to someone else in the team who can deal with it. At this point the customer has already provided their details and explained the problem to one person, they must now repeat this process as they are handed to a second person in the hope they can deal with it. This must happen as seamlessly as possible to avoid the customer becoming dissatisfied. In the event that the next team member is unable to deal with it, the customer will understandably become irate and annoyed.

Teamwork and Leadership

A customer support team which does not work together will make customers repeat themselves over and over again and this is one of the most annoying things for someone calling an organisation.

Excellence in customer service can only be achieved through a team effort.

Furthermore, the closer the team, the better the quality of customer service delivered.

The results of a customer service survey clearly evidence the issues which cause the greatest concern for customers approaching a customer support service.

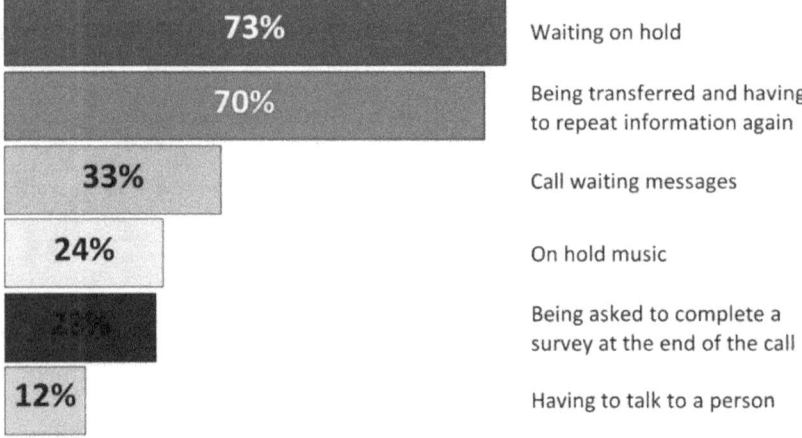

Teamwork Improves the Level of Customer Service

Teamwork is about bringing members of a group together to achieve a common goal. Team members work together with the aim of increasing productivity and performance. Some of the benefits are shown below:

Teamwork creates a smoother and more relaxed structure by developing a friendly environment. *Leaders are not trying to be bosses but rather work together with members of the team. This helps build strong bonds between the members.*

Encourages flexibility - *by working and communicating together, teams envisage broader perspectives to be considered and thus respond to problems faster.*

Enhances problem-solving - *combining different solutions, abilities, and talents into one productive unit allows ideas to flourish and goals to be achieved faster.*

Teamwork and Leadership

Improves productivity - *the performance and knowledge of an individual is limited compared to the varied skill sets of a team.*

Motivates the workforce - *people spend more time with their work colleagues than they do with their friends, so a healthy working environment is essential.*

Successful organisations encourage effective teamwork and give teams the authority to make decisions based on what they see is right. Great teamwork translates to great performance when it is managed well.

"None of us is as smart as all of us." -Ken Blanchard

Benefits of Teamwork in Customer Service

When customer service team members work together, they make each other's jobs (and the jobs of those around them) so much easier. Some of the benefits of good customer service teamwork include:

- *Customer's concerns are resolved faster*
- *75% of customers believe that it takes too long to reach a live customer service team member*
- *Team members who work closely together know exactly who they should pass customer problems on to, based on their strengths.*
- *Team members should feel comfortable asking for assistance or referring a problem that is beyond their scope of knowledge.*
- *Provides a more consistent customer service experience*
- *Each customer service team member brings different skillsets and personality.*
- *Reduces customer dependency on individual team members*

Customers expect a personal, caring customer experience. Customer service teams should strive to deliver such an experience through all of their customer service team members, not just a select few. By setting processes and expectations as a team, customer service representatives are encouraged to rise to the occasion and solve problems on behalf of every customer.

Teamwork and Leadership

Reduce Stress and Burnout

The pressure of working in a stressful environment like a customer service support centre can cause high levels of stress among the support team members. It is therefore important that organisations take steps to ensure the burden on the customer service team is strictly managed to ensure no single team member becomes overwhelmed with support requests.

Working in customer service, means there is a great deal of individual responsibility. 74% of call centre customer service representatives state that they are going through or are on the verge of burnout.

Burnout will cause employees to become disgruntled or cause them to leave.
The more evenly and appropriately customer queries are distributed, the fairer it is for the team—and it keeps stress levels low. (*more experienced customer service team members get more difficult queries*)

Work should be evenly distributed which will allow the team to handle a higher volume of support queries. If one team member is overwhelmed with a particular customer or situation, they should be able to request backup or have someone else pick up the outstanding tasks to prevent a longer queue forming which reduces waiting for customers.

This will, in turn, mean customer service representatives will not feel rushed because they will have opportunities to have meaningful conversations with customers.

Given that 70% of purchasing decisions are based on how people *feel* they are treated, a personalized service is essential.

Customer Service in the Wider Organisation.

There is a tendency to believe that customer service is a provision only for the people who buy the services or products on offer, however, as discussed earlier, customers are both internal and external to the organisation. Regardless of whether the customer is internal or external. The rules of customer service and teamwork exist all situations. The effects of a poor internal customer/supplier relationship are just as damaging as they are for external customers. It is vitally important that positive relationships exist between internal customers as it is with external customers.

External Customers

Customer service teams or departments are customarily set up for the external customers who buy goods or services from the organisation. However, there are other external customers of our business. Our suppliers are customers of the organisation too. We are certainly their customer as we buy goods and services from them, however, they are also our customer in the context that we will provide them with feedback and guidance on the performance of their products. As such, this changes the normal supplier customer

Teamwork and Leadership

relationship to one where both parties are customers and customer service levels must be reflected between both organisations.

Internal Customers

Internal customers will also have an expectation of high levels of customer service. This does not apply exclusively to the provision from the customer service department. The different departments or sections within the organisation are all customers of each other and there is a need for high levels of customer service to exist between the internal departments in the same way the organisation services its external paying customers.

Teamwork and Leadership

Developing a Team

A team takes time and effort to build. A group of people will not work together smoothly and happily from day one. It takes time for team members to settle into the structure and during that settling in period a key development is opening lines of communication. Communication between team members is very important when a team is developing.

Creating a team that you can count on and that can work together effectively is an important element of a successful business.

Bruce Tuckman conducted research on how teams develop over time and it is important to recognise that until each stage is completed the team cannot progress to the next level. It should also be noted that the initial work completed on this produced a four-stage model, but subsequent work added the fifth stage.

Team Development Stages:

Forming
The first stage is the *'Forming' Stage*. This is a relatively short stage in terms of duration and may be complete in a matter of days. Team members are getting to know each other. They are trying to understand the roles that need to be filled and the goals that must be achieved. The leader should be working together with the team members directing them as to what is expected.

Storming
The next stage is the *'Storming' Stage*. Here, conflicts arise as the pecking order among team members is established.

Team members will be uncomfortable and wary of their colleagues. There will be competition for recognition, roles and leadership. Differences in perspectives and experiences collide with each other. This stage may seem to settle quite quickly, however, there may well be underlying issues which do not immediately appear. At this point, the leader must strive to reduce tension.

Norming
The *'Norming' Stage* Is reached when members start communicating together. Trust is starting to build among them, everyone knows what their role is and their position in the team. Leaders should be developing communication between members, enabling the start of stable teamwork.

Performing
The fourth stage is the *'Performing' Stage*. A high level of communication, understanding, and trust has developed between the team members. Individuals are working together efficiently to achieve common goals. Group decision making, collaboration, motivation, and effective development have evolved. Leaders offer

Teamwork and Leadership

gratitude to the members individually and also as a team for their striving performance but otherwise will step back from a full-time, hands-on role.

Adjourning

Finally, the *'Adjourning or Mourning' Stage.* In a support team, this fifth stage is of far less significance than it might be in a team created for a short period of time. Once the goal has been achieved, there is no further need for the team. Team members will return to previous roles or seek new ones. The term mourning is included in the title because it is often considered that the dissolution of a team can trigger a grieving process which is similar to the experienced on the death of a relative or close friend. Team members will typically experience the key stages grief cycle, such is the strength of the associations and relationships formed within the team. There can be similar mourning experiences when a key or popular member of a support team leaves, however, as the majority of the team remains, the team will recover quickly.

It is important to remember that the success of the team is entirely dependent on the leadership it receives. The more closely the team members work together, the more successful the team will become.

There are many ways in which teams can be developed to become more effective and some of these can be summarised as follows:

- *Utilise the different skillsets within the team by assigning tasks based on the unique capabilities of each team member.*
- *Identify areas of need from the broad range of capability and experience already held by the team before recruiting new team members.*
- *Allow the team members to work together and support each other to achieve a faster resolution.*
- *Monitor progress but allow the team to resolve issues independently. This will improve confidence making the team stronger and more responsible with time.*
- *Thank them for their efforts which will motivate and encourage new responsibility with a positive attitude to do things even better in the future and building trust, friendship, and respect between the employees.*

Teamwork and Leadership

Leadership

The term 'leadership' can be used in many different ways.

It can be defined as:

> *the capacity to influence people to achieve a common goal*

There is, however, no single definition or concept of leadership that satisfies all situations. Leaders adopt many different approaches to each task and can operate at any level. As a result, identifying and developing leaders can be challenging.

When leadership is skilfully demonstrated, it can bring positive outcomes for individuals, teams, organisations and wider communities. It is therefore important to develop leaders to meet the current and future needs of an organisation, as well as investing in other areas which enable leaders and teams to be effective.

What is clear is that leadership covers three integral elements:

- **Self** - *skilful expression of personal qualities.*
- **Other people** - *staff, line managers, peers but also senior management and other stakeholders.*
- **The job to be done** - *specifying, defining, clarifying, reviewing, and revising when needed, the task to be achieved.*

The leader must address the question 'what we are doing this job for.'? This identifies the purpose of the task and when purpose is shared, people become collaborators, offering insights of their own.

> *'Climb that hill!' becomes 'Climb that hill - so we can get a better view of the river'.*

When people see a point to their efforts, the work itself may become more meaningful. A leader is involved in shaping and moulding the behaviour of the group towards accomplishment of organisational goals.

> *There is no best style of leadership. Leadership is linked to the situation. Successful leadership depends on tackling the problems appropriately, which each situation presents.*

A leader must have many and diverse qualities, skills and traits to ensure they are effective in all situations. The following are some of the pre-requisites needed to be a good leader:

Teamwork and Leadership

- **Physical appearance** - A leader must have a pleasing appearance. Physique and health are very important for a good leader.
- **Vision and foresight** - A leader cannot maintain influence unless they exhibit that they are forward looking. They must visualise situations and thereby frame logical programmes.
- **Intelligence** - A leader should be intelligent enough to examine problems and difficult situations. They should weigh up the pros and cons and then summarises the situation. A positive frame of mind and mature outlook is very important.
- **Communicative skills** - A leader must be able to communicate the policies and procedures clearly, precisely and effectively. This can be helpful in persuasion and stimulation.
- **Objective** - A leader has to have an open outlook which is free from bias and which does not show any favouritism towards a particular individual. They should develop their own opinion and should base any judgement on facts and logic.
- **Knowledge of work** - A leader should know the nature of the work of those they lead so they can win the trust and confidence of the people they lead.
- **Sense of responsibility** - A leader must have a sense of responsibility towards organisational goals in order to gain maximum benefit from their endeavours. Thy must be able to motivate themselves in order to motivate team members to give their best.
- **Self-confidence and will-power** – Self-confidence helps to earn the confidence of those they lead. A leader should be trustworthy and should handle challenging situations with the will power self-confidence brings.
- **Humanist** -This is essential in a leader. They deal with human beings and need to have close interpersonal contact with them. They must address the personal problems of those they lead with great care and attention. Therefore, treating the human beings at a humanitarian level is essential for building a relaxed, comfortable, working environment.
- **Empathy** - This is very important because fairness and objectivity comes from the ability to see issues from another person's perspective. A leader must be able to understand the problems and complaints of employees and be able to recognise the needs and aspirations of the employees. This helps in improving human relations and personal contacts with the employees.

Recognising the need for these qualities in a leader, underpins the scope of leadership and its importance for a business. A leader cannot have all of these qualities, skills and traits all at one time, but having at least some of them, helps in achieving effective results.

In summary, a good leader needs to:

1. **Provide Guidance.** Guidance involves training, instructing team members along with the vision or goal of the organisation, and ensures no deviation from the vision or goal even though it may be challenging.

Teamwork and Leadership

2. **Encourage Creativity.** Good leaders abandon their egos and give room for their subordinates to express themselves in order to encourage new ideas, innovations that can trigger an organisation to new levels of success.
3. **Motivate.** Motivation is vital to the achievement of an organisation. A good leader ensures team members' energy is high to perform the job to the very best of their ability.
4. **Communicate.** Co-ordination of work in an effective and efficient manner requires excellent communication between the team leaders and team members.
5. **Foster Good Values.** The exhibition of good values is vital to the achievement of an organisation.
6. **Resolve Conflict.** A productive leader manages the conflicts that pose a threat to the unity of team members, productivity, and motivation.

Teamwork and Leadership

Leadership in Teamwork

Leadership is a key element in teamwork. Teams need far less management than many other types of team, especially if it has clearly defined targets and goals to work towards, which motivates and drives the team. Leadership is still needed, however, as there are decisions to be made and directions to be taken.

Every team needs to be led and that role should be taken by an individual who may have been recruited to the role or preferably, has been elected to the role from withing the team. A leader that cannot work with a team, is a failure!

Effective leaders have two things that they do well:

- *high emotional intelligence*
- *ability to provide a clear vision for the team.*

Team members on the other hand need only high emotional intelligence. This is a distinct quality common to both roles.

The leader will naturally have influence over the team, both in the way it performs but more importantly, the culture it creates. The leader must ensure that the is a positive attitude towards customer service and the resolution of issues, rather than a negative stance where responsibility is directed elsewhere. This negative attitude will spread through the support team and service standards will collapse leading to negative customer satisfaction, loss of business and in the longer term, possible closure of the organisation. Their high levels of emotional intelligence should engender problem solving from the customer perspective. They should encourage empathy in the process and proactive resolution by customer service staff.

It should be emphasised that this is emotional intelligence and not intellectual intelligence. Emotional intelligence is the ability to understand, use, and manage one's own emotions in positive ways to relieve stress, communicate effectively, empathise with others, overcome challenges and defuse conflict.

Teamwork and Leadership

Leadership Styles

"Great leaders are born, not made?"

The early hypotheses on the leadership of people were based on the presumption that "great leaders were born" and could not be created by any other method. As a result of this the "Great Man Theory" evolved during the 19th century and was highly regarded for some time. This, of course, has proven to be completely incorrect and there is an abundance of evidence to show that the reverse is actually true!

Much of this mistaken belief was due to early research on leadership which looked at people who were already successful leaders. These individuals were often aristocratic rulers who achieved their position through birth right. People of lesser social status had fewer opportunities to practice and achieve leadership roles and therefore the idea that leadership is an inherent ability was formed.

Research has subsequently shown that leadership is a surprisingly complex subject and that numerous factors influence how successful a particular leader may or may not be. Characteristics of the group, the leader in power, and the situation all interact to determine what type of leadership is needed and the effectiveness of this leadership.

"Leadership style" refers to a leader's behaviours when directing, motivating, guiding, and managing people.

Great leaders can inspire political movements and social change. They can also motivate others to perform, create, and innovate.

If you think about some of the people who are thought of as great leaders, it is clear there are vast differences in how each person leads. Researchers have now developed different theories and frameworks that allow a better understanding these different leadership styles.

Teamwork and Leadership

Lewin's Leadership Styles

In 1939 psychologist Kurt Lewin set out to identify different styles of leadership. This early study was very influential and established three major leadership styles and these have been a steppingstone for more defined leadership theories.

Lewin assigned schoolchildren to one of three groups with an authoritarian, democratic, or laissez-faire leader. The children participated an arts and crafts project while their behaviour in response to the different styles of leadership was observed. The researchers found that democratic leadership tended to be the most effective at inspiring the children to perform well.

Autocratic Leadership (Authoritarian)

The phrase most associated with an autocratic leader is "Do as I say." Generally, they believe they are the smartest person at the table and know more than others. They make all the decisions with little input from team members.

Autocratic leaders provide clear expectations of what needs to be done, when it should be done, and how it should be done. This leadership style is strongly focused on both command by the leader and control of the followers. Authoritarian leaders make decisions independently, with little or no input from the rest of the group. This command-and-control approach is typical of leadership styles of the past, but it does not have much credibility with the employees of today.

Autocratic leadership can still be appropriate in certain situations. For example, when crucial decisions need to be made on the spot, the leader has the most knowledge about the situation. Similarly, when dealing with inexperienced and new team members and there is no time to wait for team members to gain familiarity with their role.

An authoritarian leader will:

- *make all the important decisions*
- *not consider input from team members*
- *dictate all the working methods and processes*
- *not trust your team members with important decisions*
- *have a highly structured working environment*
- *discourage creativity and out-of-the-box thinking*
- *want to instigate rules and make sure everyone follows*

The Negative Effects of Autocratic Leadership

While autocratic leadership has some benefits, it also has some serious issues which certainly cannot be ignored. People who are autocratic leaders tend to be bossy and dictatorial in nature.

Teamwork and Leadership

Being bossy is great for some situations; however, it can create some strong resentment among team members. They have no input or no say in how things are done. This can become problematic when highly skilled and fully capable members are left feeling that their experience and information is undermined.

Some common problems with autocratic leaders are:

- *It discourages group input*
- *It has a detrimental effect on the morale of the group*

Using an authoritarian style

The authoritarian style can be beneficial in some settings, but also has its shortcomings. If this tends to be your dominant leadership style, there are things that you should consider whenever you are in a leadership role.

Listen to the team
You might not change your mind or implement their advice, but team members need to feel that they can express their concerns. Autocratic leaders can sometimes make team members feel ignored or even rejected. Listening to people with an open mind can help them feel like they are making an important contribution to the group's mission.

Define the Rules
If you want team members to follow your rules, you need to ensure that guidelines are clearly established and that each person on your team is fully aware of them.

Provide Training
Once the team understand the rules, you need to be sure that they have the education and capability to perform the tasks you set. If they need additional assistance, offer training to fill in this knowledge gap.

Reliability
Inconsistency can quickly lead to the loss of respect of the team. Enforce the rules you have defined. Establish that you are a reliable leader, and your team is more likely to follow your guidance because you have built trust with them.

Recognise Success
The team will quickly lose motivation if they are criticised when they make mistakes but never recognised for their successes. Try to recognise success more than pointing out mistakes. By doing so, the team will respond much more favourably to the correction.

While autocratic leadership does have some potential pitfalls, leaders can learn to use elements of this style selectively. For example, an autocratic style can be used effectively in

Teamwork and Leadership

situations where the leader is the most knowledgeable member of the group or has access to information that other members of the group do not.

Instead of wasting valuable time consulting with less knowledgeable team members, the expert leader can quickly make decisions that are in the best interest of the group. Autocratic leadership is often most effective when it is used for specific situations. Balancing this style with other approaches including democratic or transformational styles can often lead to better group performance.

Participative Leadership (Democratic)

Lewin found that participative leadership, also known as democratic leadership, is commonly the most effective style. Participative leaders offer guidance to group members, but they also participate in the group and allow input from other group members. Lewin found the children in this group were less productive than the members of the authoritarian group, but their contributions were of a higher quality.

This type of leadership can be applied to any organisation, from private businesses to public bodies and the third sector.

Everyone is given the opportunity to participate, ideas are exchanged freely, and discussion is encouraged. While the democratic process tends to focus on group equality and the free flow of ideas, the leader of the group is still there to offer guidance and control.

Participative leaders are more likely to ask, "What do you think?" They share information with employees about anything that affects their work responsibilities. They also seek employees' opinions before approving a final decision.

Participative leaders encourage group members to participate in decision making, but retain the final say in the decision-making process. Group members feel engaged in the process and are more motivated and creative. Democratic leaders tend to make followers feel like

Teamwork and Leadership

they are an important part of the team, which helps foster commitment to the goals of the group.

There are numerous benefits to this participative leadership style. It can develop trust, promote team spirit and cooperation from employees. It allows for creativity and helps employees develop. A participative leadership style gets people to do what needs to be done but in a way that they *want* to do it.

The democratic leader will decide who is in the group and who gets to contribute to the decisions that are made. Researchers have found that the democratic leadership style is one of the most effective types and leads to higher productivity, better contributions from group members, and increased group morale.

Some of the primary characteristics of democratic leadership include:

- *Group members are encouraged to share ideas and opinions, even though the leader retains the final say over decisions.*
- *Members of the group feel more engaged in the process.*
- *Creativity is encouraged and rewarded.*

Research suggests that good democratic leaders possess specific traits that include honesty, intelligence, courage, creativity, competence, and fairness. Strong democratic leaders inspire trust and respect among followers.

These leaders are sincere and make decisions based on their morals and values. Followers tend to feel inspired to act and contribute to the group. Good leaders also tend to seek diverse opinions and do not try to silence dissenting voices or those that offer a less popular point of view.

Strengths of Participative Leadership

Because group members are encouraged to share their thoughts, democratic leadership can lead to better ideas and more creative solutions to problems. Group members also feel more involved and committed to projects, making them more likely to care about the end results. Research on leadership styles has also shown that democratic leadership leads to higher productivity among group members.

- *More ideas and creative solutions*
- *Group member commitment*
- *High productivity*

Weaknesses of Participative Leadership

While democratic leadership has been described as the most effective leadership style, it does have some potential downsides. In situations where roles are unclear or time is of the

Teamwork and Leadership

essence, democratic leadership can lead to communication failures and uncompleted projects.

In some cases, group members may not have the necessary knowledge or expertise to make quality contributions to the decision-making process. Democratic leadership can also result in team members feeling like their opinions and ideas are not considered, which may lower employee satisfaction and morale.

- *Communication failures*
- *Poor decision-making by unskilled groups*
- *Minority or individual opinions overridden*

When to use Participative Leadership

Participative Leadership works best in situations where group members are skilled and eager to share their knowledge. It is also important to have plenty of time to allow people to contribute, develop a plan, and then vote on the best course of action.

Participative Leadership is usually effective because it allows lower-level employees to exercise and use authority they will need in future positions. In a team meeting, a democratic leader might give the team a few decision-related options, they could then discuss each option. After discussion, the leader might take the teams thoughts and feedback into consideration or may open the decision to a vote.

Delegative Leadership (Laissez-Faire)

Under delegative leadership, Lewin found that children were the least productive. The children also made more demands on the leader, showed little cooperation, and were unable to work independently.

Delegative leaders offer little or no guidance to group members and leave the decision-making up to group members. Lewin also noted that laissez-faire leadership created groups

Teamwork and Leadership

that lacked direction, members blamed each other for mistakes, refused to accept personal responsibility, made less progress, and produced less work.

The laissez-faire leadership style is at the opposite end of the scale to the autocratic style. Of all the leadership styles, this one involves the least amount of control. The autocratic style leader stands as firm as a rock on issues, while the laissez-faire leader lets people swim with the current.

On the surface, a laissez-faire leader may appear to trust people to get on with the task, but it can also leave the disassociated leader appearing aloof. Whist it is beneficial to give people the opportunity to spread their wings, with a total lack of direction, people may unwittingly drift in the wrong direction - away from the critical goals of the organisation.

This style can work however, if the team comprises highly skilled, experienced employees who are self-starters and motivated. To be most effective with this style, monitor team performance and provide regular feedback.

Characteristics of Laissez-Faire Leadership

- *Hands-off approach*
- *Leaders provide all training and support*
- *Decisions are left to employees*
- *Comfortable with mistakes*
- *Accountability falls to the leader*

Pros and Cons of Laissez-Faire Leadership

Laissez-faire leadership means the leaders has a hands-off role and allows group members to make the decisions. This leadership style has been found to deliver the lowest productivity among group members.
However, this leadership style can have strengths as well as weaknesses.

There are certain settings and situations where a laissez-faire leadership style might be the most appropriate.

Strengths of Laissez-Faire Leadership

Like other leadership styles, the laissez-faire leadership style has its advantages:

- **It encourages personal growth.** Because leaders are so hands-off in their approach, employees have a chance to be hands-on. This leadership style creates an environment that facilitates growth and development.
- **It encourages innovation.** The freedom given to employees can encourage creativity and innovation.

Teamwork and Leadership

- **It allows for faster decision-making.** Since there is no micromanagement, employees under laissez-faire leadership have the autonomy to make their own decisions. They can make quick decisions without waiting weeks for an approval process.

To benefit from these strengths, certain preconditions must be met. The team should be full of highly skilled and experienced people, capable of working on their own, meaning they are capable of accomplishing tasks with very little guidance.

This style is particularly effective in situations where group members are more knowledgeable than the group's leader. The laissez-faire style allows them to demonstrate their deep knowledge and skill surrounding that subject. This level of autonomy can be motivating to some group members and help them feel more satisfied with their work.

Weaknesses of Laissez-Faire Leadership

Because the laissez-faire style depends so heavily on the abilities of the group, it is not very effective in situations where team members lack the knowledge or experience, they need to complete tasks and make decisions.

This is leadership style is also not suitable for situations where efficiency and high productivity are the main concerns. Some people are not good at setting their own deadlines, managing their own projects, and solving problems on their own. Under this leadership style, projects can go off-track and deadlines can be missed when team members do not get enough guidance or feedback from leaders.
Weaknesses of the laissez-faire style include:

- **Lack of role clarity:** The laissez-faire style leads to poorly defined roles within the group. Since team members receive little or no guidance, they might not really be sure about their role within the group and what they are supposed to be doing.
- Poor involvement with the group: Laissez-faire leaders are often seen as uninvolved and withdrawn, which can lead to a lack of cohesiveness within the group. Since the leader seems unconcerned with what is happening, followers sometimes pick up on this and express less care and concern for the project.
- **Low accountability:** Some leaders take advantage of this style to avoid responsibility for failure. When goals are not met, the leader can blame members of the team for not completing tasks or living up to expectations.
- **Passivity:** At its worst, laissez-faire leadership represents passivity or even an outright avoidance of true leadership. In such cases, these leaders do nothing to motivate followers, do not recognise the efforts of team members, and make no attempt at involvement with the group.

If team members are unfamiliar with the process or tasks, leaders are better off taking a more hands-on approach. They can switch back to a more delegative approach as team members gain more experience.

Teamwork and Leadership

Where Laissez-Faire Leaders can Succeed

Working in a creative field, where people tend to be highly motivated, skilled, creative, and dedicated to their work, can be conducive to obtaining good results with this style.

Laissez-faire leaders typically excel at providing information and background at the start of a project, which can be particularly useful for self-managed teams. By giving team members all that they need at the outset of an assignment, they will then have the knowledge they need to complete the task as directed.

A leader with this style may struggle in situations that require oversight, precision, and attention to detail. In high stake and high-pressure work settings, where every detail needs to be perfect and completed in a timely manner, a more authoritarian or managerial style may be more appropriate. Using a laissez-faire approach in this scenario can lead to missed deadlines and poor performance.

Famous Laissez-Faire Leaders

There have been several well-known political and business leaders throughout history who have exhibited characteristics of a laissez-faire leadership style.

Steve Jobs was known for giving instructions to his team about what he would like to see but then leaving them to their own devices to figure out how to fulfil his wishes. Former U.S. President Herbert Hoover was famous for taking a more laissez-faire approach to governing, often by allowing more experienced advisors to take on tasks where he lacked knowledge and expertise.

Teamwork and Leadership

Other Leadership Styles and Models

In addition to the three styles identified by Lewin and his colleagues, researchers have described numerous other characteristic patterns of leadership. A few of the best-known include:

Strategic Leadership Style

Leaders must first understand their organisation's mission to be strategic. This means fully grasping why the company exists, who its customers are and how exactly it can provide value for them.

Then, strategic leaders need to create a vision of what that mission will look like at a specified time in the future.

Finally, leaders must craft a strategy to put that vision into action. The strategy should map out the steps a company needs to take or the changes it needs to make to get from its current state to its desired state.

Strategic leaders sit at the intersection between a company's main operations and its growth opportunities. He or she accepts the burden of executive interest while ensuring that current working conditions remain stable for everyone else.

The main objectives of strategic leadership are to streamline processes, boost strategic productivity, promote innovation and cultivate an environment that encourages employees to be productive, independent and to push forward their own ideas. Strategic leaders sometimes make use of rewards or incentive programs to encourage employees and help them reach their goals.

Strategic leadership can be defined as utilising strategy in the management of employees. Strategic leaders create organisational structure, allocate resources and express strategic vision.

This is a desirable leadership style in many organisations because strategic thinking supports multiple types of employees at once. However, leaders who operate this way can set a dangerous precedent with respect to how many people they can support at once, and what the best direction for the company really is, if everyone is always getting their way.

The main objective of strategic leadership is strategic productivity. Another aim of strategic leadership is to develop an environment in which employees forecast the organisation's needs in context of their own job. Strategic leaders encourage the employees in an organisation to follow their own ideas.
Strategic leaders make greater use of reward and incentive systems for encouraging productive and quality employees to show much better performance for their organisation.

Functional strategic leadership is about inventiveness, perception, and planning to assist an individual in realising his objectives and goals.

Teamwork and Leadership

Strategic leadership requires the potential to foresee and comprehend the work environment. It requires objectivity and potential to look at the broader picture.

Key Traits of Strategic Leaders

> *Strategic leaders are visionary, open, focused, courageous, and prudent.*

What are the distinguishing characteristics of a strategic leader? How do you recognise one? And how do you acquire the traits of a strategic leader? Based on experience, the following five traits may be considered essential for strategic leadership:

Vision
Great strategic leaders have a clear and compelling vision that is going far beyond the current reality. These leaders can communicate their vision in an effective and inspiring way to mobilise commitment within their organisation and sector.

There have been several strategic leaders with such a clear and compelling vision such as Steve Jobs and his vision of the iPod and iPhone.

Openness
Strategic leaders are attuned to the fast pace of change and recognise that they cannot know it all. Their antennae are always on, as a seemingly minor detail may challenge their current strategic plans and be the trigger for changing the strategy for the organisation or department.

Strategic leaders are open to learn about new trends in their own or other sectors as well as about developments within their organisation. Their openness promotes a culture of openness in their whole organisation, which in turn facilitates the flow of information and the capacity of the organisation to adapt to a changing environment and turn challenges into opportunities.

Focus
Strategic leaders can focus their attention and energy on what they perceive as the most important activities and projects. Apple co-founder Steve Jobs is a prime example of a leader with a relentless focus. Instead of producing a range of smartphones, he insisted on just having one iPhone model. Keeping it simple and focusing on making one product the best on the market at the time it was launched, had incredible benefits for product management and marketing.

There is no conflict between openness and focus. Openness is required in the decision-making phase. Once a decision is taken there is a need to focus relentlessly on implementation.

Teamwork and Leadership

Courage
In the face of complexity and uncertainty, a strategic leader can never be sure if their strategic decisions will be successful, despite all the information gathering and due diligence. The strategic leader therefore needs to have the courage to act and push for changes they consider necessary, even if their decisions are not popular with some stakeholders.

An example of a leader having the courage to make unpopular decisions is Marissa Mayer, President and CEO of Yahoo Inc. In November 2013, she introduced a performance review system based on ranking of employees by managers, with employees at the low end of the scoring being fired. Employees complained about the process, and the media criticised her, too. She had the courage to stick to her decision.

Prudence
Strategic leaders must act prudently. While being ready to take calculated and courageous risks, they avoid gambling and strive to minimise risks where possible.

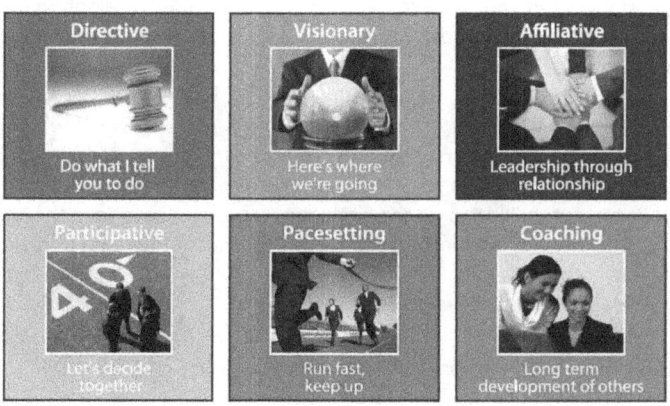

Transformational Leadership Style

Transformational leadership is often identified as the single most effective style. This style was first described during the late 1970s and later expanded upon by researcher Bernard M. Bass.

> *Transformational leaders can motivate and inspire followers and direct positive changes in teams.*

These leaders tend to be emotionally intelligent, energetic, and passionate. They are not only committed to helping the organisation achieve its goals, but also to helping team members fulfil their potential.

Teamwork and Leadership

Research shows that this style of leadership results in higher performance and more improved group satisfaction than other leadership styles. One study also found that transformational leadership led to improved well-being among group members.

Transformational Leadership Characteristics

The following are some of the characteristics of transformational leaders:

Keep their ego in check
In transformational leadership, it is important for the leader to keep their ego under control and not let it interfere with the best interest of their team or the organisation. By keeping their ego in check, the transformational leader can put the organisation before their own personal gain and obtain the best performance from others.

Self-management
Transformational leaders need little direction from others and manage themselves well. They are highly motivated and use it to direct the organisation to the right path. These leaders do what they love, and those values align with those of the organisation that they lead.

Ability to take the right risks
The transformational leader will trust their instinct, and use the intelligence gathered by team members to make informed decisions. A transformational leader's team is right behind them and is ever willing to do the necessary research to evaluate the situation appropriately. The transformational leader seeks inputs from the team to make risky decisions that facilitate growth.

Make difficult decisions
Transformational leaders do not shy away from difficult decisions. They make their decisions with a clear focus on the values, vision, objectives, and goals of the organisation.

Share organisational awareness
A transformational leader understands and shares their awareness of the entire organisation. This makes them particularly attuned to the feelings of their team members and gives them a clear idea of what actions to take to elicit the desired actions from the employees.

Since they have a complete awareness of the organisation, they can make decisions that stimulate growth, and create a shared vision for the organisation that all employees feel a part of.

Inspirational
People want to be inspired and transformational leaders are perhaps the most inspiring of all. They can motivate others to rise to the occasion. The inspiration is not just limited to formal acknowledgement of a job well done, they will treat each employee as a valued individual and take the time to understand what motivates them.

Teamwork and Leadership

Entertain new ideas
Transformation cannot be achieved if the leader is not open or receptive to new ideas. Transformational leaders understand that success is dependent on the effort of the entire team, and growth happens only in an organisation with a culture of openness to new ideas from all levels. A transformational leader makes deliberate efforts to solicit new ideas from team members and use their insights in making decisions.

Adaptability
The transformational leader knows that it is vital to constantly adapt to changing market conditions to keep moving forward. They are always willing to adapt to new situations and seek creative ways to respond to the dynamic business environment.

Proactive
The transformational leader is proactive in their approach. These leaders take risks and take an active role in growing the organisation.

Lead with vision
Transformational leaders set a realistic and achievable vision for the organisation. They then communicate the vision to their followers and inspire a sense of commitment and purpose. By getting everyone to buy into the common vision, transformational leaders can drive the organisation in the direction that they want.

Transformational leadership is always "transforming" and improving the organisation. Employees might have a basic set of tasks and goals that they complete every week or month, but the leader is constantly pushing them outside of their comfort sone.

When starting a job with this type of leader, all employees might get a list of goals to reach, as well as deadlines for reaching them. While the goals might seem simple at first, this manager might pick up the pace of deadlines or give you more and more challenging goals as you grow with the company.

This is a highly encouraged form of leadership among growth-minded companies because it motivates employees to see what they are capable of. But transformational leaders can risk losing sight of everyone's individual learning curves if direct reports do not receive the right coaching to guide them through new responsibilities.

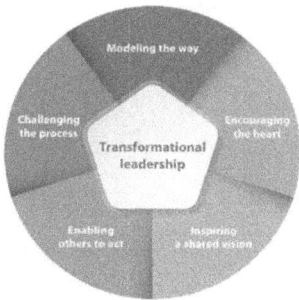

Teamwork and Leadership

Cross-Cultural Leadership

As workforces become increasingly multicultural and businesses continue to expand overseas, the homogenous workforce has become a thing of the past. In such a global economy, cross-cultural leadership skills are critically important. Many companies today operate on international projects with multi-cultural teams located in multiple countries. It is also common to find these are led by managers who come from many different countries that adds diversity to the teams and creates a need for a greater amount of collaboration and need for leadership at multiple levels.

The ability of a leader to motivate diverse teams to manage change effectively is a critical issue in the international environment. It cannot be assumed that a manager who is successful in one country will be successful in another.

Cross-cultural leadership involves the ability to influence and motivate people's attitudes and behaviours in the global community to reach a common organisational goal.

Implicit Leadership Theory (ILT):

This theory asserts that people's underlying assumptions, stereotypes, beliefs, and schemas influence the extent to which they view someone as a good leader. Since people across cultures tend to hold different implicit beliefs, schemas and stereotypes, it would seem only natural that their underlying beliefs in what makes a good leader differ across cultures.

Hofstede conducted a study into Cross Cultural leadership and identified what he calls Cultural Dimensions. This is one of the most prominent and influential studies to date regarding leadership in a globalised world. The study reveals similarities as well as differences across cultures and emphasises the need to be open-minded to understand the differences in other cultures. As per this theory, there are five dimensions of culture to compare cultures, to help leaders with an understanding of how to adjust their leadership styles accordingly.

- *Individualism/Collectivism*
- *Feminine/Masculine*
- *Power Distance*
- *Uncertainty Avoidance*
- *Long Term/ Short Term orientation*

Teamwork and Leadership

Traits of a Cross-Cultural Leader

Given below is a list of traits found to be associated with successful international executives by different researchers:

- General Intelligence
- Business Knowledge
- Interpersonal Skills
- Commitment
- Courage
- Ease in dealing with cross-cultural issues
- Open Personality

- Flexibility
- Drive
- Language Skills
- Multicultural Perspective Taking
- Knowledge and cognition
- Cultural Awareness
- Cross-cultural Schema
- Cognitive Complexity

An effective cross-cultural leader must have a well-rounded skillset and understanding of the differences that exist among people from different backgrounds.

Facilitative Leadership Style

Facilitative leadership is about aligning people in the same direction, so they can achieve a shared goal.

What makes facilitative leadership different from the other forms of leadership is the involvement of others at the decision-making stage. Traditionally managers, team leaders, or bosses decide on their own and then introduce it to the group. Facilitative leadership is different. The decisions are made together as a group.

A facilitative approach recognises the synergy of bringing together the different strengths of individuals.

The three key benefits of facilitative leadership are

- Commitment
- Alignment
- innovation

Strengths of Facilitative Leadership

- Enables self-leadership
- Helps employees see and understand the big picture
- Increases employee motivation and commitment via participatory decision making

Teamwork and Leadership

- *Helps employees align tasks*
- *Facilitated meetings can help create innovation and new ideas*
- *Very effective in dealing with complexity*

Weaknesses of Facilitative Leadership

- *Allows idea creation by employees and may seem chaotic*
- *Requires group facilitation skills to deal with the chaos of group decision making*

This concept of facilitative leadership is captured in the words accredited to Mother Theresa:

"You can do what I cannot do.
I can do what you cannot do.
Together we can do great things."

Facilitative leadership is particularly important with teams. Whether it is a team meeting, an away day, a conference, a team set up to solve a significant problem, or a continuous improvement team, their effectiveness is often determined by how well they are facilitated. This can make all the difference.

Think about the value gained when:

- *Everyone feels involved and engaged in a meeting on how to take things forward*
- *Ideas flow at a meeting*
- *You leave a meeting feeling it had purpose and direction, and it achieved something*
- *A clear set of actions are agreed, and everyone feels motivated to make them happen.*

Facilitative leadership brings people together to help them achieve more.

A facilitative leadership style involves:

- **Building rapport** – *establishing credibility to enable people to contribute with ease.*
- **Communicating effectively verbally and non-verbally** – *Being supportive and engaged*
- **Active listening** – *demonstrating your interest by your body language*
- **Questioning techniques** – *you can use questions as a very powerful facilitation skill: check understanding; seek clarification, or for a view to be expanded.*

Teamwork and Leadership

The Potential of a Facilitative Leadership Style

Too often the knowledge and potential that exists in a team is not recognised. In many cases knowledge of how to solve a problem or identify an innovative solution is already there in the team. The skill to unlock that knowledge and expertise is often found in form of facilitation.

Transactional Leadership Style

The transactional leadership style views the leader-follower relationship as a transaction. By accepting a position as a member of the group, the individual has agreed to obey the leader. In most situations, this involves the employer-employee relationship, and the transaction focuses on the follower completing required tasks in exchange for monetary compensation.

The "transaction" usually involves the organisation paying team members in return for their effort and compliance on a short-term task. The leader has a right to "punish" team members if their work does not meet an appropriate standard.

Transactional leadership is present in many business leadership situations, and it does offer some benefits. For example, it clarifies everyone's roles and responsibilities. Because transactional leadership judges team members on performance, people who are ambitious or who are motivated by external rewards – including compensation – often thrive.

The downside of this style is that, on its own, it can be chilling and amoral. It can lead to high staff turnover. It also has serious limitations for knowledge-based or creative work. As a result, team members can often do little to improve their job satisfaction.

One of the main advantages of this leadership style is that it creates clearly defined roles. People know what they are required to do and what they will be receiving in exchange. This style allows leaders to offer a great deal of supervision and direction, if needed.

Transactional leaders are common today. These managers reward their employees for precisely the work they do. A marketing team that receives a scheduled bonus for helping generate a certain number of leads by the end of the quarter is a common example of transactional leadership.

When starting a job with a transactional boss, you might receive an incentive plan that motivates you to quickly master your regular job duties. For example, if you work in marketing, you might receive a bonus for sending 10 qualified marketing emails. On the other hand, a transformational leader might only offer you a bonus if your work results in a large amount of newsletter subscriptions.

Transactional leadership helps establish roles and responsibilities for each employee, but it can also encourage bare-minimum work if employees know how much their effort is worth all the time. This leadership style can use incentive programs to motivate employees, but they should be consistent with the company's goals and used in addition to *unscheduled* gestures of appreciation.

Teamwork and Leadership

Situational Leadership style

Situational leadership theories stress the significant influence of the environment and the situation on leadership. Hersey and Blanchard's leadership styles are one of the best-known situational theories.
First published in 1969, it describes four primary styles of leadership, including:

- **Telling:** *Telling people what to do*
- **Selling:** *Convincing followers to buy into their ideas and messages*
- **Participating:** *Allowing group members to take a more active role in the decision-making process*
- **Delegating:** *Taking a hands-off approach to leadership and allowing group members to make the majority of decisions*

Blanchard later developed the original Hersey and Blanchard model to emphasise how the developmental and skill level of learners influence the style that should be used by leaders. Blanchard's SLII leadership styles model also described four different leading styles:

- **Directing:** *Giving orders and expecting obedience, but offering little guidance and assistance*
- **Coaching:** *Giving lots of orders, but also lots of support*
- **Supporting:** *Offering plenty of help, but very little direction*
- **Delegating:** *Offering little direction or support*

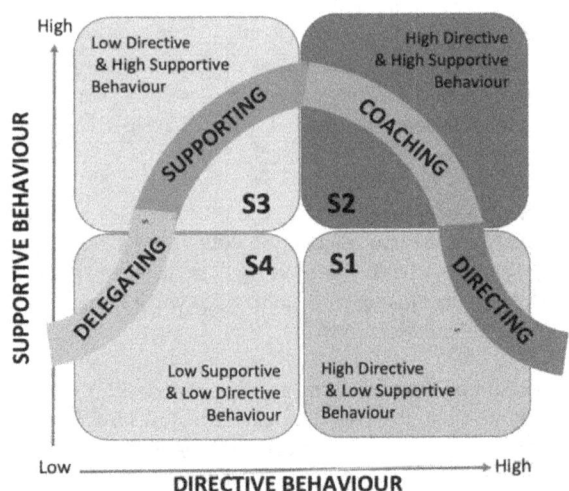

Teamwork and Leadership

Bureaucratic Leadership Style

Bureaucratic leaders go by the book. This style of leadership might listen and consider the input of employees - unlike autocratic leadership - but the leader tends to reject an employee's input if it conflicts with company policy or past practices.

Bureaucratic leadership still exists especially at a larger, older or traditional company. When a colleague or employee proposes a strong strategy that seems new or non-traditional, bureaucratic leaders may reject it. Their resistance might be because the company has already been successful with current processes and trying something new could waste time or resources if it does not work.

Employees under this leadership style might not feel as controlled as they would under autocratic leadership, but there is still a lack of freedom in how much people are able to do in their roles. This can quickly close down innovation and is not encouraged for companies who are chasing ambitious goals and quick growth.

As a style it is widely regarded as outdated and is seldom successful.

Coaching Leadership Style

A coaching leadership style implies there is a "consider this" approach. A leader who coaches views people as a reservoir of talent to be developed and seeks to unlock that potential.

Like a sports coach, a coaching leader focuses on identifying and nurturing the individual strengths of each member of the team. They focus on strategies that will enable their team to work better together.

This style offers strong similarities to strategic and democratic leadership but places more emphasis on the growth and success of individual employees.

Rather than forcing all employees to focus on similar skills and goals, this leader might build a team where each employee has an expertise or skillset in something different. In the long term, this leader focuses on creating strong teams that can communicate well and embrace each other's unique skillsets to get work done.

Teamwork and Leadership

A manager with this leadership style will help employees improve on their strengths by giving them new tasks to try, offering them guidance, or meeting to discuss constructive feedback. They might also encourage one or more team members to expand on their strengths by learning new skills from other teammates.

Affiliative Leadership Style

A phrase often used to describe this type of leadership is "People come first." Of all the leadership styles, the affiliative leadership approach is one where the leader gets up close and personal with people.

This type of leadership was first developed by famous D. Goleman in the early 21st century. He said that an affiliative category is designed for managers who are well-versed in the situation and can recognise the maturity levels of their staff. Rewards or sanctions recede into the background in comparison to the inner satisfaction that wage-earners receive from realising their potential and creative capabilities.

Under this style employees are spared constant monitoring and are trying, independently, to find ways to reach the desired objectives within the framework of the delegated powers. They do not accept that the boss has already thought of everything necessary for success or provided the necessary conditions for the process.

A leader practicing this style pays attention to and supports the emotional needs of team members and strives to bridge the gap between themselves and their team.

Ultimately, this style is all about encouraging harmony and forming collaborative relationships within teams. It is particularly useful, for example, in smoothing conflicts among team members or reassuring people during times of stress.

Traits of Affiliative Leaders

Affiliative Leadership refers to emotional supervision because it directly affects the feelings of team members. An affiliative leader will typically display the following characteristics.

Teamwork and Leadership

- **Focus on conflict-free.** *Strive to eliminate hostility and create an atmosphere of calm.*
- **Constructive criticism.** *Provide constructive feedback to maintain focus.*
- **A skilled psychologist.** *Strong emotional intelligence awareness*
- **The flexibility of thinking.** *Create a trusting relationship between staff and managers, it is necessary to be kind-hearted about new ideas and procedures that are offered by to relieve tension and contribute to creativity.*
- **Faith in an initiative**. *Affording team members the right to adjust the company's strategic aims meaning they cooperate with maximum efficiency, without fear of mistakes or punishments*
- **Persistence.** *Effective leadership in stressful or extreme conditions when the morale of the team is significantly affected.*
- **An empathic connection.** *Demonstrate empathy when dealing with issues.*

Affiliative leadership could be considered one of the most effective ways of creating a reliable team of like-minded people truly interested in the organisation's prosperity. It will help to cope with a low level of morale due to stress or other factors. It is not effective on its own and should be combined with authoritarian and democratic methods as well.

Charismatic Leadership

Charismatic leadership resembles transformational leadership: both types of leaders inspire and motivate their team members.

The difference lies in their intent. Transformational leaders want to transform their teams and organisations, while leaders who rely on charisma often focus on themselves and their own ambitions, and they may not want to change anything.

Charismatic leaders may believe that they can do no wrong, even when others warn them about the path that they are on. This feeling of invincibility can severely damage a team or an organisation, as was shown in the 2008 financial crisis.

Teamwork and Leadership

Servant Leadership

A "servant leader " is someone, regardless of level, who leads simply by meeting the needs of the team. The term sometimes describes a person without formal recognition as a leader.

These people often lead by example. They have high integrity and lead with generosity. Their approach can create a positive corporate culture, and it can lead to high morale among team members.

Supporters of the servant leadership model suggest that it is a good way to move ahead in a world where values are increasingly important, and where servant leaders can achieve power because of their values, ideals, and ethics.

However, others believe that people who practice servant leadership can find themselves "left behind" by other leaders, particularly in competitive situations.

This style also takes time to apply correctly: it is ill-suited to situations where you must make quick decisions or meet tight deadlines.

Teamwork and Leadership

Identifying a Leadership Style

At first glance, we may think that some leadership styles are better than others. The truth is that every leadership style has its place in the leader's toolkit. The prudent leader knows to flex from one style to another as the situation demands.

There are many tests online which can be used to identify your natural leadership style. This is the style you will use naturally and tend to revert to when placed under pressure.

It is important that you know what this natural leadership style is so you can understand how your style may be regarded and interpreted by those who report to you or by those who oversee what you do. That does not mean that you will live or die by your natural style – remember we know great leaders are not born!

Knowing your natural leadership style is a key step in the process to become a more effective and efficient leader. If you know the benefits of your leadership style, you can use these to your advantage. Similarly, if you are mindful of the weaknesses of your natural style, you can ensure that you do not use this style in situations where it can have a negative effect, but rather adopt an alternative style which is better suited to the situation.

Choosing Leadership Styles

Knowing which of the leadership styles works best for you is part of being a good leader. Developing a signature style with the ability to stretch into other styles as the situation warrants may help enhance your leadership effectiveness.

Know yourself
Start by raising your awareness of your dominant leadership style. You can do this by asking trusted colleagues to describe the strengths of your leadership style. You can also take a leadership style assessment.

Understand the different styles
Get familiar with the repertoire of leadership styles that can work best for a given situation. What new skills do you need to develop?

Practice makes a better leader
Be genuine with any approach you use. Moving from a dominant leadership style to a different one may be challenging at first. Practice the new behaviours until they become natural. In other words, do not use a different leadership style as a "point-and-click" approach. People can smell a fake leadership style a mile away—authenticity rules.

Develop your leadership agility.
Traditional leadership styles are still relevant in today's workplace, but they may need to be combined with new approaches in line with how leadership is defined for the 21st century.

Teamwork and Leadership

Today's business environments are fraught with challenges due to the changing demographics and the employee expectations from a diverse workforce. This may call for a new breed of leader who is an amalgam of most of the leadership styles discussed here.

As the Chinese proverb says:

> *the wise adapt themselves to circumstances, as water moulds itself to the pitcher.*

Over time and as you become more aware and experienced, you will begin to use the benefits of more leadership styles eliminating the negative aspects, as necessary. An agile leadership style may be the ultimate leadership style required for leading today's talent

Benefits of Effective Teamwork in Customer Service

The benefits of teamwork in customer service cannot be overstated. The professional, seamless, handling of customer queries and problems elevates the standards, reputation and performance of the whole organisation.

Teamwork motivates unity
An effective teamwork environment promotes an atmosphere that fosters friendship and loyalty. Close-knit relationships can form and these motivate employees and align them to work harder, cooperate and be supportive of one another. The individuals within the team possess diverse talents, weaknesses, communication skills, strengths, and habits and it is this diversity that increases the strength and effectivity of the team.

Teamwork offers differing perspectives and feedback
Good teamwork structures provide the organization with diversity of thought, creativity, perspectives, opportunities, and problem-solving approaches. A proper team environment allows individuals to brainstorm collectively, which in turn increases their ability to problem solve and arrive at solutions more efficiently and effectively.

Effective teams also develop innovation, in turn creating a competitive edge to accomplish goals and objectives. Sharing differing opinions and experiences strengthens accountability and can help make effective decisions faster, than when done alone.

Team effort increases output by having quick feedback and multiple sets of skills come into play to support work. The process of designing, planning, and implementation is much more efficiently when a team is functioning well.

Teamwork improves efficiency and productivity
Teamwork strategies allow the workload to be shared, reducing the pressure on individuals, and ensure tasks are completed within a set time frame. It also makes goals more attainable, enhances the optimization of performance, improves job satisfaction and increases work pace.

Teamwork and Leadership

When a group of individuals work together, compared to one person working alone, they create a more efficient work output and are able to complete tasks faster due to more minds focussing on the same goals and objectives of the business.

Teamwork provides learning opportunities
Working in a team enables members to learn from one another's mistakes. This eliminates future errors, helps gain insight from differing perspectives, and learn new concepts from more experienced colleagues. In addition, individuals can expand their skill sets, discover fresh ideas from newer colleagues and therefore ascertain more effective approaches and solutions towards the tasks at hand.

Teamwork promotes synergy
Mutual support, shared goals, cooperation and encouragement provide workplace synergy. Team members feel a greater sense of accomplishment, are collectively responsible for outcomes and feed each other with the incentive to perform at higher levels.

Chapter 5: Governance and Compliance

Governance and Compliance

Governance and Compliance

All businesses must have Policies, Processes and procedures which apply Governance and Compliance to its operations.

Compliance is the term used for the way the organisation complies with the legal aspects of its operation, whilst governance refers to the systems by which it is directed and controlled.

Aims of Governance and Compliance

Organisations need to operate in compliance with a wide variety of financial rules, regulations and legislation that vary according to the type of organisation and the activities it undertakes.

There will be internal governance to ensure compliance with the requirements set out in the organisation's policies and procedures, for example:

- *how sales need to be recorded*
- *how often reports need to be generated*
- *how to use systems that track banking activities*
- *information needed for monthly reports sent to head office*
- *how to prepare quarterly reviews for shareholders*
- *systems to check and monitor compliance*

Issues that governance and compliance aim to avoid and mitigate

Broadly speaking, governance and compliance aim to avoid and mitigate issues such as:

- **fraud** – *e.g., procedures to shred documents to prevent identity theft*
- **theft** – *e.g., using CCTV to monitor staff using a cash till*
- **tax evasion** – *e.g., procedures to make sure that cash payments are declared*
- **criminal activity** – *e.g., taking bribes or trafficking workers*
- **misuse of funds and resources** – *e.g., monitoring budgets closely to reduce waste and unnecessary spending*
- **inefficiency** – *e.g., from not monitoring waste or opportunities to steal cash or goods*
- **money laundering** – *e.g., disposal of large sums of money which have been derived from illegal activity*

Governance and Compliance

Sometimes actions are deliberate and have a criminal intent – e.g., knowingly employing people who are illegal immigrants or those who have been trafficked, stealing products or cash.

Some actions are due to negligence and ignorance – e.g., from someone not realising that they need to provide workplace pensions for their employees; under-declaring VAT due to lack of knowledge about the rules.

There many legal requirements imposed by external stakeholders which must be complied with. It is a requirement of all organisations to satisfy these legal requirements by, for example:

- **paying the right amounts of tax** – *e.g., PAYE tax and national insurance, VAT or corporation tax*
- **paying the correct level of minimum wage**
- **making contributions to workplace pensions** – *e.g., to comply with the Pension Regulator's requirements*
- **keeping adequate records** – *e.g., audited accounts for large companies*
- **using, storing and disposing of financial information correctly** – *e.g., in accordance with the General Data Protection Regulations 2018 (GDPR)*
- **submitting accurate returns on time** – *e.g., to HMRC or Companies House*
- **avoiding making bribes** – *e.g., to conform with the Bribery Act 2010*
- **satisfying industry-specific requirements** – *e.g., FCA requirements for financial services organisations*

There can also be costs associated with compliance – e.g., accountancy fees for preparing and submitting accounts; consultancy fees for compliance advice and strategy making and audit fees for verification. In order to achieve compliance with legislation, organisations need good governance – the systems by which organisations are directed and controlled, imposed by management such as a board of directors or trustees.

Financial governance is necessary to enable organisations to:

- *keep up to date with new legislation and stakeholder expectations*
- *increase efficiency and revenue*
- *lower the costs of compliance*
- *avoid fines and penalties*
- *avoid damage to their reputation*

Governance and Compliance

Compliance

All organisations must comply with the laws and regulations which relate to its industry, environment, legal entity and circumstances. Financial compliance must be demonstrated through the accounts of the business and the financial returns it makes to the necessary enforcement bodies.

The following are just a small sample of the laws which apply to every business in the UK.

- Health and Safety Act
- Financial Laws including tax laws
- Employment law
- General data Protection Regulations (GDPR)
- Freedom of Information Act
- Privacy and Electronic Communications Regulations
- Copyrights, Design and Patents Act
- Human Rights Act
- Equality Act

In addition, there is also the legislation which defines how a business should conduct itself.

These can include:

Legislation	Purpose
Companies Act	Defines the duties of the Directors of all companies registered in the UK
Financial Services and Markets Act	Regulates shares and securities
Financial Services Act	Applies criminal offences for making false claims or misrepresentation and creating false impressions
Insolvency Act	Governs the winding up of companies including liquidation and bankruptcy
Consumer Credit Act	Protects credit cards, loans and hire purchase agreements
Consumer Rights Act	Protects and assigns rights to the consumer including the right to compensation
Misrepresentation Act	Protects consumers from false or fraudulent claims
Payment Services Regulations	Protects consumers who are victims of fraud
Unfair Terms in Consumer Regulations	Defines the terms which are considered unfair in consumer agreements
Consumer contracts Regulations	Protects customers when buying items online

Governance and Compliance

The type and nature of the legislation which must be complied with, will vary from organisation to organisation. Not all legislation will apply to all business, however, a few do and include employment law, equality law, data protection and health and Safety.

The Health and Safety Act 1974

The thought of being hurt at work is not very appealing but on average, 300 people a year lose their lives at work in Britain. In addition, around 158,000 non-fatal injuries are reported each year and an estimated 2.2 million people suffer from ill health caused or made worse by work. Some £16 billion is lost each year through accidents and injuries.

Accidents don't happen. They are caused!

The Health & Safety at Work Act 1974 applies to all employees, the self-employed, government offices and in some circumstances the general public.

Its main concept is that employers have a duty to protect their employers and members of the public affected by their work and must inform them about matters relating to their health, safety and welfare.

Naturally, the heaviest burden of responsibility falls to the employer.

When it was introduced, the Act did three things.

- *Introduced the concept of criminal liability.*
- *Introduced the concept of you are guilty until proven innocent.*
- *Gave wide, sweeping, powers to Health & Safety Inspectors to enter businesses at any time that work is in progress, carry out inspections and if necessary, serve notice that practices are dangerous.*

Health and Safety – Your Duty

It is a legal requirement that employers provide healthy and safe working conditions for all employees by implementing safe working practices.

The employee and employer share a legal obligation under the Health & Safety at Work Act 1974 to maintain a healthy and safe work environment.

All employees must familiarise themselves with all health & safety procedures. It is your legal duty to take care of your own health and safety together with that of your colleagues. Failure by an employee to comply with these procedures will be considered an act of gross misconduct and will result in disciplinary action.

Governance and Compliance

Employees must familiarise themselves with all the requirements in the organisations staff handbook and pay particular attention to the contents of any statutory warning notices displayed in the workplace.

Employees must:

- *Work safely in the interest of both themselves and any others who may be affected by their working activity.*
- *Comply with Health and Safety procedures and standards.*
- *Making appropriate use of equipment, and personal protective clothing.*
- *Reporting any hazards, accidents and near misses.*

Good health and safety practices help make the workplace safe for everyone. Most health and safety practices are common sense. Many accidents can be avoided by simply being careful. Some hazards are obvious. For example, when there is a spillage on the floor the quickest, easiest and safest solution is to mop it up straight away. Other hazards are harder to spot. People do not always realise the risk involved in everyday activities. For example, lifting and moving heavy loads incorrectly can be very dangerous.

The following are some of the common hazards:

- *Slippery floors*
- *Electrical equipment*
- *Boiling water*
- *Uneven floors*
- *Damaged carpets*
- *Manual Handling*

Health and Safety – Employer Duty

The Health and Safety at Work Act 1974 states:

> *"All employers are requires to have a health and safety policy, carry out risk assessments and provide health and safety training for their employees."*

Under the Health and Safety at Work Act 1974 all employers have a legal responsibility to:

- *Provide healthy and safe premises, machinery, systems and working conditions*

Governance and Compliance

- Provide all necessary personal protective equipment (PPE) needed to ensure safety – free of charge
- Provide safe methods of handling, storing and transporting materials
- Provide adequate information, training, instruction for all employees in matters concerning health and safety
- Provide adequate means of safe access and exit from buildings and places of work
- Draw up a health and safety policy statement, including the health and safety organisation and arrangements in force and bring it to your attention
- Appoint a representative of management to have specific responsibility for health and safety in each place of work
- To report certain injuries, diseases and dangerous events to the enforcing authority which, in this case, is the Environmental Health section of your local council.

Health and Safety Policy Statements

All employers are required by law to have a Health and Safety Policy. If there are five or more employees, including any owners who work in the business, this policy must be in written form.

Health and Safety Policies are very important documents. They set out the aims and objectives of the company in terms of how it intends to provide and maintain safe and healthy working conditions, safe systems of work, equipment and plant for all its employees and how it will provide information, instruction, training and supervision for all its employees. It will also set out how it will ensure that all its legal requirements are met, how the policy shall be made known to its employees and how it will be monitored and regularly reviewed to make sure that its aims and objectives are achieved.

Health and Safety Policies also contain valuable information about the nature of the business. It also describes who in the company is responsible for what aspects of Health and Safety as well as stating any company specific Health and Safety Rules that apply to all employees.

Although it is your employer's legal responsibility to make you aware of its Health and Safety Policy, it is equally your responsibility to make sure you fully understand it!

You are strongly urged to adopt a positive approach to working safely, to be aware of hazards, correct anything that might cause an accident (unless this would involve risk) and report it to your manager or Supervisor.

Governance and Compliance

Any employee who contravenes or fails to observe relevant health and safety rules could normally expect to be subjected to disciplinary action by their employer.

Workplace Welfare

Workplace welfare involves the employer ensuring not just the safety of the employees, but also providing support as needed to ensure their welfare. Toilets and handwashing facilities along with a rest area where staff can eat their meals is a minimum requirement, but the requirement may be more far reaching.

Some tasks are known to cause problems for some people and steps must be taken to minimise this or make provision to limit the exposure to the problem.

What you need to know poster

A Health and Safety Law Poster is a brief guide to health and safety law and provides a list of the key point's employees and employers have to know.

> *Every business in the UK must display a copy of this poster, regardless of the number of staff they employ.*

This poster is available to purchase on the HSE website.

Governance and Compliance

Equality and Diversity

The term equality and diversity has become a watch word in both the workplace and society. It is vital that everyone is aware of the implications, especially for those in a Customer Service role.

Equality & Diversity is about being fair to all:

- *fair to men and women*
- *fair to those from other countries*
- *fair to those from other communities or groups*
- *fair to those with disabilities*
- *fair to those with religious beliefs*

Equality
Equality in the workplace means equal job opportunities and fairness for employees and job applicants.

In the wider world, you must not treat people unfairly because of reasons protected by discrimination law ('protected characteristics'). For example, because of a person's sex, age or race. This applies particularly in a Customer Service role.

Diversity
Diversity is the range of people in your workforce. For example, this might mean people with different ages, religions, ethnicities, people with disabilities, and both men and women. It also means valuing those differences.

Inclusion
An inclusive workplace means everyone feels valued at work. It lets all employees feel safe to:

- *come up with different ideas*
- *raise issues and suggestions to managers, knowing this is encouraged*
- *try doing things differently to how they have been done before, with management approval*

An inclusive workplace can help lower the risk of bullying, harassment and discrimination.

Equality & Diversity at Work

Diversity is the uniqueness of all individuals, which encompasses different personal attributes, values and organisational roles. Equality and diversity management is the process of creating and maintaining a positive environment where the differences of all employees

Governance and Compliance

are recognised, understood and valued so that they can reach their full potential and maximise their contributions.

It has also been described as:

> *"promoting equality of opportunity for all, through diversity, giving each individual the chance to achieve their potential, free from prejudice and discrimination."*

Responsibilities

The principles of legislation have to be applied at work and in all dealings with other people. This means that customers and colleagues alike must be treated fairly and equally by you. It is important that you are clear about your personal responsibilities and liabilities under equality legislation and any relevant codes of practice.

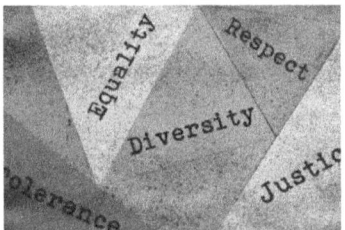

Failure to comply with equality legislation could lead to legal action against you or your organisation. You should have been made aware of these when you joined your organisation. If you are unsure of any of your responsibilities it is important that you clarify them with your manager or equality and diversity representative.

Once you are clear about your responsibilities, if you wish to find out more about these responsibilities there are hundreds of books on the subject of equality and diversity in the workplace as well as websites you can search on.

An important aspect of good customer service is the fair and equal treatment of all customers no matter who they may be

Working successfully as a team with your colleagues depends upon all parties involved behaving in a fair and equal manner towards one another.

This does not mean you have to like everyone, but you must respect others and not treat people differently because of their individual characteristics and preferences.

Behaviour

It is important that information regarding equality and diversity is available to all employees. Some organisations may choose to have a written equality and diversity policy. It is important that this policy is communicated quickly and clearly to the relevant people in your area of responsibility e.g., all employees, visitors and contractors.

Equality and diversity training should be communicated at the induction as soon as possible after the employee has joined the company.

To avoid bullying, harassment or discrimination, employers should make sure:

Governance and Compliance

- employees understand what is protected by discrimination law
- what is expected under discrimination law is actually happening in the workplace
- changes are made if what is expected is not happening, e.g., stepping up staff training
- employees understand the benefits of having a range of people with different background

There are a number of ways that equality and diversity induction training can be delivered e.g., videos, talks, leaflets, and games etc. Whichever way it is delivered; it is important that it is communicated effectively so that employees can understand it and put it into practice.

No matter what your personal views are, your behaviour at work should not be based upon them. A good employee always behaves professionally.

Professional behaviour means you must be:

- *Respectful towards others in your dealings with them*
- *Consistent in your treatment of others at all times*
- *Honest in your communications with others*

If you require any information regarding equality and diversity your first point of call should be your manager, HR or equality and diversity representative if one exists in your workplace. They should be able to answer the majority of your questions and have all the up-to-date information around relevant legislation.

Treat others as you would expect them to treat you!

Employee Rights

Employee rights are not always made clear when starting a new job but knowing about them is important. Not only to protect yourself but also so you can support and stand up for others in the workplace.

Statutory rights ensure all workers are treated fairly by their employers under law. Here, we share some of the most important rights. They apply to most though not all workers. If you are a freelancer, or you are self-employed or working for an agency, you may not have the same rights.

The only universal rights for every worker are the right to minimum wage and to not be discriminated against.

UK workers have 8 key legal rights

Governance and Compliance

The Right to Maximum Working Hours
Employees cannot be forced to work more than 48 hours in one week so must agree to put in additional hours in writing. Workers also have a legal right to paid holiday every year. Full-time employees can get up to 5.6 weeks (depending on the company) and part-time workers get pro rata holiday.

Workers can also legally take unpaid time off for reasons such as additional training, taking part in trade union activities, and for emergencies, like looking after dependants.

What people often do not realise is if you have been working somewhere for six months you have the right to submit a request for flexible working. The business does not have to accept your request but must give a compelling reason why not if so.

The Right to Equal Pay and Minimum Wage
UK workers must be paid at least National Minimum Wage. All employees should receive a payslip breaking down their pay and deductions soon after starting, and employers cannot make any illegal wage deductions.

Under the Equal Pay Act 1970, unequal treatment between men and women over pay and employment conditions became completely prohibited. It was repealed but then many of its provisions were replicated in the Equality Act 2010. It is important to distinguish between unequal pay – which is illegal – and the issues surrounding the gender pay gap, where one sex is earning more than the other within a company because one dominates the higher up positions, which is not illegal but is an issue many businesses are tackling.

The Right to Health and Safety at Work
Health and safety laws state every worker has a legal right to daily and weekly time off. This means anyone working more than six hours must have a break of at least 20 minutes and everyone must get at least one day off in every seven days.

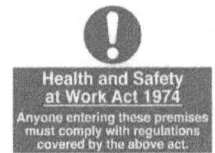

All workers also have a right to work in an environment where any risks to their health and safety are properly dealt with and controlled. This is the duty of the employer, who must also ensure they communicate with employees on all health and safety matters. The responsibility includes, for example, ensuring staff have a clean environment to work in, any necessary protective clothing, water for drinking, and first aid equipment.

The Right to Parental Leave
Every woman who has a baby is entitled to up to a year of maternity leave, no matter how long they have worked for the company. Statutory leave for fathers is currently only two weeks and the fathers must have worked for the company for at least 26 consecutive weeks by the end of the 15th week of the pregnancy.

Governance and Compliance

Leave is very different to pay, which can be more complex and varies depending on how long you have worked for a company.

Fathers qualifying for paternity pay must earn at least £113 a week before tax and the rate is either £140.98 a week or 90% of your weekly earnings, whichever is lower.

Mothers are only entitled to pay for 39 weeks of their leave, and this changes over time. They get 90% of their pre-tax weekly earnings for the first six weeks, £145.18 a week or 90% of their earnings if it is less for the next 33 weeks and nothing after that.

Shared Parental Leave is a recent ruling which allows both parents to share up to 50 weeks of leave and 37 weeks of pay between you. (*Please check the accuracy of these details before using them as they change frequently*)

The Right to Trade Union Membership
Trade unions are organisations of workers who join together to achieve a common goal, like improving wages and working conditions and protecting their trade's integrity.

Employees have the right to belong to a trade union, join or not join a trade union, and leave or remain a member of one at any time during their employment. Employers are not allowed to treat you unfairly or dismiss you because you do any of these things. Workers decide to join trade unions because they give you the power to negotiate a better deal through collective bargaining.

The Right to Not be Discriminated Against
Under no circumstances can anyone be discriminated against at work for gender, sexuality, age, background, race, religious beliefs, marriage and partnership, pregnancy, or disability. Examples of how this could happen include not choosing someone for a job or promotion, not paying them the same, and it could even occur indirectly through rules which put certain employees at a disadvantage.

Employers can actively prevent discrimination from occurring by ensuring they recruit inclusively, have an equal opportunities policy, and ensuring all staff follow these practices, by providing training on this topic, encouraging universal respect, and dealing with any complaints quickly. There is no situation when it is legally acceptable to harass or victimise anyone at work if they complain or expose a wrongdoing.

The Right to Fair Dismissal
Employees must usually give employees at least the notice stated in their employment contract or the legal minimum notice period, whichever is longer.

Governance and Compliance

An employer can only dismiss a worker without notice if it considers someone to have done something which constitutes gross misconduct, for example committing fraud or being violent. Employers must always pursue the fair procedure when considering dismissal.

If you are threatened with or receive what you consider to be unfair dismissal, you can get help from a third party to solve the issue by mediation, conciliation, and arbitration. Trade union members can speak to their unions. You must have worked for the company for a minimum period before you have the right to claim unfair dismissal, and this completely varies depending on when you started working for the company and how long you have worked there, due to changes in the law.

The Right to Reasonable Adjustments

Under the Equality Act 2010 employers must also ensure there are reasonable adjustments so that workers with disabilities are not disadvantaged, neither in the job application process or in the job itself. A person is classed as disabled under this law if they have a mental or physical impairment which has a substantially adverse and long-term impact on whether they can do day-to-day activities.

Reasonable adjustments remove or minimise disadvantages disabled people face and, while some businesses will spend a lot on expensive equipment, this does not have to happen. Examples of reasonable adjustments include a keyboard for someone with arthritis, a wheelchair ramp, changing performance targets, and a phased return to work after a period off sick.

Governance and Compliance

Harassment
No one should be deliberately harassed at work. Neither should they be bullied or made to feel bad. Employees do not have to put up with it!

Harassment can take many forms such as:

- *Threatening or abusive language*
- *Insulting language or behaviour*
- *Disorderly behaviour*
- *Displaying any writing, sign or other visible representation that alarms or distresses and was intended to do so*

Sexual Harassment
It is perfectly acceptable to court and pay attention to someone if it is wanted or invited, but it is illegal to pester people.

If you are told once 'No, I don't like it', but you do it again, you are in danger of breaking the law, both Civil and Criminal. No one has to put up with sexual harassment at work. Be careful and think. Even a thoughtless comment may cause offence.

- *It might be OK for a man to say to a woman, 'You look smart today'*
- *But it might not be so good to say, 'I like that top you are wearing'*

Bullying
Bullying at work can also take many forms such as:

- *Aggressive or violent behaviour*
- *Threatening postures*
- *Putting you in a position where if you do not do something a threat of some kind hangs over you*
- *Excluding you from a group by intimidation*

If you feel that you are being harassed or bullied at work, you should inform your supervisor

Remember, there are laws that exist to protect you, such as:

- *Sex Discrimination Act 1975*
- *Race Relations Act 1976*
- *Protection from Harassment Act 1997*
- *Gender Reassignment Regulations 1999*
- *The Human Rights Acts of 1948 and 1998*

Governance and Compliance

Equality, Diversity and Employment Laws

Gender Balance

The idea is to get equal numbers of men and women in jobs regardless of the trade or profession involved. This had led to more women in construction and computing and more men in administration and hairdressing, for example. Never be put off applying for any job or promotion because of your sex

Advertising and Employment

The Anti-discrimination laws lay down specific requirements upon firms when they advertise for staff or when marketing product, such as:

- *Adverts must not make gender an issue. Using words like 'salesgirl' or 'barman' in an advert encourages discrimination and is banned*
- *Adverts should encourage both men and women and people of all races to apply for a job*
- *Any illustrations or pictures should not show only one sex doing a job*
- *Adverts can be targeted towards the sex or racial group if they are selling a product or service for that sex or group*

When it is Legal to Discriminate

It is sometimes legal and necessary to discriminate over certain issues such as gender, for example:

- *If a man or woman is needed to act in a particular role in a play*
- *The job is one of two to be held by a married couple*
- *The work is in a single sex prison or hospital ward*
- *Carers for the mentally ill must be of the same sex*

Governance and Compliance

The Human Rights Act

This Act is designed to provide legal protection to all human beings. It embraces all other Equality & Diversity Acts and ensures human rights are protected in areas not covered by them.

Human Rights Act 1998

The Human Rights Act was set out and agreed in 1948. It was reaffirmed by all nations on its 50th anniversary in 1998 and led to the introduction of the European Convention on Human Rights.

It came into force as law in the UK on 2nd October 2000.

The Human Rights Act declares that:

'All human beings are born free and equal in dignity and rights. They are endowed with reason and conscience and should act towards one another in a spirit of brotherhood.'

It also states that 'Everyone is entitled to all the rights and freedoms set forth in the declaration, without distinction of any kind such as race, colour, sex, language, religion, political or other opinion, national or social origin, property, birth or other status'.

In an equal and fair society all people have rights and these are protected by legislation

For example:

- *The right to be treated as equal as human beings regardless of sex or race*
- *The right to be treated properly at work*
- *The right to be free from discrimination*
- *The right not to be bullied or harassed*
- *The right to be healthy and safe at work*

Two key pieces of legislation relating to Equality and Diversity are those of Equal Pay and Sex Discrimination.

Governance and Compliance

Employment Legislation

Employment law, while designed to protect the rights of the employee, covers most of the aspects regarding the relationship between the employer and the employee. The business must comply with all aspects of employment law to avoid the negative impact of not doing so, including costly fines, employment tribunal's, adverse publicity and loss of their brand reputation, for example.

There are several pieces of legislation that can be connected with the delivery of work including:

- *Employment Rights Act 1996*
- *Equality Act 2010*
- *Working Time Regulations*
- *The General Data Protection Regulation 2016*
- *Health and Safety at Work Act 1974*
- *Other legislation and regulations*

Employment Rights Act 1996

The main employment legislation in the UK is the Employment Rights Act 1996. This law is very detailed and deals with a huge number of aspects about employment. Some of the main points covered by the Act are:

- *the employee's right to have a statement or contract of employment*
- *the employee's right to have an itemised pay statement*
- *protection of wages*
- *protection from suffering detriment in employment from taking time off work* – e.g., taking time off for jury service, family reasons or antenatal care
- *sickness*
- *maternity, paternity and adoption payments and leave*
- *suspension from work*
- *procedures for discipline, grievance, dismissal and redundancy*
- *Sunday working and time off*

Employment law is constantly under review and revision, with additions and changes happening every year, so it is important for managers and their organisations to keep up to date with the latest legislation and regulations.

Governance and Compliance

It helps if line managers are aware of their rights, and those of their team members, so that they can apply disciplinary processes fairly, and act if the employer does not comply with this Act.

Equality Act 2010

The Equality Act 2010 is the current legislation that deals with equality and discrimination in the UK. The Act gives individuals rights as it is unlawful to discriminate against anyone because of a protected characteristic:

- **age** – all people over 18 are protected at work or in work training
- **disability or impairment** – organisations must make 'reasonable adjustments' to accommodate staff, customers and visitors with disabilities
- **gender** – equal pay, training and opportunity for males and females
- **gender reassignment** – people changing from male to female, or female to male
- **marriage or civil partnership** – preventing discrimination on the grounds of being married or in a civil partnership, at work or in work training
- **pregnancy or maternity (including breastfeeding)** – only reasons of safety are not covered – e.g., equality may not be possible for pregnant women in some circumstances if the activity could harm them or the baby
- **race** – wherever they were born, their parents' and their own race, colour, ethnicity are protected
- **religion or beliefs** – any religion, lack of religion or personal belief is protected
- **sexual orientation** – heterosexual, gay, lesbian and bisexual people are covered

If there are special operational reasons, such as carers in a nursing home needing to be able to lift residents, there are exceptions to the rule, but the employer must take great care to be as fair as possible.

There are many things that organisations need to observe. For example, employers have a responsibility to:

- *avoid discriminating against employees, trainees and job applicants on the grounds of any of the protected characteristics*
- *make 'reasonable adjustments' to accommodate staff, job applicants, trainees, customers and visitors with disabilities or impairments*
- *make sure that discrimination is not tolerated, and take steps to deal with bullying, harassment, victimisation or other forms of discrimination in the workplace*
- *give men and women equal pay and treatment in the terms and conditions of their employment contract if they are employed to do work that is the*

Governance and Compliance

same, broadly similar or of equal value in terms of effort, skill or decision-making
- train and monitor their workforce, and put in place policies and procedures for dealing with problems and complaints
- make sure that all employees, customers, job applicants and visitors know where to find information about their equality policies and procedures
- avoid asking job candidates about their health, age, absences due to pregnancy-related illnesses etc. during the application and interview processes – health questions can only be asked after a job offer has been made

Employees also have a responsibility to make sure that they do not breach their employer's equality and diversity policies, codes of conduct or guidelines. The law requires each individual to take responsibility and avoid discrimination, and the employer needs to give clear guidelines in contracts of employment, equality and diversity policies, training sessions and so on.

If an individual fails to follow the guidelines, the organisation can implement disciplinary action or claim breach of contract (the employment contract).

Working Time Regulations

The Working Time Regulations generally provide rights for employees to have:

- a limit of an average 48-hour working week, although individuals may choose to work longer by 'opting out'
    - weeks of paid leave a year
- 11 consecutive hours' rest in any 24-hour period
- a 20-minute rest break if the working day is longer than 6 hours
- 1 day off each week
- a limit on the normal working hours of night workers to an average 8 hours in any 24-hour period, and an entitlement for night workers to receive regular health assessments

There are special regulations for young workers, which restrict their working hours to 8 hours per day and 40 hours per week. The rest break is 30 minutes if their work lasts more than 4 and a half hours, and they are entitled to 2 days off each week.

Governance and Compliance

Other Employment legislation and regulations

There are numerous other regulations and pieces of legislation that apply to certain industries or circumstances. Employees and management need to check the organisation's policies and procedures to find out which ones affect them, and what their responsibilities might be. These might include, for instance:

- *Trade Union and Labour Relations (Consolidation) Act 1992* – the ACAS code is issued under this Act
- *National Minimum Wage Act 1998* – dealing with the minimum wage for different age groups
- *Pensions Act 2014* – dealing with contributions to occupational pension schemes and state pensions
- *Modern Slavery Act 2015* – dealing with people trafficking and slavery
- *Part-Time Workers (Prevention of Less Favourable Treatment) Regulations 2000*
- *Fixed-term employees (Prevention of Less Favourable Treatment) Regulations 2002*
- *Statutory Paternity Pay and Statutory Adoption Pay (General) Regulations 2002* – and later amendments
- *Work and Families Act 2006*
- *Enterprise and Regulatory Reform Act 2013*

Operational Legislation

The Data Protection Act 2018

The Data Protection Act 2018 controls how your personal information is used by organisations, businesses or the government.

Data Protection Act 2018

The Data Protection Act 2018 is the UK's implementation of the General Data Protection Regulation (GDPR).

Everyone responsible for using personal data has to follow strict rules called data protection principles. They must make sure the information is:

- *used fairly, lawfully and transparently*
- *used for specified, explicit purposes*
- *used in a way that is adequate, relevant and limited to only what is necessary*
- *accurate and, where necessary, kept up to date*

Governance and Compliance

- *kept for no longer than is necessary*
- *handled in a way that ensures appropriate security, including protection against unlawful or unauthorised processing, access, loss, destruction or damage*

There is stronger legal protection for more sensitive information, such as:

- *race*
- *ethnic background*
- *political opinions*
- *religious beliefs*
- *trade union membership*
- *genetics*
- *biometrics (where used for identification)*
- *health*
- *sex life or orientation*

There are separate safeguards for personal data relating to criminal convictions and offences.

Rights

Under the Data Protection Act 2018, you have the right to find out what information the government and other organisations store about you. These include the right to:

- *be informed about how your data is being used*
- *access personal data*
- *have incorrect data updated*
- *have data erased*
- *stop or restrict the processing of your data*
- *data portability (allowing you to get and reuse your data for different services)*
- *object to how your data is processed in certain circumstances*

You also have rights when an organisation is using your personal data for:

- *automated decision-making processes (without human involvement)*
- *profiling, for example to predict your behaviour or interests*

Governance and Compliance

The General Data Protection Regulation 2016

GDPR stands for General Data Protection Regulation. The GDPR is a regulation from the Data Protection Act and covers any information related to a person or data subject that can be used to directly or indirectly identify them. It can be anything from a name, a photo and an email address to bank details, social media posts, biometric data and medical information. It also introduces digital rights for individuals.

When it came into effect on May 25, 2018, the GDPR set new standards for data protection, and kickstarted a wave of global privacy laws that forever changed how we use the internet.

The Purpose of GDPR
Personal data is highly valuable — in fact, it supports a trillion-dollar industry. Companies like Facebook and Google make their profits by selling personal information to advertisers. With this much money at stake, do you trust them to have your best interests at heart? The GDPR defines what companies of all sizes can and cannot do with customer information.

What Is Classified as Personal Data Under GDPR?
Personal data is information that can be used to identify you. Put simply, it is any private details that you would not want to fall into the wrong hands.

Here are some examples of personal data:

- Name
- phone number
- address
- social media posts
- geotagging
- health records

- date of birth
- bank account
- passport number
- race
- religious and political opinions

Think of personal data like a jigsaw. One piece alone might not say much but connected together they reveal a vivid picture of your life.

What Is a 'Breach' Under GDPR?
Any incident that leads to personal data being lost, stolen, destroyed, or changed is considered a data breach. Unfortunately, breaches happen all the time.

Here are some newsworthy examples from before the GDPR started cracking down:

- *Almost half the population of the US had their name, date of birth, and social security number stolen from credit reporting agency Equifax as the result of a data breach.*

Governance and Compliance

- *Political consulting firm Cambridge Analytica secretly took information from 50 million Facebook profiles and gave it to the 2016 Trump campaign.*

Both of these incidents illustrate how data breaches have serious real-world consequences. This is exactly what GDPR and similar laws hope to regulate.

Penalties for Violating the GDPR
The GDPR threatens would-be violators with some severe penalties. To make sure companies handle your personal data in a legal, ethical way, the fines for noncompliance are:

Up to £18 million or 4% of annual global turnover.

Some big names have already been hit with these noncompliance fines:

- **British Airways — £165 million.** *The UK airline set the record for fines when the booking details of 500,000 customers were stolen in a cyberattack.*
- **Marriott — £90 million.** *After buying the Starwood Hotels group, Marriott failed to update an old system belonging to the group. This system was hacked, revealing information about 339 million guests.*
- **Google — £40 million.** *Important information was hidden when users set up new Android phones, meaning they did not know what data collection practices they were agreeing to. The Google GDPR fine shows even tech giants are not immune to GDPR enforcement.*

Although smaller businesses would not be hit for such high amounts, they are held to the same standards.

A business owner now has to make sure their operations comply with the GDPR.

The only thing most people will need to do is read the cookie consent banners that now appear on websites and click agree (or not). The GDPR affects everything people do online, but it is mostly working behind the scenes.

Governance and Compliance

Freedom of Information Act 2000

The Freedom of Information Act 2000 provides public access to information held by public authorities.
It does this in two ways:

Freedom of Information Act 2000

- *public authorities are obliged to publish certain information about their activities*
    and
- *members of the public are entitled to request information from public authorities.*

The Act covers any recorded information that is held by a public authority in England, Wales and Northern Ireland, and by UK-wide public authorities based in Scotland. Information held by Scottish public authorities is covered by Scotland's own Freedom of Information (Scotland) Act 2002.

Public authorities include government departments, local authorities, the NHS, state schools and police forces. However, the Act does not necessarily cover every organisation that receives public money. For example, it does not cover some charities that receive grants and certain private sector organisations that perform public functions.

Recorded information includes printed documents, computer files, letters, emails, photographs, and sound or video recordings.

The Act does not give people access to their own personal data (information about themselves) such as their health records or credit reference file. If a member of the public wants to see information that a public authority holds about them, they should make a data protection subject access request.

Digital Economy Act (2017)

The Digital Economy Act 2017 (the Act) makes provision about electronic communications infrastructure and services, including the creation of a broadband Universal Service Order (USO), to give all premises in the UK a legal right to request a minimum standard of broadband connectivity, expected to be 10 megabits per second (Mbps). The Act also introduces reform of the Electronic Communications Code and provides greater clarification on data sharing between public bodies.

Digital Economy Act 2010

The Digital Economy Bill was introduced in the House of Commons on 5 July 2016, completed its parliamentary stages and received Royal Assent, becoming law, on 27 April 2017.

The Bill followed an announcement made in the Queen's Speech to introduce legislation seeking to make the United Kingdom a world leader in the digital economy.

Governance and Compliance

The Act is made up of six parts as follows:

1. *Access to digital services*
2. *Digital infrastructure*
3. *Online pornography*
4. *Intellectual property*
5. *Digital government*
6. *Miscellaneous.*

Other Legislation and Regulations

There are numerous other regulations and pieces of legislation that apply to certain industries or circumstances. Managers need to check their own organisation's policies and procedures to find out which ones affect them, and what their responsibilities might be. These might include, for instance:

- **Trade Union and Labour Relations (Consolidation) Act 1992** – *the ACAS code is issued under this Act*
- **National Minimum Wage Act 1998** – *dealing with the minimum wage for different age groups*
- **Pensions Act 2014** – *dealing with contributions to occupational pension schemes and state pensions*
- **Modern Slavery Act 2015** – *dealing with people trafficking and slavery*
- **Part-Time Workers (Prevention of Less Favourable Treatment) Regulations 2000**
- **Fixed-term employees (Prevention of Less Favourable Treatment) Regulations 2002**
- **Statutory Paternity Pay and Statutory Adoption Pay (General) Regulations 2002** – *and later amendments*
- **Work and Families Act 2006**
- **Enterprise and Regulatory Reform Act 2013**

Governance and Compliance

Consumer-Related Legislation in Customer Service Delivery

Whenever goods or services are provided to customers there are expectations from both the supplier and the customer of the goods and/or services being provided.

There is a minimum expectation that the goods or services will be fit for purpose.

A window cleaner that does not leave clean windows will not have many happy customers nor will they be in business for long. The customer, however, will have paid to have their windows cleaned and if they are not clean, they have a right to demand a refund of the monies paid.

Similarly, promises made by suppliers must be met in full – A new sofa in your home before Christmas is a common message on TV advertising, they are making a promise that they will achieve the delivery deadline – if they do not, they will be in breach of contract and the purchaser can make a claim against them for failing to fulfil the contract.

All these rights are defined and covered by The Consumer Rights Act which came into force on 1 October 2015 and replaced a number of old laws which had become outdated.

The law is now clearer and easier to understand, meaning that consumers can buy with confidence and businesses can sell to them with similar confidence.

On the rare occasions when problems arise, disputes can now be sorted out more quickly and cheaply.

Alternative Dispute Resolution, for example through an Ombudsman, offers a quicker and cheaper way of resolving disputes than going through the courts. The changes are relevant to all consumers and every business which sells directly to them.

UK consumers spend £90 billion a month across all sectors. This new, clear, statement of consumer rights helps them to make better choices when they buy and save both time and money.

The Consumer Rights Act

The Consumer Rights Act came into force on 1 October 2015 which meant from that date new consumer rights became law covering:

Consumer Rights Act 2015

- *what should happen when goods are faulty*
- *what should happen when digital content is faulty*

Governance and Compliance

- *how services should match up to what has been agreed, and what should happen when they do not, or when they are not provided with reasonable care and skill*
- *unfair terms in a contract*
- *what happens when a business is acting in a way which is not competitive?*
- *written notice for routine inspections by public enforcers, such as Trading Standards*
- *greater flexibility for public enforcers, such as Trading Standards, to respond to breaches of consumer law, such as seeking redress for consumers who have suffered harm.*

Most of these changes were important updates to existing laws. But two new areas of law were also introduced.

- For the first time, rights on digital content has been set out in legislation. The Act gives consumers a clear right to the repair or replacement of faulty digital content, such as online film and games, music downloads and e-books. The law here has been unclear, and this change has brought us up to date with how digital products have evolved.
- There are now also new, clear rules for what should happen if a service is not provided with reasonable care and skill, or as agreed. For example, the business that provided the service must bring it into line with what was agreed with the customer or, if this is not practical, must give some money back.

In terms of what is covered by the new Act, the old standards remain, and these are as follows:

- **Claims about goods** - *It is an offence for the business or any member of staff to issue false statements about services, accommodation and facilities, or to give misleading information about prices, discounts or special offers.*
- **Description of goods** – *Examples are labels such as 'home-made', 'made in France', 'fresh vegetables', etc. There is still a sale by description even where the customer selects the goods, for example, in a self-service restaurant, if he or she relied in some way on the description.*
- **Satisfactory Quality** – *Goods must be fit for the purpose for which they are usually bought*
- **Fitness for a particular purpose** – *Reasonable fitness for a purpose known to the seller*
- **Samples** – *Ensuring that goods when sold correspond with samples*

Governance and Compliance

Governance

Good corporate governance is about effectively supervising the management of a company. It is necessary for the effective, entrepreneurial and prudent management that can deliver the long-term success of an organisation.

The term Governance refers to the action taken by those who run the organisation by using and regulating influence to uphold the company's integrity, achieve more open and rigorous procedures and ensure legal compliance.

Ultimately it should also promote good relations with stakeholders, including shareholders and employees.

It is the exclusive responsibility of the 'governing body', the person, or group of people accountable for the performance and conformance of the organisation. In a commercial organisation, this is the Board of Directors.

There is a code of governance which is enshrined in company law for organisations listed on the London Stock exchange. This sets a code of practice for the governance of financial matters; however, governance is required in all organisations and is also across the spectrum of activities.

Governance along with compliance aim to avoid and mitigate against:

- **fraud** – e.g., procedures to shred documents to prevent identity theft
- **theft** – e.g., using CCTV to monitor staff using a cash till
- **tax evasion** – e.g., procedures to make sure that cash payments are declared
- **criminal activity** – e.g., taking bribes or trafficking workers
- **misuse of funds and resources** – e.g., monitoring budgets closely to reduce waste and unnecessary spending
- **inefficiency** – e.g., from not monitoring waste or opportunities to steal cash or goods
- **money laundering** – e.g., Disposal of large sums of money which have been derived from illegal activity

Accountability

An organisation is not just accountable to HMRC, it is also accountable to its Shareholders, Stakeholders, Investors, Suppliers, Customers and the staff within the organisation.

Internal stakeholders who need to be satisfied about how an organisation looks after its financial procedures could include, for example:

Governance and Compliance

- **business owners** – e.g., sole proprietors or partners who need to know the levels of profit and cash flow
- **shareholders** – e.g., employees or others who own shares in a company who need to keep an eye on their investment
- **employees** – e.g., who rely on the organisation to operate payroll and bonus systems

External stakeholders could include, for example:

- **banks and other lenders** – e.g., who provide business loans to the organisation
- **national and local government agencies** – e.g., who collect taxes and provide grants
- **external customers** – e.g., individuals and companies who buy and use the organisation's products and services
- **charity commission** – e.g., who examine accounts and regulate registered charities

By ensuring an organisation is compliant with legislation and is governed fastidiously and fairly, everyone involved with the business will have confidence in the way the business is being operated and satisfied that the business is being managed equitably and legally.

Sometimes actions are deliberate and have a criminal intent – e.g., knowingly employing people who are illegal immigrants or those who have been trafficked, stealing products or cash. Some actions are due to negligence and ignorance – e.g., from someone not realising that they need to provide workplace pensions for their employees; under-declaring VAT due to lack of knowledge about the rules.

A system of governance needs to be created for every organisation and this can be created through the design, implementation and ensuring compliance with the five functions of governance.

These are:

Determining the objectives of the organisation
These are expressed through the vision and mission statements and implemented through its strategic plan. The objectives define the purpose of the organisation and describe how the purpose will be fulfilled.

Determining the ethics of the organisation
Defining what aspects of behaviour are really important. How much importance is genuinely given to factors such a sustainability, corporate social responsibility and stakeholder engagement over profits and short-term movements in the share process? Ethics are based on morals and values and define the rules or standards governing the conduct of people within the organisation.

The ethical standards of any organisation are set by the behaviours of people at the top and cascade down the hierarchy.

Governance and Compliance

Creating the culture of the organisation
This is a more subtle process and deals with the way people interact with each other. The governing body decides on the culture it wants and influences the operating culture of the organisation through the people it appoints to executive positions.

'Governmentality', the willingness of people to 'be governed' and to support the governance system is at the centre of an effective culture. Other aspects include how supportive the organisation is, how innovative, how risk seeking/averse, how open and transparent, how mature and professional, and how tolerant it is. It is impossible to have a culture of innovation and sensible risk taking if the organisation is intolerant of failure.

Ensuring compliance by the organisation
Governance is implemented to ensure the organisation meets its regulatory, statutory and legal obligations, as well as ensuring its management and staff work towards achieving the organisation's objectives, while working within the ethical and cultural framework defined by the governing body.

Designing and implementing the governance framework for the organisation.
The governing body is accountable for the performance of the organisation and retains overall responsibility for the organisation it governs; however, in most organisations the governing body cannot undertake all of the work of governance itself.

To ensure the efficient governance of the organisation, various responsibilities need to be delegated to people within the organisation's management. The governance framework defines the principles, structures, enabling factors and interfaces through which the organisation's governance arrangements will operate by delegating appropriate levels of authority and responsibility to managers and other entities, and ensuring accountability.

In summary, the governing body appoints, provides direction to and oversees the functioning of the organisation's management and makes the 'rules' the organisation's management and staff are expected to conform to. Management's job is to achieve the objectives of the organisation; working within its ethical and cultural framework, while complying with the 'rules' and providing assurance back to the governing body that this is being accomplished.

The governance system and the management system are derived from each other. The management system is dependent on the governance framework and the governance system is driven by the management. A well-governed organisation allows these two systems to work together to the benefit of the organisation's overall stakeholder community.

A good system of corporate governance will strive to:

- *Ensure that the management of an organisation considers the best interests of everyone*
- *Help organisations deliver long-term corporate success and economic growth*

Governance and Compliance

- *Maintain the confidence of investors and as consequence organisations raise capital efficiently and effectively*
- *Has a positive impact on the price of shares as it improves the trust in the market*
- *Improves control over management and information systems (such as security or risk management)*
- *Gives guidance to the owners and managers the strategy of the company*
- *Minimises wastages, corruption, fraud, risks, and mismanagement*
- *Helps to create a strong brand reputation*
- *Most importantly – it makes organisations more resilient.*

Creating a framework for the governance of an organisation can be immensely challenging. You need to spend only a few moments thinking about the number of policies and procedures which are followed each day within one department to realise scale of the task of producing a framework for the governance of a whole organisation. In order to begin to make sense of the process it can be broken down into four elements often known as the four Ps'

These are:

- *People*
- *Purpose*
- *Process*
- *Performance*

People
People come first in the Four Ps because people exist on every side of the business equation. They are the founders, the board, the stakeholder and consumer and impartial observer.

People are the organisers who determine a purpose to work towards, develop a consistent process to achieve it, evaluate their performance outcomes, and use those outcomes to grow themselves and others as people.

This is a cyclical process, but it has to start with people.

Purpose
Purpose is the next step. Every piece of governance exists for a purpose and to achieve a purpose. The 'for' is the guiding principles of the organisation. Their mission statement. Every one of their policies and projects should exist to further this agenda.

Governance and Compliance

The 'achieve' is the small step on the road to completing that large goal. It might seem pointless to type up minutes for a meeting that felt irrelevant, but those minutes and all the other governance from that meeting contribute to making the business effective at achieving its stated purpose.

Process

Governance is the process by which people achieve their organisation's purpose, and that process is developed by analysing performance. Processes are refined over time in order to consistently achieve their purpose, and it is good practice to constantly review the governance processes.

Can they be streamlined? Are they efficiently achieving their purpose? It takes work to make your processes function, but once they do you will quickly see how they can help your company grow.

Performance

Performance analysis is a key skill in any industry. The ability to look at the results of a process and determine whether it was successful (or successful enough), and then apply those findings to the rest of the organisation, is one of the primary functions of the governance process.

The analysis of these performance results should then be used to identify developmental needs in order to refine the process. The question to be asked regularly is: Governance: is it performing?

Examples might include:

- *how sales need to be recorded*
- *how often reports need to be generated*
- *how to use systems that track banking activities*
- *information needed for monthly reports sent to head office*
- *how to prepare quarterly reviews for shareholders*
- *systems to check and monitor compliance*

Developing Governance

The leaders of organisations will not sit around a boardroom table and begin to discuss which policy or procedure of governance they will start with, it is very much more likely to be an organic process.

At day one of the organisation there will probably be only a few people involved and one or two people will be able to manage all

Governance and Compliance

four elements listed above so the need for detailed, documented Governance will be negligible.

As the organisation grows, volumes will increase, more staff will be required and suddenly the business needs far more controls. New policies and procedures will be required and existing ones will need to be reviewed. Organisations will continue of this cycle designing, developing, documenting and implementing new policies and procedures as the needs of the business require.

The key word here is documenting. If an organisation relies on word of mouth to implement new standards, governance is immediately under threat as it is open to interpretation or omission and people will not follow the prescribed processes.

It may seem that the number of policies an organisation has is excessive, however, it should be remembered that many policies and processes will not apply to all departments.

The key policies will be those that are directly linked to ensuring compliance with legislation. There will then be a number of policies and procedures which relate specifically to a department or team. These will be developed to ensure consistency in behaviour and performance and it is essential that those people affected by the policy adhere to it.

An example might be an escalation policy. A problem which cannot be dealt with by a junior team member will need to be escalated to someone in a more senior role, but who is the appropriate person?

This will be defined in the process. If it is a supply issue, it may be directed to an identified member of a sales team. If it involves a quality issue it may need referring to a defined member of the production team. If the issue relates to a refund, it may need a certain level of authority to authorise the refund.

If the staff member knows this policy or has immediate access to it, they can explain to the customer how they will deal with the problem and pass the query on quickly, to the right person, to ensure a speedy resolution.

It is important that all staff are conversant with the policies which relate to their job role to ensure problems are resolved in a standardised manner to protect all stakeholders involved.

Typical Framework
A framework for governance will necessitate the creation of policies and procedures or processes. These reflect – how a process should be performed in practice – and can be a separate document or a section of the same. It is often worth trying to be clear, as a policy change may or may not alter the procedure, while a necessary change in procedure should not be allowed to change the policy by default. It should be clear in a procedure which policy or policies it relates to.

Governance and Compliance

Basic Requirements

- **Health and Safety Policy and Procedure. Could include:**
    - Workstation assessment procedure.
    - Fire safety.

- **Equal Opportunities Statement of Intent. Could include:**
    - Harassment.
    - reference to Recruitment procedure.
    - Confidentiality Policy (including Data Protection).

Staff

- Basic terms of employment
- Expenses Policy (with due regard to Inland Revenue rules)
- Staff Disciplinary procedure.
- Staff Grievance procedure.
- Staff Appraisal procedure.
- Supervision.
- Staff loans (travel, cycle, car).
- Union recognition Policy.
- Sick Leave Policy and procedure
- Leave policy and procedure.
- Time off in Lieu Policy and procedure.
- Public Duties.
- Recruitment Procedure.
- Redundancy policy.
- Induction Procedure and Checklist.
- Exit interviews.
- Job evaluation.
- Retirement policy.

Office Management

- Green Office Policy/Environmental Impact.
- E-mail/internet use policy.
- Personal, or associated group, use of office facilities.
- Security.

Ethics, Empowerment, Improvement

- **Complaints Procedure** (for members, service users, public).
- Service user/member involvement.
- Training policy.
- Quality/monitoring policy
- Staff involvement policy.
- Ethical Investment Policy.
- Whistleblowing.
- Child/vulnerable adult protection – 'safeguarding'.

Governance and Compliance

External

- *Partnership working.*
- *Media Handling* – who is authorised to say what
- *Supplier selection*

Finance

- *Insurances*
- *Other accounting policies often part of audit process* (e.g., valuation of assets).
- *Financial Policies and Procedures.*

Governance

- *AGM procedures.*
- *Committee Procedures* (standing orders).
- *Management Committee/Board (and sub-committee) Terms of Reference.*
- *Job descriptions for directors / board members – chair, secretary and any others.*
- *Conflicts of Interest*

Implications of Unresolved Governance and Compliance Issues

There can be serious implications if governance and compliance issues are unresolved. Failure to address governance and compliance can cause internal issues that, for example:

- **result in theft and loss of income** – e.g., if sales and transactions are not monitored correctly
- **cause longer-term financial problems for the organisation** – e.g., from paying compensation and having to repay money that has been taken; from a drop in share value as investors lose confidence
- **lead to a breach of contract** – e.g., being sued for releasing information
- **cause a security problem** – e.g., a personal attack or terrorist threat if security arrangements are leaked; passwords and access codes being used by unauthorised people
- **cause embarrassment** – e.g., if personal details or financial records are made public
- **give competitors an advantage** – e.g., from gaining access to confidential operational data
- **increased compliance costs** – e.g., restructuring costs as a consequence of prosecution or loss of reputation

Governance and Compliance

- ***increased staff turnover and related costs*** – *e.g., from staff not wanting to work for an employer with a poor reputation*

There can also be serious implications if an organisation's external stakeholders act in response to governance and compliance failures – e.g., government agencies or customers who take enforcement or legal action. Actions could, for example:

- ***result in fines and penalties*** – *e.g., from paying insufficient tax*
- ***result in compensation payments*** – *e.g., to customers when financial data has been mishandled*
- ***result in the organisation losing customers*** – *e.g., from having a bad and unprofessional reputation*
- ***cause financial problems for customers*** – *e.g., if their bank accounts are hacked as a result*
- ***lead to prosecution of the employer and/or employees*** – *e.g., under the Data Protection Act, Bribery Act or Money Laundering regulations*

The consequences of failure can seriously affect an organisation's ability to survive and thrive due to additional costs and loss of reputation.

www.ingramcontent.com/pod-product-compliance
Lightning Source LLC
Chambersburg PA
CBHW070940230426
43666CB00011B/2503